The Best of the Review – 7

Edited by David L. Fleming SJ

Praying
as a
Christian

Acknowledgments
The publisher gratefully acknowledges:

The use of "Spiritual Dryness: Some Practical Guidelines" by Eamon Tobin. Republished from *Prayer: A Handbook for Today's Catholic*, by Rev. Eamon Tobin. Reprinted with permission of Liguori Publications, Liguori, Missouri 63057. No other reproduction of this material is permitted.

The use of "Listening as the Foundation for Spirituality" by Robert P. Maloney CM. Republished from *He Hears the Cry of the Poor: On the Spirituality of Vincent de Paul*. Reprinted with permission of New City Press.

The use of the cover photograph with permission of the photographer, Vincent Hovley SJ.

Review for Religious
3601 Lindell Boulevard
St. Louis, Missouri 63108

ISBN 0-924768-08-8

Foreword

*R*eview for Religious has been nourishing the prayer life of its readers for close to sixty years. Consistently over the years since its first issue in January 1942, the journal has presented articles exploring the various approaches which spring forth from the rich spiritualities within the Christian tradition. *Praying as a Christian* (The Best of the Review – 7) brings together in one volume some twenty-eight of these articles.

The authors are women and men—religious, cleric, and lay—who, for the most part, are not well-known theologians or writers, but who desire to share their insight and grace from experience in the hope that others may also find profit. I believe that the authors chosen for this volume are representative of the many excellent contributors to our ongoing discovery of our relationship with God expressed in prayer.

The Best of the Review – 7 has been the result of a number of requests that have come to me to put together such a volume on prayer. The members of the Review for Religious Advisory Board added their own impetus to my efforts. Because of the topic and because of the large number of articles to select from, it was a work of love. The difficulty has come in the selection. The articles are grouped within some basic themes that seem to be a part of a prayer life that is seriously worked at. The first theme is titled "Scripture" since our way of praying in the Judeo-Christian tradition is in response to the word of God expressed in our sacred writings. The final theme of the book is titled "Prayer Apostolate" since, for a Christian, praying is always more than just developing a personal relationship with God; prayer as a ministry is a part of our evangelizing mission as Christians. I attempt in the intervening theme divisions to present areas of common interest for all of us who continue to desire to grow in our personal prayer life. All of the articles have been previously published in Review for Religious except for my Introduction. I have tried to set the stage of our study of prayer by suggesting a way of always finding God in the dailyness of life.

I express my gratitude to all the authors who graciously agreed to the inclusion of their articles in this volume. I owe a special debt of gratitude to Father Philip Fischer SJ, Mary Ann Foppe, and Tracy Gramm—my fellow staff members—who always add to their usual duties when I decide to bring together articles for another book. I thank also Sister Barbara Soete SSND, who did final proofreading and corrections, and to Father Vincent Hovley SJ for his contribution of photography which graces the cover of this book.

Just as God's grace touches us in our desire to pray, so may it fuel our prayer's fervor through the articles that make up this book.

David L. Fleming SJ

contents

contemplative living

darkness

prayer forms

personal paths

prayer apostolate

DAVID L. FLEMING

Praying:
Recognizing God Within

What does it mean for us to pray? Most of us would acknowledge that we do pray. At least we would agree that we go to Mass and that we say some prayers. However, many of us, if not most, would admit to feeling that we do not know really how to pray or that we do not pray nearly enough. What does it mean for us to pray? We may give some various answers: It means a feeling of inadequacy; it means a sense that we are still praying just as we prayed as a kid; it means a fantasizing that some one person or some one book is going to solve our praying problems and help us to pray like Teresa of Avila.

What Does It Mean to Pray?

In praying we need to face the reality that God takes us where we are, not where we think we should be. Consequently, we pray from where we are. We all have some ability to pray; it is a God-given ability. Prayer in many ways is like conversation. If someone were to ask us how we make conversation, we would find it rather difficult to answer. It is not intellectually difficult to answer, but conversation seems so natural, so commonplace, so daily, so much a part of our being that we find it hard to put into words. Yet the question about conversation is similar to the question about praying. Prayer is like conversing—with God. Some of us are better conversationalists than others. Some talk too much and never let anyone else get a word in. We can do the same to God. Some talk only pleasantries, and the friendship can grow only as deep as the "sweet nothings" we share. So the conversation between God and us can remain only at the level of "sweet nothings." Some people do not talk because they do not want to invite another into their lives. We can do the same with God.

Perhaps we might complain that God does not keep up his end of the conversation very well. Our unease depends on whether we really hear the word of God as the "word of God." How does God's word in the privileged area of Scripture engage us in conversation? Then again, how does God's word spoken in events, through people, in the reading of daily newspapers and various magazines, in our work, and in the entertainment that we seek out—how does this word stimulate the conversation with us? Bluntly said, prayer as conversation with God contends with all the difficulties that conversation with my fellow human beings does. Maybe we need to remind ourselves that conversation does not always come easy in daily life, and conversation with God may not always come easy either. Yet, just as we all have our ways of carrying on a conversation, so too we have our own ways of praying. We can learn to be better conversationalists, and we can learn to be better pray-ers. Granted that we can grow in our ease in praying, God and we always enter into the conversation from where we are.

Jesus' sharing with us out of his experience, is key to our hearing how Jesus experienced the closeness of God.

Of course, praying is more than just actual conversation. We all know that we communicate in many ways—even sitting together side-by-side in a car for long stretches of a journey can be a communication, with little or nothing being said. Presence, gestures, music, art, dance—there are many ways to communicate. And so we find praying bigger than just saying words or thinking thoughts. Our meeting and dealing with God, then, comes more than just in our so-called prayer times. Our ways of praying, our meeting with God, can happen in silence, in an incidental conversation, in appreciating the beauty of a day, in observing birds or dogs or any of God's creatures. Our meeting with

God happens not just in the silence of our room, not just in a church, but also in dealing with one another, in meals together, in solitary walks, in listening to music, and in and through the myriad of other activities that fill our everyday life.

What Does It Mean to Recognize God?

These reflections lead right into another "what does it mean" question. What does it mean "to recognize God"? It is akin to our previous question: How do we pray to God? How do we recognize God? What does it mean to recognize God? When do we see the face of God?

In the Gospels, Jesus points the way to our seeing, our recognizing, God in our life. Jesus talked a lot about how God is all around us and enters into our lives in daily ways. Usually he told simple stories about ordinary life and made the application to God's dealings with us. But there is an especially famous and longer talk by Jesus which in the Gospel of St. Luke is referred to as the Sermon on the Plain. This sermon, so key to Jesus' program for life, provides us with a rich gold mine of how God is so present to our everyday life. We find Jesus giving us hints how we might more easily recognize God.

Jesus has come down from the mountain and is now on a level stretch when he begins to talk to his disciples and a large crowd which has gathered to hear him and be healed of their diseases. Jesus' speaking on level ground intimates that Jesus identifies with us and our ordinary ground-level experience. He is not talking down from a mountain top or from a pulpit; he is speaking to us on our level. Perhaps Luke wants to highlight that Jesus shares with us out of his own human experience. Jesus' sharing with us out of his experience, I think, is key to our hearing how Jesus experienced the closeness of God. That closeness of God to us in every aspect of life, both in good times and in bad, is Jesus' gift to us to help us to see and recognize God's presence.

> And raising his eyes toward his disciples he said: Blessed are you who are poor, for the kingdom of God is yours. Blessed are you who are now hungry, for you will be satisfied. Blessed are you who are now weeping, for you will laugh. Blessed are you when people hate you, and when they exclude and insult you, and denounce your name as evil on account of the Son of Man. Rejoice and leap for joy on that day! (Luke 6:20-23)

In his Sermon on the Plain, Jesus declares people blessed in four situations: being poor, being hungry, being in sorrow, and being hated or insulted. Every situation seems to be a paradoxical take on what a blessing is. In fact, for the people of Jewish faith, God's favor was to be seen in prosperity, in success, and in good reputation. The world in which we now live says the same thing and advertises these as its values. And they are values— good gifts that we can strive for—prosperity, success, and a good reputation. But the question looms before us: Do we mistake the gifts of God for God? Do the gifts become identified with God, so that their absence means the absence of God?

Jesus emphasizes that God can be near to us in every human situation. For example, God is close to those who feel empty and are called poor. Their very emptiness and poverty allow God to break through and make shine out for them the deeper-down reality present in our world—the kingdom of God, the reign of God, God's nearness. Is not their real richness their very relation with God—being sons and daughters—something no one gives them but God, and no one can take away from them? It is truly the poor who share this blessing of true human dignity with us. We sometimes think that we, in our rich generosity, are gifting the poor, and instead we find them gifting us. Thus enlightened, we can recognize that our own moments of poverty, our times of emptiness, can truly be graced, for they are moments of knowing God's nearness and God's inalienable gift of dignity.

The neediness, the deprivation, the sorrow is not what Jesus is declaring a great blessing. Jesus is saying, from his experience, that God wants to be especially close to us at these very moments. That is a great blessing. Our human poverty is the emptiness that opens us to God. Poverty in all its forms symbolizes the "hole" in us, the hollow, that only God can fill—and thereby hallow. The ache is a call to recognize God. We are being taught how to look for and so see God.

> But woe to you who are rich, for you have received your consolation. But woe to you who are filled now, for you will be hungry. Woe to you who laugh now, for you will grieve and weep. Woe to you when all speak well of you, for their ancestors treated the false prophets in this way. (Luke 6:24-26)

When Jesus declares a "woe" on these experiences that are the opposite of poverty, he is not saying that riches or feasting or laughter are not good things. He is reminding us that we can feel self-satisfied and think that we no longer need God. Then why seek God? We have our own satiety in whatever form it takes—food, wealth, friends, travel, even wanderlust. Being full, we will get in touch with God if we feel the unlikely inclination. It is an attitude of "don't call us; we will call you." That is why good times can—as often as not—not be good for us at all. They do not become times for us to turn our eyes to God in gratitude for the gifts and goodness that we are enjoying. In fact, they actually become barriers for us, preventing us from seeking and finding God.

There is no use identifying ourselves as people of faith when we do not live with faith.

What does it mean to act like a son or daughter of God? To act in ways similar to the ways that God acts, Jesus says. As Jesus keeps trying to impress upon us, God is merciful, God is compassionate, God is good to the ungrateful and wicked, God has the sun come down upon the good and wicked, and so too the rain. How difficult it is to live out the kind of evenhandedness that God shows to us! And yet Jesus challenges us: What kind of faith do we live if we are good only to those who are good to us, if we always expect to give only insofar as we get something in return? Isn't this the way of the world—needing no God? But do we not sense God's presence when we reach out so as to be God's hand, when we speak out a word of support or consolation and realize it is God's voice coming from within us? We experience God working right with us. Or, we should more correctly say, we experience ourselves working with God.

There is no use identifying ourselves as people of faith when we do not live with faith—maybe the very reason for our not seeing God. There is no use saying that we are good people if good deeds do not flow from our heart so that we see God's grace being the link in our interchange with others—so that we see God in them. Jesus says that we can easily mouth the words "Lord, Lord" without knowing who it is that we are addressing. We do not recognize God's face before us.

Finding God Within

Our attitude towards life has a lot to tell about our recognizing God or not. What is our life about? Where does our life come from? How do we go about making choices that give us life?

> He said to his disciples, Therefore I tell you, do not worry about your life and what you will eat, or about your body and what you will wear. For life is more than food and the body more than clothing. Notice the ravens: they do not sow or reap; they have neither storehouses nor barn, yet God feeds them. How much more important are you than birds! Can any of you by worrying add a moment to your life-span? If even the smallest things are beyond your control, why are you so anxious about the rest? Notice how the flowers grow. They do not toil or spin. But I tell you, not even Solomon in all his splendor was dressed like one of them. If God so clothes the grass in the field that grows today and is thrown into the oven tomorrow, will he not much more provide for you, O you of little faith? As for you, do not seek what you are to eat and what you are to drink, and do not worry anymore. All the nations of the world seek for these things, and your Father knows that you need them. Instead seek his kingdom, and these other things will be given you besides. Do not be afraid any longer, little flock, for your Father is pleased to give you the kingdom. Sell your belongings and give alms. Provide money bags for yourselves that do not wear out, an inexhaustible treasure in heaven that no thief can reach nor moth destroy. For where your treasure is, there also will your heart be. (Lk 12:22-34)

Listen to Jesus: Jesus points out that God is truly a God of life. Who feeds the birds, who clothes the lilies in such beauty? If birds and flowers and grass of the field are held in such care by God, what does God do for those he calls his sons and daughters? Jesus asks us to question ourselves: Who is the God of our life? the God of our whole and total life, day in, day out, all night, all day? Who is the God of everything that makes up the complex of what we call our life? If we act on the reality that God is the God of our life, then God is very close. We find that we more readily recognize God in a daily way.

Finally Jesus gives us the most precious key to our recognizing God within. He says very simply: "Wherever your treasure is, there your heart will be." If God is our treasure, our heart will always know how to find him. Just as our heart knows, and our heart has its reasons, so too we can say that our heart sees. Seeing with our hearts, we are never far from God. For God fills our days and our nights with his presence and power. We recognize his face, feel his touch, sense his presence. We are growing to be people who find God in all things.

Yes, we are people who take time to pray regularly. Better yet, we are becoming people who have an ease in making contact with God in the ordinary flow of our day. As we enter into Jesus' experience of God and let his words form us, we are becoming—like him—contemplatives-in-action. We are caught up in prayer because we are finding God within all things.

The God of the Scriptures:
An Invitation to Passionate Prayer

scripture

We all have them. Most of us have learned to control, even ignore them. But for some they appear unasked for, and when they do they are tolerated with all the patience we have for a head cold. They are our emotions, our deep seated emotions, the dark and passionate side of our human nature.

We enjoy them when, at sports activities, we give ourselves permission to act outraged or triumphant and they suit our moods. We like it when they sneak out quietly in the form of tears at the end of a touching movie. They may also try to make their presence known during prayer, but here they are often considered most distracting and least desired. And yet, if there is a time for emotion, if there is a time for passion at all, it is during prayer.

Prayer is a naturally revealing activity. It is natural that passionate emotions should arise within us during prayer. They are conduits to the parts of ourselves God wishes most to go. It is little wonder we should find them straining to emerge. Could it be that they are even called forth by a God eager to touch this part of ourselves so seldom shared?

Unfortunately, they are the parts of ourselves we least of all like. Most often, they are corridors to the side of ourselves we fear. They lead into the cauldron of emotion we have not yet learned to control. We may not be really sure what lurks there, but we are fairly confident that God has no part of it, that it is best shielded from

God, that what surges there is best atoned for in secret, not something to be proud of and shared openly with God.

But are passionate emotions like anger and jealousy and lust called forth during times of prayer so that we can "confess" to them? Or are they summoned at God's own invitation? Can it be, might it be, that God can desire a passionate prayer as well and as much as a prayer that is contemplative, tranquil, and serene? Might it be that the God who appears throughout the pages of the Bible speaks to us best and can identify with us most through the part of ourselves we keep most hidden?

The God of the Scriptures is indeed a passionate God. This article is an exploration of that theme and of the constructive relationship that exists between passion and prayer.

The Passionate Nature of God

Pascal was right when he said that there seemed to be two Gods: the God discussed by philosophers and the God of Abraham, Isaac, and Jacob, the God of the Scriptures. Most people prefer the philosophers' God. That Being is reasonable, controlled, logical. The God of the philosophers thinks, plans, orders, foresees. There is, of course, a "feeling" side to this God too. God does, after all, feel compassion and love for creation. But those "feelings" are held well in check and are dispensed coolly and properly. This God seems to resemble a fine Victorian gentleman/scholar. And, very often, especially here in the Western world, that is the image we would like to have of ourselves. That is the standard and goal we set for ourselves.

The point is not that this image of God is false. But is it all there is? Is it only one side of a much more complex personality? Do we, with a too exclusively philosophical model of God, lose some of God's mystery because we fail to pay proper attention to God's emotion and passionate nature?

Perhaps such a theology is no more complete than an anthropology that deliberately ignores the emotional and passionate side of human beings? The point of human growth is to integrate and harmonize the parts of our nature into one. To ignore our emotions is to ignore half of our selves. In addition to being rational, thinking creatures, human beings also love, feel anger and jealousy, crave revenge, yearn, and feel pity. We are indeed complex beings. Can we dare imagine a God who is any less? Moreover, if we are so thoroughly emotional and if we were made in God's own image and likeness, what can we conclude about God?

Scripture tells us that "God is love." Love is, to be sure, more than an intellectual attitude or disposition toward life. Love is an emotion. People in love are known sometimes to do strange things, spontaneous things, unpredictable things. Or so they seem to us. But to them, following the "logic of love," their actions have a rationality, a purpose, an order. Finding it, though, and seeing the reasoning behind such actions can be almost as hard as finding the sense and reason behind some of God's actions in our lives. God is not illogical nor is God emotionally unstable. God is simply love. God is simply *in* love with us and with all of creation. God is a Being of great and passionate emotion. That, at least, is what the Scriptures tell us.

Perhaps, to beg the question a bit, that is why God chose the Jews in the first place as recorders of divine revelation. The Jews, and all Near Eastern people for that matter, were extremely emotional and passionate people. Check the papers—they still are. But if you were God, would you have chosen them to write the record of your revelation?

Many people would probably have preferred the Greeks. Their philosophical bent would more likely have appealed to us. And indeed, they would probably have done an admirable job at revealing God's mind. But could they have matched the Jewish brilliance for revealing God's heart? The Jewish passion for life was a most fitting medium for the manner of God's message. For the Scriptures reveal, in emotional and passionate imagery and terms, the heart as well as the mind of God.

Maybe, we argue, the Jewish people were simply transferring their own emotional nature onto God and that God no more has passionate feelings than God has legs with which to walk around in the garden of Eden. Yet, even though they were not meant to be read literally, all the images and words do reveal and communicate something about God. To glean this, though, the Scriptures must be read with an open mind and heart.

God's Emotional Involvement in Life

What do the Scriptures tell us about God? The Bible reveals a God who is very much alive and near. The biblical God does not observe the glories and follies of creation from afar. This is not a

God who aloofly administrates creation and human history. Rather, this is a God who *ministers*, to it and within it. The God of the Bible is *pastorally* involved in human life. We know that because the Scriptures reveal a God who is *emotionally* involved in human life.

There are levels and degrees of involvement in community, in family, in politics, in everything regarding life. One criterion for measuring or determining the depth of involvement is the amount of emotional investment shown. In community living, for example, it is easy enough to state one's involvement in community affairs. One may even show up at community meetings and functions. But does that person's words and presence communicate an active involvement or a benign disinterest? Does body language alone, for instance, tell the others present that "I am here to observe. Really, I couldn't care less what happens. It is somewhat interesting, even humorous though. Just continue and pretend I'm not here"? No words may communicate that. But the message is sent, communicated through posture, through sleepy eyes and flaccid facial expression. On the other hand, is the person very much involved in the proceedings? Like the other, this person says not a word. Yet, through all the same means, the message communicated is much different. This person exhibits interest through a tense body, through a face that while silent is red with anger or aglow with satisfaction. The eyes hold an interest, the palms sweat, a leg fidgets nervously. This person is truly and pastorally present and alive. Why? Because the person is visibly emotionally involved. And that is what we want from each other and from God.

If we are so thoroughly emotional and if we were made in God's own image and likeness, what can we conclude about God?

Similarly, why do we become upset with the "professional" pastor who runs the office well and administrates the parish efficiently but who cannot feel his people's pain, who cannot rejoice at someone's birth or mourn at another's death? Why do we feel cheated? Why does the person seem pastorally out of touch and somehow less a priest than the pastor who is able and willing to be emotionally present to the people? Why does the emotionally uninvested pastor seem to communicate less of God's presence? Why do we feel disappointed? For what reason do we feel we should be able to expect and receive more?

All of this speaks to an image or a set of expectations we have about God. Because God cares, God's ministers should also care. Because God is able to and does feel with the people, so should God's priests and pastoral workers. We want and need to feel God present in our lives and feel cheated by those who serve in God's name if somehow we cannot sense from them a deeper presence of God than the merely physical. We want and feel a right to expect an emotional presence and involvement. We want our pastoral workers to be passionately present and active. We want and expect that because we feel God is passionately present and active.

But why? Does that expectation and feeling originate within us alone? Or is that the image of God that is mysteriously and boldly communicated through almost every page of the Bible? Indeed, God is most emotionally present and involved in the lives of the Jewish people. That is true from exodus to exile, from restoration through resurrection. God communicates through the Scriptures a presence and involvement that is intensely passionate.

The Passionate God of the Prophets

Nowhere is this more evident than in the writings of the prophets. Within the prophetic books we see a picture of a God at wits' end. The people had rebelled from God's love and were running headlong toward destruction. We hear a response from God that is the emotional equal of what is politically, socially, and spiritually at stake.

Read with the emotion befitting the texts Amos 8:4-8 or 4:1-3 or Hosea 11:1-11 or Jeremiah 7:1-20 or Isaiah 54:7-8 or any of the other prophets, and you find the words of a person on the edge, the words of a person who is not at all detached or only mildly interested. In those words and so many others, we receive a message of a God filled with passion for the welfare of his people, a God who is truly emotionally involved in the life, past and future, of his people.

If there is anger in God's words, it is the anger of a parent or lover, the passion of someone who cares tremendously about another. It is an anger born of frustration and love. Who has been in love without feeling anger? Love is a powerful emotion that opens us up to other equally powerful feelings. And what of the energy invested in both love and anger? Passion has a high price in emotional energy that is paid only by those truly sincere about what they feel. The quality and quantity of God's emotion so naked and strong throughout the prophets is testimony to the sincerity of God's passionate love.

Moreover, it is a passion and sincerity that God expects in return. Love that is deep and intense expects a return in kind. One of our ways of showing love is through our prayer, both private and liturgical. Note, then, in Isaiah 1:11-16 and Amos 5:21-25 and Jeremiah 7:21-28, the reaction of God to worship that is liturgically correct but void of sincerity and feeling. God expects a worship from the heart, a worship that is a reflection of our love. To be proper and true to the rubrics is not enough, not even the most important thing. What God seeks is what God gives, a prayer that is emotionally sincere. What God "hates" and "detests," what is "loathsome" to God is prayer empty of affect.

God expects a worship from the heart, a worship that is a reflection of our love.

That does not mean that worship must be a wild and ecstatic affair. However, it must be sincere; it must reveal an authentic human warmth. Worship, prayer, is more than so many words or lack of them. We can meditate quite correctly and all without opening our hearts in love. A prayer that is emotionally flat and cold is the sacrifice displeasing to God.

Perhaps that is why Paul tells us that because "we do not know how to pray as we ought, the Spirit makes intercession for us with groanings that cannot be expressed in speech" (Rm 8:26). That is an invitation to pray our feelings, to pray from and with our emotions. That is what God asks for and longs to share, for it is that which is most truly in our hearts. The Spirit helps us to raise what we are feeling in prayer, even if it can be expressed in no other way than by a groan.

Since we are to live as we pray, God expects from us a life that is emotionally honest and open. How often we repress our feelings and hold in check our passion. We refuse to allow ourselves to feel and that prevents us from being as effective and compassionate as Jesus was and calls us to be. The "cry of the poor" is too painful to hear so we learn to close to the poor not only our ears but also our hearts. We dull our ability and willingness to feel and so lose a major motivating force behind Christian action. Pity is not the issue here, rather compassion and justice.

Perhaps it was because Jesus was a man of such strong emotions that he was as compassionate and sensitive as the Scriptures say. Yet not only did Jesus have strong feelings, he was willing to live with them and feel them. Because he did not repress what he felt but lived what he felt, he could be moved enough to touch and heal the leper (Mk 1:41) and raise the widow's son (Lk 7:11-17). If Jesus was the troublemaker and lawbreaker the Pharisees claimed, it was because he allowed his emotions to so move his charity and inspire his faith that he saw not simply the law but the people the law did not and could not serve.

God's Call for a Passionate Faith

Jesus' emotion is most manifest in his faith. Many people were raised to believe that faith is something we do with our minds, that faith is an intellectual act of agreement or obedience to a tradition or set of beliefs. While it may be that, it is not only that. This is clear from the way Jesus lived and how he believed. For Jesus, faith was an emotion that gripped not only his mind, but his heart and body as well.

Oftentimes one emotion is held in check by another. A boy, for instance, may want to introduce himself to a girl. The "love" he feels for her is held in check, though, by his "fear" of being rejected. He decides to say nothing. Fear has overruled his young love. Similarly, a person may feel inclined to speak out on a justice issue. That person too feels fear. But this time the person's convictions on the matter, the person's belief, is the stronger of the two and bids the person to speak out. Here faith overruled fear.

All of us know what fear is, all of us have felt it. Reflect for a moment what happens when you feel fear. The mind freezes, it becomes difficult or even impossible to think. The entire body is also affected. Knees shake, palms sweat, the mouth runs dry. If the fear is sharp enough, we may even close our eyes and prefer to block out the cause of our fear. Fear, to be sure, is a powerful emotion. It would require, then, an equally powerful emotion to counter it.

Only two emotions give us the courage to overcome fear: love and faith—although the two are intimately related. A mother stands terrified at the sight of her burning home when she hears the cry of her child from within. Her fear of the flames and smoke cause her to stand for a moment paralyzed until love for her child overpowers the fear and forces her in to rescue him. Jeremiah the prophet stands equally terrified before the people gathered at the temple. He too, however, hears—or rather *feels*—an inner voice, the call of God bidding him to speak in God's name. For a moment his fear prevails before the faith within his heart overwhelms it and causes him to cry out.

How many of us have had our faith compromised by fear? By closing ourselves to our feelings, by repressing our emotions, we have been eliminating a source of strength that could well empower our faith to rival that of the prophets. If our faith is solely intellectual it is but half, at best, of what it could be. Faith is authentic when it flows from our hearts, when it flows from our love for God.

Jeremiah, for example, and Jesus after him, may have seemed like people without faith because they spoke against the traditions and customs of the people. They could rightly be asked, "Have you no faith, Jeremiah, in the temple and the promise God made to dwell in it always? Why is it so hard for you to have faith in what our traditions teach? Why can't you agree with them?" Faith in this sense is an act of the intellect. But for Jeremiah, for the other prophets, and for Jesus, faith was an act of love; its motive force was an intuition of God's abiding presence within. They felt God's love and returned it as they could (that is, they believed), and it was that faith in God's love that enabled them to stand up and say what their hearts could not deny.

The love they felt empowered them, gave their faith the spirit of courage. All of us are given the gift of that love. All of us have within ourselves the courage to truly use our faith. But so often in closing ourselves to our emotions, in denying them, we deny ourselves the grace, the love, that gives us the courage to truly believe. Jesus and the prophets before him were not ashamed of their emotions. Indeed, they prayed with them (Jeremiah's lamentations, for example) by bringing them before God instead of hiding them in the dark recesses of their spirits. By so doing, they provide for us all an example of authentic living and prayer.

Praying with Our Emotions

Oddly enough, it is the emotion of fear that most inhibits us from bringing our other emotions to prayer. As mentioned earlier, prayer is a naturally revealing activity. In prayer the love and union we share with God is revealed and made known to us. We may receive the revelation of truths and intuitions about questions and problems we may have, as well as insights into God and ourselves. It is this that often scares us into emotional and spiritual repression.

In the quiet, centering communion of prayer with God, we forget to maintain many of the blocks and barriers we place between our conscious selves and our more disquieting emotions. Suddenly and quite unexpectedly we can find the composure of our prayer compromised by unwelcome feelings. The person whose thoughts continue to center upon feelings of passion for a lover, the religious whose heart is suddenly filled with anger and resentment toward a superior, the person who becomes aware of his or her jealousy and envy—all of these people find the rewarding calm of prayer ruined by the onslaught of emotions.

In each of these cases, whether or not prayer has been ruined depends upon whose agenda is being followed. Prayer is a dialogue. However, especially with meditation, prayer can become a monologue of silence. Our meditation can be but another way of saying, "Listen God, there are just some things I'd sooner not think about. Why don't we just sit here quietly and ignore them together." Our prayer agenda calls for some peace and quiet, a bit of reprieve, a break in the action of confrontation. Yet we find ourselves continually pestered by thoughts and feelings we have decided not to share. Might it be, however, that their continual interruption is an effort on God's part to make it part of our prayer? Might God have an agenda too? And might that agenda include the very feelings we are so desperate to ignore?

It might do well, then, since prayer is a dialogue, to "ask" God about what should be shared. One way of doing so is by beginning our prayer with a bit of soul-searching journaling. We might record what and how we are feeling, any significant encounters we have had with people, good and bad. The point is not to dwell on any of them. Rather we acknowledge what is already inside of us. We acknowledge it to God and to ourselves. Then, having done that, we set it aside and open ourselves to God. Yet the very action of having been honest with ourselves about what we are feeling has already invited God into our deepest selves. We have laid everything bare and have effectively told God, "Well, now that you know, what do you say?" Then, if our prayer is quiet, perhaps God is saying, "Let it rest for now," and so we should. If, however, we find the emotions returning, perhaps we should pay them some prayerful attention.

It is one matter to continually harp on a feeling and another to attend to one that finds its way to the surface. Yet it is here that fear can overcome all else and totally inhibit our communion with God, not to mention any communion with ourselves. We are afraid of what may come if we allow our emotions to flow. We are afraid of what God may think if we stood before God with emotions bare. Perhaps most of all, we are afraid of what we would have to admit about ourselves if we allowed our spiritual vision to focus upon our feelings. Especially in times of stress, when we need prayer most, we are most reluctant, most afraid to pray because the emotions we so fear are so close to the surface, so hard to dispel.

It is the emotion of fear that most inhibits us from bringing our other emotions to prayer.

In such cases the fear and shame we so strongly feel should be the opening movement of our prayer. But here is the test. Have we the faith to share what we fear? Here we become the shy person struggling to talk to a friend. Here we become the mother rooted in fear or stirred by love into action. Here we find the revelation, not of God but of ourselves, that prayer so powerfully conveys. Here we find a truth about ourselves. Prayer is a dialogue. Has God been speaking, shouting through hands pressed tight against our ears, trying to get through?

Summary

We can repress our prayer and weaken our faith because we are unwilling to face the passion of our own emotions. Why? Is it God's rejection or wrath that we fear or is it facing the truth about ourselves? Some people are simply ashamed that they are emotional people at all. Somewhere many of us have learned that we should be rational at the expense of being emotional. Emotions are something to master, signs of weakness, occasions for sin. To be holy is to be emotionally controlled. Perhaps. To be sure, some emotions need to be held in check. Some need to be confessed. But not all.

Our emotions are occasions for grace, provided we let our God work through them. They can be conduits leading to deeper prayer. They can be the means for facing and overcoming our fear of living. For, indeed, without emotions we are less than human. We were made in the image and likeness of a living, feeling God who is revealed in the pages of Scripture as a truly passionate lover, a God who, for example, is quite honest about being "jealous." We were made to have feelings and to use our emotions to feel and act alive. If Jesus was not ashamed of the force of his emotions, why should we be ashamed?

As Christians we are called to become fully alive. That means learning to live with and harness our emotions. Truly, our emotions are gifts from God, gifts to be enjoyed, gifts for which we can be grateful. But, before any of that can happen, our emotions must first be accepted.

Desire, Asking, and Answers

*P*rayer, as St. Thomas Aquinas said, is the articulation of our desire before God.[1] That is the way we teach our children their first practical lesson in religion: we teach them to ask God for what they want. As people grow in spiritual life, they can never outgrow the spirit of their beginnings, if for no other reason than that the highest reaches cannot exist without the lowest attainments. There is reason, then, not to abandon altogether the early, petitionary stage of spiritual life, but to continue to experience its varying moods and movements.

Here biblical personages at once spiritual and earthy can be illustrative and illuminative. The recorded experiences of Hannah, David, and Job are relevant. They are all apparently of marked spirituality, notably above the ordinary. Yet in their dealings with God they do not remain always ethereal. Possessed of human desires, too, as down-to-earth people, they approach God openly with the desires of their heart. That is to say, they are simple enough not to be shamming but to move with the tide of their life. Spiritually oriented people will neglect this basic lesson only to their cost.

Not much is known of Hannah, surely; but the little that is known of her reveals her womanly spiritual fiber. Her husband, Elkanah, less known than herself, is religious too, but in the usual way, performing the regular practices like yearly pilgrimage. Perhaps part of his routine spirituality is his seeming resignation to God's disposition regarding Hannah's barrenness. But Hannah herself would not be resigned to her situation. She burns with desire for a son as much as, or even more than, she is resentful and in distress because of the taunts of the other wife, who is not barren. All this compounded desire of her heart she pours out to her God, completely oblivious of her surroundings, and she keeps on beseeching him for a son till—that is the important point here— she is assured that she will get what she has painfully longed for. She has not supplicated in vain. No wonder she knows peace in her heart.

David is great in every way, in particular in his spiritual gifts. He attains spiritual heights on certain occasions when God surprises him with choice favors. But he also knows low spirits and even falls. Then he prays, staying where he is. One such occasion is when he realizes that he has to pay for his adultery by the death of the child of adultery. Though he owns his sin, still he wants the son his sin produced. How he prays for the life of the child, struck by God with a grave illness! He pleads with God for his child, fasting and lying on the ground for days together. He prays with all his energies, hoping against hope till he realizes that the child has died. He has supplicated in vain and still, surprisingly enough, seems to find unusual peace in his heart.

Job is an exceptional figure who manages a happy blend of his wealth in the world with his godly life. If he has enjoyed all the prosperity in the world, still he seeks and humbly keeps his integrity before his God. Such a man, however, meets with one disaster after another. Even then he allows no curse to cross his mind or lips; on the contrary, he walks humbly with God, blessing him still. However, in the prolonged anguish of his final disaster, made worse by his three friends preachifying to the effect that every sufferer must be necessarily a sinner, he is stung to the quick and so driven to defend his honor. He argues with them point by point, personally convinced that there is no sin that would explain his suffering. In between he puts the matter before God, too, quite unafraid, now lamenting his plight, now complaining to him, now appealing to him, now reasoning with him, now challenging him, then yearning to reach him, all the while wanting to vindicate his stand that he is innocent, whatever the traditional doctrine of retribution may be. He has supplicated alone and in company, aloud and in silence, passing through the struggle of it all, only to be surprised at the end by the mysterious and yet overwhelmingly peaceful vision of God clearing up all the agonizing questions and difficulties.

The three biblical episodes may be compared to one another with respect to three elements common to them. First, the three protagonists experience an urgent desire. Second, they take it up in their prayer, making it indeed their whole prayer, however long drawn out it may be. Third, they attain something positive.

First, then, they are alike in experiencing desires, however various the desires may be. Hannah desires a son. Her desire is natural, normal, proper, appropriate, and worthy inasmuch as she wants only the full enjoyment of her marriage as willed by God right from the beginning. David desires that the son of his passion, born of another man's wife, should live and not die. His desire, too, is natural and normal and yet perhaps not especially worthy, if only because the circumstantial will of God is for the child of adultery to die. Job desires an answer to the puzzle of his undeserved suffering. His desire, too, is normal and natural and yet only dubiously proper against the background of the common traditional belief that every suffering implies some sin in the sufferer. While Hannah's desire is in every way agreeable, David's and Job's are not particularly so. David resists the apparent mind of God regarding the fruit of his sin, and Job's honest and frank desire is naively bold because it seems to put God in the wrong.

Second, however one evaluates the three desires, they are nevertheless real and candid; the persons know and feel their desire as only they can. They find it so urgent that they do not fight shy of voicing it before other people and even before God. They do not simply pray about it, but make it their sole and constant prayer. Without any distracting self-consciousness, they simply present themselves before God as they experience their desire consuming them, not minding or caring whether they might come across to casual observers as strange or surprising or suspect. Possessed by their sole burning desire, they beseech God persistently without any thought of circumspection or shame or seeming propriety till something good happens to them—which leads to my third point. ◯

In Hannah's case, what happens is just what she has desired and prayed for. She gets a son and calls him Samuel since, as she says, "I asked Yahweh for him" (1 S 1:20). In David's case, what happens is just the opposite of his lingering desire and prayer. His ill-gotten child whom he wants to see saved dies of illness. But David—note well—comes alive after the whole ordeal of praying, pining, and fasting. He bathes, anoints himself, dresses up, goes to the sanctuary, then sits down to a meal, and finally even consoles his forlorn Bathsheba. In Job's case, what happens is not just what he agonizingly wanted to find, for he finds far more than he has dared ask. He has asked only for a vindicating proof of his undeserved suffering, but he is given to see God himself, the answer of all possible problems and puzzles.

It may appear at first sight that the prayer arising from and suffused with unquenchable desire turns out to be a success for Hannah, a failure for David, and a mere struggle for Job. But further reflection would show that the reality or radicality of their experience is not that simple. The feverish desires of David and Job may not have ended in natural, ordinary, and expected satisfaction as in the case of Hannah. But they too have their definite, unmistakable denouement, with their desires set at rest. Indeed, they attain what may be called the resolution of their desires, a positive ending to their experience of desire in and through and by means of prayer.

Despite the obvious differences in their desires, Hannah, David, and Job all end up with positive experiences through prayer.

Here is a lesson for life. Despite the obvious differences in their desires, Hannah, David, and Job all end up with positive experiences through prayer. Their prayer experience has something in common: making their desire transparent to God or, better, living their desire before God in all its urgency. The experience of any urgent desire is itself a sort of struggle till its fulfillment. This is only accentuated when the fulfillment of desire depends, not on oneself, but on the good pleasure of another—in the present context, God.

So Hannah prays in an unusual manner, speaking under her breath, giving room for suspicion that she is drunk. So too does David, to the surprise of his officials, covering himself with sacking, lying on the bare ground, and keeping a strict fast. So too does Job, confounding and shocking his onlookers by his unorthodox stand that, though he has been afflicted with the worst of sufferings, he cannot be accused of having really sinned. Even if he occasionally concedes, for the sake of argument, that he has sinned, he challenges God outright: "Suppose I have sinned, what have I done to you?" (Jb 7:20). But the burden of his prayer runs now and again in such words as these: "I shall say to God, 'Do not condemn me, but tell me the reason for your assault. Is it right for you to injure me, cheapening the work of your own hands and abetting the schemes of the wicked?'" (Jb 10:2-3).

He ends his apologia daringly with no apology whatever: "I have had my say, from A to Z; now let Shaddai answer me" (Jb 31:35). How acute must be the struggle of the man who, in his dire straits, makes bold to speak to God without mincing words about what he wants. If Hannah and David, too, definitely pass through quite a struggle in their prayer seeking what they want, theirs would seem to be nothing compared with the struggle of Job for God's own vindication of his innocence.

Generally speaking, the struggle experienced in prayer as people keep on imploring God for what they want is proportionate to the intensity of their desire. The surpassing struggle Job goes through in his prayer reveals how hard he desires. There is, if one may put it this way, truth in his desire. That is to say, his desire is so true and so truly possessing and consuming him that he needs must seek its fulfillment by every means possible, even if it should entail a gigantic struggle.

Here may be raised a very important question concerning prayer. If people pray and complain that they do not get an answer to their prayer, it may be asked whether their prayer arises out of truth, the truth of their desire in the sense suggested above. People may be accustomed to and satisfied with bland preferences, with mere velleities, and thus may not have true desire even if they know, or seem to know, what they desire. Certainly velleities are *paltry* desires. It is worth noting in this context that Job with his ruling desire and passionate prayer is a fictitious figure, unlike Hannah and David. From this may one not infer that people like Job are seldom found in real life, that rarely are real people moved by strong, ardent, fervent, and in a word *true* desire?

But without desire there can be no prayer, for desire is part and parcel of prayer. St. Thomas said so (as I have indicated above), and St. Augustine had said something similar much earlier. Writing to Proba on prayer, he pointed out that, if the Lord wants us to pray even though he certainly knows independently our wants and needs, it is because "he wants our desire to be exercised in prayer, thus enabling us to grasp what he is preparing to give."[2] He added: "We pray always in faith, hope, and love, with uninterrupted desire. But at certain hours and seasons we also pray with words. We use these signs of realities to rouse ourselves, to become aware of the growth of our desire, and to strongly move ourselves to increase it. . . . What do the Apostle's words, 'Pray constantly,' mean, if not that we must constantly desire. . . ?"[3]

Of course, one may remark quite correctly that, in the context, Augustine had in his mind a constant desire for the blessedness of eternal life. One may observe just as correctly, however, that what we do in prayer—namely, exercise our desire—may reach out not only to eternal life, but to present life as well, with all that we want here and now. Anyhow, the very prayer that Jesus taught explicitly is not confined to holy desires connected with God and his kingdom, but, in the phrase "daily bread," makes mention of ordinary human desires and material needs. The Lord's Prayer certainly includes the gamut of human desires, from the lofty to the lowly.

Other teachings of Jesus on prayer also focus on desire experienced and expressed before God. The parables of the importunate friend and the widow (Lk 11:5-8; 18:1-8), for instance, emphasize the keenness of desire without which prayer would flag and falter. Apart from desire there can be no meaning in prayer of petition; and it is this sort of simple, straightforward prayer that Jesus mostly speaks of. His injunction regarding effective, infallible prayer is to "ask . . . search . . . knock" (Mt 7:7); and this really means that one should go on asking and searching and knocking with the growing impulse of intense desire. This reality of glowing desire may throw light even on the basic requirement—namely, belief or faith—in all such prayer. For instance, in the saying of Jesus that "everything you ask and pray for, believe that you have it already, and it will be yours" (Mk 11:24), the action of belief is as much an activity of desire as it is anything else.[4] When belief comes into play in prayer, it invariably brings desire into the foreground, the desire which was already there in the prayer right from the start.

All this is not a matter of theory but of practice, as may be seen in dealings of Jesus with people to whom he grants favors. In the case of the Syrophoenician woman, Jesus senses right from the beginning how badly she desires the healing of her daughter. His apparent reluctance to accede to her request only brings out all the more her desire, at once insistent and persistent, regarding her daughter's welfare. He takes note of it and refers to it with pleasant surprise when he finally gives his word of favor to her request (see Mk 7:24-30).[5] Just the opposite is the story of the sick man at the Pool of Bethzatha (Jn 5:1-6). When Jesus sees him and knows how long he has been ill, he asks him, "Do you want to be well again?" It is a surprising question at first, but on reflection very revealing. Jesus cannot heal the sick man unless he first desires it. As the man had been ill for so long, perhaps he no longer has any desire for healing. It is precisely to awaken this desire that Jesus puts the question to him.

Today, too, neither Jesus nor his Father can hear any prayer unless it arises in real desire and is poured out in ardent desire and sustained in unabated desire. It *matters* how much and how far we desire whatever we desire. As I conclude, I find myself wondering if social activists have an idea how much they can effect by prayer that is sharpened by the "violence" of desire. When I say violence here, I am thinking of that intriguing logion: "The kingdom of God has been subjected to violence and the violent are taking it by storm" (Mt 11:12).

Notes

[1] See Simon Tugwell, *Prayer in Practice* (Springfield, Illinois, 1974), p. 75.

[2] See *The Divine Office*, vol. 3 (London, Glasgow, Sydney, Dublin, 1974), p. 662.

[3] *Letters of Saint Augustine*, ed. and trans. John Leinenweber (Liguori, Missouri: Triumph Books, 1992), p. 172.

[4] The Markan version lends itself to such an interpretation, unlike the Matthean parallel 21:22 with its connotation of faith as a matter of not doubting about what is prayed for.

[5] Here again Mark is different from Matthew. Mark tells the plain story of the woman with her heart's desire whereas Matthew stylizes it in terms of faith (Mt 15:21-28).

Learning to Curse

Daily recitation of the psalms continues to occupy a prominent place in the spiritual practices of religious as well as in the lives of many lay Christians. These hymns are a wellspring for spirituality, expressing the awe, anguish, gratitude, and longings of our individual and communal lives. The psalms strengthen our participation in the rich tradition of the Judaeo-Christian past. They join us in prayer with the communion of faithful throughout the world. Moreover, the power of these familiar hymns surpasses their own recitation. In times of spiritual oasis, their formulaic lines inspire our own spontaneous prayer to burst forth. In times of spiritual wilderness, these solemn hymns provide words when our own words fail us.

Despite the richness it contributes to our spirituality, praying the psalms is not without peril. Many lines of these hymns disrupt and distract our reflection. Especially troublesome are the many texts with inflammatory language toward one's enemies. Graphic images of violence characterize many of the psalms: "Slaughter them God . . . strike them down" (Ps 59:11); "O God, break the teeth in their mouths" (Ps 58:8-10); "Strike their loins with chronic palsy" (Ps 69:23). Sentiments of hatred and vengeance charge these hostile expressions.

The frequency with which one encounters these negative outpourings poses a serious problem. The difficulty unfolds on two fronts. First, we find the negative sentiments toward enemies at odds with Christian tradition. The teachings of Jesus not only contradict but rule out such curses. Jesus requires us to love our enemy (Mt 5:44; Lk 6:27) and pray for those who persecute us (Mt 5:44). These mandates are not invitations to naive or uncritical behavior. The morality which Jesus sets forth grows out of a consciousness and context of justice. The recognition of evil and evildoers is a critical first step. The response to this recognition distinguishes the ethics of Jesus from the response to enemies in the psalms. In Jesus' teaching, the response to a recognized enemy must be an appropriate expression of love—healing, forgiveness, prayer, instruction. In the final moments of his life, Jesus recognizes his own enemies with precisely this kind of gesture. He prays for their forgiveness (Lk 23:34). In sharp contrast, lines from the psalms suggest a different course of action toward one's enemy. "May his children be orphans and his wife a widow" (Ps 109:6), and "let them vanish like water that runs away" (Ps 58:7). In these and many other psalms, the psalmist's recognition of the enemy evokes a curse. Such curses or imprecations are characteristic of many of the psalms.

How are religious and all Christians to claim the psalms for contemporary spirituality? Should we ignore the inflammatory lines? Or do we select only certain psalms for prayer?

Second, in the contemporary context of our prayer, the expression of hatred and revenge toward the enemy is especially disquieting. It is no secret that the precarious future of humanity rests in the bosom of our nuclear-ensnared world. In our time, pleading to God for the destruction of the enemy evokes images of the monstrous consequences associated with contemporary warfare. Prayer which begs the obliteration of the enemy ignores the ethics incumbent on our era. From moment to moment, the survival of humanity hinges on our ability to resolve conflicts peacefully within society, across borders, and everywhere on the planet. Ultimately, we must constantly commit ourselves to the long and arduous process of redefining the enemy as sister and brother.

So then, how are religious and all Christians to claim the psalms for contemporary spirituality? Should we ignore the inflammatory lines? Or do we select only certain psalms for prayer? Moreover, are such decisions defensible? Is it theologically shortsighted or, perhaps, theologically conscientious to exclude whole psalms or specific verses of these hymns from our spiritual practices?

Over the centuries whole denominations such as the Eastern Orthodox communities and the Calvinists have recited every line of the Psalter. Until recently, Roman Catholic communities recited all one hundred and fifty psalms as well. In 1970 the Apostolic Constitution on the Divine Office explained why the revision of the Divine Office excluded many texts which cursed one's foes. A few of the psalms and the verses of others had been omitted because they were "somewhat harsh in tone . . . especially in the vernacular celebration." It seems that the revised edition intended to spare religious the offense of what they previously had prayed in Latin but had not understood. The exclusions include three lengthy laments (Ps 58, 83, 109) and selected verses from nineteen other laments. The deleted lines consist primarily of the curses against the enemy occurring in the laments.

Uttered in the context of prayer, the curse becomes a vehicle for catharsis.

Laments make up forty percent of the Psalter. They express the depths of anguish and fear in individual or communal travail. At the same time, they give voice to an undying confidence that Yahweh hears the cry of the oppressed. Biblical scholars identify the lament as a particular form of prayer among the psalms. Each lament consists of characteristic elements that include: 1) a cry for help; 2) a complaint that addresses three subjects—God, the sufferer, and the enemies; 3) a confession of trust that God will act on behalf of the sufferer; 4) a petition for God to take action against the enemy; 5) a declaration of assurance that God has heard the prayer; and 6) a vow of praise.

The curse or imprecation is situated in the complaint or the petition. It expresses a wish for the defeat, deprivation, deportation, desolation, or death of the enemy: "Let them go down to Sheol in silence" (Ps 31:18); "Let their attacks bring shame to them" (Ps 109:28); "May their eyes grow dim so that they cannot see" (Ps 69:23). These imprecations are a characteristic element of the lament. To exclude them distorts the form of the hymns. Moreover, such alterations may jeopardize the theological integrity of the prayers. Hence, the solution to such troublesome language may not reside in their selective omissions or in the revisions of the texts. Rather, it may entail a revision of our understanding of a curse.

Catharsis

In West Semitic use, curses uttered between individuals had the power to bring about what was said. The spoken word was endowed with a potential to pursue its subject inexorably. With this in mind, Balak, king of Moab, brought the seer Balaam to curse Israel (Nb 22:5). Similarly, David curses those who drive him into exile where he must worship foreign deities (1 S 26:19). The curse language in the psalms bespeaks a different reality and dynamic. The psalmist recites the curse against a foe *before* God in the context of prayer. Uttered before God, the curse assumes its power from divine intervention. God could act to bring about the curse; God could render it ineffective (Nb 23:8); or God could even return the curse upon the one who recited it (Gn 12:3; 27:29). The actualization of the curse remains a divine prerogative. The expression of malediction toward the other is placed in the hands of God. It is God's decision alone to act upon it. When vengeful retaliation is surrendered to God, the curse assumes a different force.

Uttered in the context of prayer, the curse becomes a vehicle for catharsis. Recitations of these imprecations acknowledge the desperate emotions Israel felt before its captors in exile, before the militia that slaughtered its children, or before the hegemonic rulers who confiscated the land of its peasants. In the same way, reciting these curses against a foe allows us to express the objectionable but nevertheless real sentiments we harbor toward those who cheat us in the workplace, toward those who harm our children, toward those who commit violence in our city, or toward those whose actions further impoverish the most vulnerable members of society. The candor, robustness, and intensity of our outcry gives voice to honest, undeniable emotions. Such cursing in the psalms not only gives voice to what otherwise might be suppressed hostility; its cathartic outcome also serves the more important end of paving a path to our own conversion.

Conversion

Human sinfulness is present everywhere in our world. Cursing is our initial response when we experience the pervasiveness of evil and our own helplessness in the face of it. Daily, the front pages of our newspapers suggest that the candidates for our curses are legion. But the imprecations in the psalms not only provide occasion to confront and damn the iniquity of our age; the recitation of the curse also makes us face the potential for sin in ourselves. By cursing our enemy, we give voice to our own capacity to hate, to do harm, and to desire ill for another. To censor these expressions of anger and hatred in prayer risks bypassing an important step on the road to conversion: the ability and honesty to detect sinfulness in ourselves.

Jesus called us to a change of heart whereby we love our enemies. To eliminate or pass over these curses where we express hatred of our foes impoverishes our potential to love them. Our ability to bless another is diminished if we cannot or are incapable of cursing. Similarly, our desire to love our enemies is impossible if we do not first acknowledge our hostility and feelings of hate toward them. The curse in the psalms provides an acceptable expression of these sentiments as we move toward this change of heart in our prayer.

Communion

"O Lord, you have probed me and you know me" (Ps 139:1). Human life is an open book before God. The One who created life searches and knows its depths and abysses. Can anything be hidden from the mind and heart of God? God knows all before we pray. Our prayer need not be scrutinized or sanitized. Praise, thanks, anguish, tears, lament, and cursing are all admissible before the divine. To omit expressions of anger and outrage and to bypass recitations that bespeak our potential to hate and desire vengeance threaten the integrity of our relationship with God.

Moreover, cursing our enemies in prayer surrenders our option to act in an ungodly manner. Such prayer is the act of those who choose to place vengeance in the hands of God rather than to act vengefully themselves. In the form of a curse we recite before God feelings that we choose not to act upon. In so doing we acknowledge that the divine assessment of evil and justice surpasses all human judgment. The deepest faith yields all power to God, in trust that God will do justice in God's own way.

Cursing in the context of prayer becomes an admission of our own finiteness and shortsightedness before God. The inhumane and immoral action we urge is the product of an undeniably human reaction. The curse is an expression of our emotional ensnarement, the concomitant distorted perceptions, and hence, our inability to act justly. At the same time, it is an outcry of one who comes before God with the certainty of getting a hearing. It is a testimony of faith that we can tell God what is in the deepest recesses of our hearts and still believe that we will not be scorned or turned away. It is an act of utter confidence that we can rant and rave, express deadly sentiments, disclose the darkest side of our own interiority—and still be loved by God.

Like thanksgiving, praise, and expressions of need, curses in the psalms are a legitimate form of prayer. But they are not where prayer ends. The lament psalms that house curses against the enemy conclude with a statement of divine assurance or sometimes even a vow of praise. Hence, cursing is not a place we stay in our prayer. It is a stage we pass through on route to a more important destination where we partake of comfort and communion with the divine:

> I look to no one else in heaven,
> I delight in nothing else on earth.
> My flesh and my heart are pining with love,
> my heart's Rock, my own, God for ever!
> (Ps 73:25-26)

The One Prayer of Jesus

The power to praise is itself your gift.

E very prayer is ultimately some shadow and some part of the praise of God. To be able to praise God, of course, is itself God's gift. The fact is we do not pray on our own strength; we pray out of discovering a strength within us. We just hope that our presence, our attempt, is itself prayer. In other words, we come with a tremendous sense of humility into the act of prayer. We hope that our effort at doing certain things really is prayer offered to God.

There is only one "pray-er": that is Jesus. Anything we do is a participation in the one prayer addressed to God through Jesus. When we go to pray, we can be mindful of the Japanese Buddhist in a shrine in Kyoto, or the Hindu taking care of a poor man on the streets of Calcutta, or all the people of the world wanting to pray. In the light of the Gospel, we believe that we all share but one prayer: the prayer of Jesus. All the prayer of the whole world reaches God through Jesus because God's ultimate revelation to the human is Jesus, the Christ.

We enter into a stream, a wide stream of life. We can have a great sense of solidarity with our human family of brothers and sisters throughout the world as each tries to pray in his or her respective way. Somehow or other, the prayer of each is nudged this way and that, is celebrated this way or heard that way. Somehow or other the prayer of each is taken by Jesus and offered to the Father. When we pray we hope that we have heard the prayer of Jesus and that we are releasing his prayer into the world. As we enter into prayer, his prayer is released through us into all the nooks and crannies of this huge, complicated world of human beings.

"The power to pray is itself your gift." Who is this gift of God? Jesus! The power to pray is Jesus. Theologians speak about the "anonymous Christian" and about the convergence of all things towards God as the "omega point." We, even with our feeble efforts, are a part of that wide drama. Sometimes it is hard to keep our footing in this marvelous procession through Jesus to the Father. We want to bail out. But we were never asked to succeed. Rather we have been invited to become part of the prayer who is Jesus. "Accept my effort, Good God, and make it part of the prayer of Jesus." Deep down we know that all we do is to offer ourselves. The point is made clearly each time we pray at the Eucharist: "Pray, brothers and sisters, that our offering may be acceptable. . . ." Our offering is united to the offering of Jesus. The offering of Jesus is lovingly accepted by the Father. It becomes a sacrifice. We do

All the many ways we pray are efforts to enter the prayer of Jesus.

not presume to call *our* offering a sacrifice. Only God makes holy. Only God makes a sacrifice. Only God's action accepting our offering makes it a sacrifice. Jesus' prayer, acted out in his loving self-donation on the cross, is totally and completely acceptable to God. Jesus is God's gift. Jesus is God's power to pray. Only in his power do we pray to God. Only his prayer fully resonated with the Father's desire to redeem the world.

Perhaps all of us experience problems with prayer. These can be problems of all shapes and makes; at times, problems of faith, at other times, problems of discipline. It will help to solve some problems to underscore the humility and honesty with which we come to prayer. We place ourselves in the presence of the praying Jesus. The evangelists portray Jesus in prayer with the intention of inviting us to be with him. The simple statement: "I prayed this morning," may in fact be too proud. All I did was place myself alongside of the only pray-er there is, Jesus. This is the most exciting and beautiful part of prayer.

Recall the scene in Luke's gospel where the Pharisee and the publican pray. One of them trots up to the front of the temple and pours out his prayer, while the other one is depicted as hanging back, terribly conscious of the small offering that he is making; he knows that this whole thing of praying could fall apart in his hands at any moment. I suggest that this reaction is central to the experience of prayer. "I must decrease, he must increase." We come to pray with a deep sense of our frailty but secure in our awareness that Jesus is the pray-er to whom God has responded. God raised Jesus from the dead, sure sign that God heard the prayer of Jesus. His whole life was prayer because his whole life led to the response of God in raising him up. In prayer we are asking that we be heard as was Jesus. This brings a beautiful unity to our prayer and a deep consolation.

All the many ways we pray are efforts to enter the prayer of Jesus. It would be unwise to evaluate the various ways of praying and declare one way better than another. Each comes from our broken lives at a particular moment and is offered through Jesus who likewise knew many ways to pray to his Father. We give a very concrete interpretation to the idea that we should pray always. Many persons have experienced a whole new creativity in prayer by choosing to call upon this gift of God in a whole variety of situations. The gifts of God are not to be compared but only identified as God's gift for this time and in this place and in these circumstances of my life. So it is wise not to compare gifts of prayer but to marvel at the way in which God enables us to pray as we need at any given time. This is true also of the prayer of dryness, even the "prayer of distraction" if we are permitted to coin such a term.

Distractions in prayer are a big problem. The problem is not, however, that we have distractions but how we handle them. When we find ourselves distracted, we must reread the distraction. We must put ourselves in touch with the feelings that were experienced in the distraction. It could be that the distraction is what God wants us to bring to consciousness and surrender to him in this prayer. When we offer our distractions to God often we are offering our real selves at that moment. We are "praying from the gut." That is what God wants. God wants our real lives, here and now made part of ever-being-prayed prayer of Jesus. Our distractions are putting flesh on the prayer of Jesus now. How? We are enfleshing his prayer in the midst of that distraction. We are taking the prayer of Jesus and allowing it to become part of our world. It may mean praise, it may mean glory, it may mean healing, it may mean contrition.

All the more powerfully therefore do we conclude our time of prayer with the simple refrain: "through Jesus Christ our Lord." As I conclude my prayer with this refrain I am greatly consoled.

It is not just a nice way to end a prayer; it is the only way both to begin and to end. Often I am distracted during those prayers at the Eucharist when we recall all those for whom we pray. And before I know where I am we are praying the final doxology. If I trust Jesus praying in me, I can abandon myself in that final sweep as our prayer reaches out to God in the outstretched arms of Jesus: "Through him, with him, in him, in the unity of the Holy Spirit, all honor and glory is yours, almighty Father, for ever and ever." As the Amen of the community resounds in my ears, I can let go of my frailty and recognize again that all our strength comes from our being rooted in God. If God could be so "distracted" as to take up his abode in our midst, we can see our distractions as an invitation to take up our abode in God.

So our issue then is to be very much in touch with the prayer of Jesus, to believe deeply that we are baptized into his prayer. That prayer is going on inside of us constantly. To take time to pray is to tap into that deep vein, that deep thrust of life which is going on inside. We are in Christ. We are profoundly in Christ. We are far more in Christ than we shall ever imagine. To pray is to come home to ourselves in the depth to which we are being plunged into Christ.

Jesus' purpose in preaching the kingdom of God was to direct people again to the community of praise.

To live is to belong to the community of praise.

Now what is Jesus Christ doing in his prayer in the midst of us? He is leading us into the community of the praise of God. We become part of his prayer because his prayer is access to the community of praise. In the imagery of the Letter to the Hebrews, it can be said that Jesus leads us into the Holy of Holies. We are ushered into the presence of God. The wildest dreams of the Old Testament people are fulfilled. Many longed for the joy of going to Jerusalem. Three times a year the pious Jewish person went up to the Holy City. These visits were the high points of the year. All the remainder was lived in the valleys of expectation. Hear the psalmist say it in words of unspeakable beauty:

> For a day in thy courts is better than a thousand elsewhere.
> I would rather be a doorkeeper in the house of God than

dwell in the tents of wickedness. (Ps 84:10 RSV)

For them the annual pilgrimages to Jerusalem expressed a hope that God would grant such a request: access to God's presence in the midst of the community of praise. They set out for Jerusalem hoping and praying that they could make the journey and then be found not unworthy to enter into the very presence of God. Only the high priest could enter the Holy of Holies once a year. That is what it meant to be alive: to be given access in the community of praise to the very presence of God.

This image of the community of praise is a very powerful image. To develop it I suggest a reading of the healing of the Samaritan leper in Luke's Gospel. The story is known to all:

> On the way to Jerusalem he was passing along between Samaria and Galilee. And as he entered a village, he was met by ten lepers, who stood at a distance and lifted up their voices and said, "Jesus, Master, have mercy on us." When he saw them he said to them, "Go and show yourselves to the priests." And as they went they were cleansed. Then one of them, when he saw that he was healed, turned back, praising God with a loud voice, and he fell on his face at Jesus' feet, giving him thanks. Now he was a Samaritan. Then said Jesus, "Were not ten cleansed? Where are the nine? Was no one found to return and give praise to God except this foreigner?" And he said to him, "Rise and go your way; your faith has made you whole." (17:11-19 RSV)

A painful part of being a leper was that one was denied access to the community of praise. Jesus sent the lepers off to the priests to be readmitted to the community of praise. They discovered that they were healed while on the way there. The Samaritan did not need a priest to declare him readmitted. In a daring move he stepped out in faith and declared that the new situation in which he now stood was indeed the community of praise. He rejoiced and praised God.

Jesus' purpose in preaching the kingdom of God was to direct people again to the community of praise. He had come from that community of praise and he was leading people back to that community of praise. He would give us access to the community of praise to the glory of God. And the proclamation of the kingdom was to overcome the things that held us back from that community. Call it Satan, call it the reign of Satan, call it whatever you will. But he set himself very directly against those things that held back people from allowing that formula of praise to really resonate in their hearts.

It is interesting that the person healed is not only a leper; he is also a Samaritan. There was only one thing worse than being a leper in a Jew's eyes; that was being a Samaritan. Here there is one, both a Samaritan and a leper, who finds that all that Jerusalem ever stood for is right here now before him as he praises God for the gift of Jesus. It is wonderful! One finds a whole new redefinition of Jerusalem, of temple, of Samaritan, and of what it means to belong to the community of praise.

> How lovely is thy dwelling place, O Lord of Hosts. My soul longs, yea, faints for the courts of the Lord; my heart and flesh sing for joy to the living God. (Ps 84:1 RSV)

In all of the gospels, but especially in Luke, there is an emphasis put on the response of the people to a miracle performed in their midst. It is part of telling the story to underscore the reaction of the participants. Here Luke gives a story which outdoes all others in presenting this reaction of praise. The favorable reaction is proportionate to how much the person felt bound by the particular malady. Every miracle restores a person to the community of praise; the story of the Samaritan has as its special purpose to point out that Jesus restores one to the community of praise by removing the blocks that hold back people from access to God. The purpose of the miracles and the purpose of recounting the miracles is less proving that Jesus was divine than illustrating how Jesus gave access to the Divine. Only God can give access to Godself and Jesus as God's beloved Son rejoiced in giving to humankind access to his Father. Such access is life.

Jesus restored the dead to life as a pledge of the Father's power at work within him to lead us all finally to the praise of God's glory forever.

Pray Always:
John Cassian on Distractions

tradition

St. Paul encourages us to "pray always" (1 Th 5:17). Nowadays we usually take this invitation to mean that we should make a general intention to conform all our actions to the will of God. Once that intention is in place, we feel free to give our full attention to the tasks at hand. But does "praying always" mean nothing more than this? The starkness of the phrase and the appropriateness of its invitation to keep God, the meaning and goal of our existence, constantly before us seem to echo the Old Testament insistence which Jesus repeated when he gave the great commandment: "You shall love the Lord your God with your whole heart, and your whole soul, and with all your mind" (Mt 22:37; see Dt 6:5). But how can we do this when the experience of each and every one of us proves that we cannot keep our mind fixed on God even during the most solemn liturgies? A centipede racing across the floor or a bit of dust dancing in a sunbeam is all it takes to shift our attention away from Christ.

In the context of our daily life we can make work prayer, but can we pray and work? Given human nature and the multitude of distractions that bombard us, is it really possible for us to "pray always"? John Cassian (+435), whose writings about the years he had spent in the Egyptian desert before he settled in Marseilles made him an important influence on western monasticism, grappled with this problem.[1] Although Cassian had monks in mind when he wrote, I think he has something to say to anyone trying to live a life focused on God amidst the distractions of the modern world.

Distractions in the Desert

The 4th-century hermits, who set out to live for God alone in the bleak solitude of the Egyptian desert, took the command to "pray always" quite literally. They did, of course, strive to conform all their actions to God's will, but for them "praying always" meant an at-oneness with God that implied more than a general intention to make God the ultimate goal of their actions. Their ideal was to be so centered on God that, in all the events of life, love rather than concupiscence would be the spontaneous reaction of their being. They felt that only when they had been transformed by grace and brought into harmony with God through a process of moral rectification would they be able to obey the apostolic instruction to pray always. This meant that they had to enter into a long therapeutic program to heal the moral disorders that literally distracted them from God and neighbor.[2]

However, the Egyptian hermits who had left the hustle and bustle of village life to dedicate themselves to God and the healing of the wounds of sin within them were disconcerted to find that, despite their goodwill and long years of asceticism, they were still unable to focus on God. Not only did the desert have its own distractions, but the images and sounds of the past refused to be suppressed. Cassian himself complains that he cannot get the stories and verses that were drummed into him in school out of his mind. They keep popping up in his memory at inappropriate moments.[3]

All of this worry about the inability to attain an impossible ideal may seem to us to be much ado about nothing since, in our practical way, we accept ideals as exactly that and get on with the task of making the world a better place to live. But this turn toward action was not available to those who felt they had been called to be alone with God in the desert. Consequently, the senior monks or fathers had to rescue their disciples from the restlessness and despair that would inevitably follow from their inability to attain the ideal that had, in fact, led them to embrace their fiercely austere life in the first place.

The frustration that could overtake a young monk when he

began to feel that he was pursuing an impossible ideal is evident in the reply that Cassian and his traveling companion Germanus make to Abba Serenus in Conference 7 when he asks about the state of their souls. They complain that, after all this time in the desert, they should have come to perfection but that, in fact, all they have done is learn they are incapable of attaining it. They ask, therefore, "What is the good of having learned what is best, if it cannot be attained even when known?"[4] The root of their problem is the constant presence of distractions pulling them this way and that: "For when we have been feeling that the aim of our heart was directed towards what we purposed, insensibly the mind returns to its previous wandering thoughts and slips back with a more violent rush, and is taken up with daily distractions and incessantly drawn away by numberless things that take it captive, so that we almost despair of the improvements which we long for, and all these observances seem useless."[5] Indeed, distractions seem so persistently present that Cassian and Germanus despairingly conclude that they are an inescapable, built-in feature of human nature.

"What is the good of having learned what is best, if it cannot be attained even when known?"

Abba Serenus disagrees and insists that the wandering of our mind should not be blamed on God or his creatures. Although he concedes that the mind is naturally active and flits from one thing to another if it is not focused, he emphasizes that we are responsible for our thoughts. We are not helpless victims of external or demonic forces. He admits, however, that the degree of concentration Cassian and Germanus yearn for cannot be attained "without great interior labor."[6]

Can Distractions Be Overcome?

But can we ever really fix our mind on God perfectly, it being understood, of course, that nothing human is ever truly perfect? Cassian, who returns to the issue of our distracted condition perhaps more frequently than to any other topic,[7] is well aware that we must contend with a vast array of distractions. Not only does our mind move from one thing to another in an endless chain of associations, but we are subject to inexplicable mood changes and tossed this way and that by what goes on in the church and world. Even when we do manage to keep our mind on spiritual matters, the run-on association of images continues as we leapfrog from one scriptural reference to another, from one idea to the next.

The minor details which shape our life also seem to conspire to keep us off balance. It was no different in the desert. The more advanced solitaries may have developed a certain equilibrium before "the slings and arrows of outrageous fortune," but not even a desert dweller could avoid all domestic tasks. The simple work they did—usually rope braiding or basket weaving—may not have distracted them from prayer, but other tasks such as the need to build a new cell or to repair the old one required their full attention and thus interfered with their focus on God. But these disturbances were probably minor compared with the distractions of taking care of their daily needs and extending hospitality to any visitor who might happen along.

At this point we have to be careful not to let the discomfort we feel over this apparent conflict between the love of God and the love of neighbor prompt us to dismiss Cassian as a twisted ascetic whose singleness of mind kept him from grasping the interrelationship of the two great commandments. In fact, he attaches tremendous importance to hospitality and emphasizes that it is inhuman and un-Christian for a hermit to cling to his normal regime when an unexpected guest knocks at his door.[8] There are many references in Cassian's conferences to the tender regard with which the fathers cared for the guests who sought them out.[9]

Distraction and Sin

Cassian, then, is not driving a wedge between the love of God and the love of neighbor which Christ made one. He is, however, taking a hard look at the dichotomy between the call to pray always and our inability to do so. He is bluntly stating a fact: many of the virtuous and meritorious works we perform distract us from prayer. He puts this in the strongest language possible when he says that we *sin* when we attend to needs and neighbors and the business of daily life and are thereby necessarily distracted from prayer. I have italicized *sin* because Cassian makes it clear that we do not incur guilt when we do what the love of God and neighbor obliges us to do. Nonetheless, *sin* is the appropriate word here. Cassian is straining to emphasize that even in this virtuous "work" we experience the damage that sin has done to our nature. The integrity of the relationship that bound humanity simultaneously to God, neighbor, and nature in the Garden of Eden has been fragmented. As a consequence of Adam's curse (Gn 3:17-19) we cannot, in fact, turn fully toward any work that absorbs our attention without turning away from a full, conscious awareness of God.

I reiterate that Cassian makes it very clear that we sin in the normal sense of the word when we fail to help our neighbor or neglect our own physical well-being.[10] Nevertheless, when we try to do good, we discover that we are wounded, somehow, in our very nature. Even good acts are marred by our inherited inability to work without being distracted from God. In Cassian's view, the curse that turns work into a bitter, alienating business extends to all our doing. He realizes that we were made to work and that we must work to live and develop. But he also sees that it is precisely by working—by doing what is good and necessary—that we experience the inability of our fallen nature to maintain its focus on God in the midst of activity.

Does it follow, then, that the invitation to pray always and the command to love God with our whole mind, strength, and soul merely serve to keep the spectra of our sinfulness before our eyes? How Christlike can we be, how perfect (Mt 5:48), if we cannot fix our internal compass on the Father as Jesus did?

A Readjusting Formula

Given the multitude of distractions which tug at us every moment, how realistic is it to assume that we shall ever succeed in holding our mind fixed on God, the be-all and end-all of our existence? John Cassian recommends that we move in this direction by using the familiar biblical verse "God, come to my aid; Lord, make haste to help me"(Ps 70:2) in the midst of all our distractions. We have to be careful, however, to understand correctly what Cassian thinks this repetition of "God, come to my aid . . ." accomplishes.

Nowadays, because of the popularity of the Jesus prayer and John Main's promotion of the use of a mantra as a means of contemplation, a reader is likely to presume that, because Cassian recommends that we say the phrase so constantly that it vibrates in us even when we are asleep,[11] he is using the repeated biblical verse in the same way Benedictine John Main uses a mantra. (Main recommends the repetition of a freely chosen word or verse of Scripture for twenty or thirty minutes twice a day to promote interior quiet and contemplation.)[12] In this anachronistic perception of a 5th-century writer, "God, come to my aid . . ." becomes an incantation with a power of its own. But the text of Conference 10 suggests something else. For ninety-nine lines Cassian enumerates the multitude of distractions that lead us astray. Everything is here: mood changes, the ups and downs of fortune, the upsets of daily life, the pull of the passions within us. In good times and bad, winning or losing, we are in danger of forgetting God. Nothing we experience is free of this danger.

Sin is distraction writ large, and we encounter the secondary effects of sin day in and day out in the distractions which pull us off course.

Time and again, then, we need something to pull us back on course. Cassian and Germanus recognize this need, and in Conference 10 Abba Isaac offers a specific biblical quotation as a sort of "adjusting formula" they can use in all the circumstances of life. The reason the phrase is repeated over and over again is our ongoing need to be set straight.

It is important to note that the phrase does not work by itself, as it were. It is used to combat distractions and the alienation they represent. One could, I believe, make a good argument for the premise that sin, for Cassian, is whatever fractures the community of love: sin is what separates us from God and neighbor and destroys the integrity of our being. Healing, conversely, restores the integrity of our relationship to God, neighbor, and self. It is legitimate to say, therefore, that sin is distraction writ large and that we encounter the secondary effects of sin day in and day out in the distractions which pull us off course.

Cassian, remember, is not arguing that we can banish distractions by the repetition of a short biblical phrase. He is not putting forward a technique to clear the mind. He is, rather, laying down a chalk line so that we can keep ourselves straight in

Russell • Pray Always

all the meanderings of life. The specific formula works, not by virtue of its continual repetition, but because of the spiritual attitude it fosters.

What it proclaims, in fact, is the exact opposite of the independent, alienated stance of sin. In every act and experience of life, it insists upon our need of God and our filial relationship of dependence on him. It sums up the fundamental teaching of Scripture boldly proclaimed in the life and cross of Christ himself.

The formula Cassian recommends is not a poor, thin remnant of Scripture. He emphasizes, in fact, how rich it is in content and how thought provoking. It does not empty the mind; it fills it. The thoughts it drives out by a process of substitution are those which divert the mind from God. Instead of drawing attention back to a kind of mystical void, it serves as a path to the riches of Scripture. This scriptural wealth, however, is not viewed in all its variety, as happens in the ordinary practice of *lectio divina*. It is seen, instead, in terms of its essential teaching: that our relation to God is one of total dependence.

Development of a Filial Relation

This attention to Scripture's essential teaching is the exact opposite of the sinful, independent, separating tendency of distraction. It fosters a radical turnaround. By going straight to the essence of Scripture, the monk is brought to the status of the poor in spirit who have none but God on whom to rely.

Gradually the use of this "readjusting formula," which leaves no room for distractions to expand, increases a monk's filial relationship to God, inculcating in him the essential spiritual attitude of Scripture until he prays the psalms, we might say, as though he wrote them. The soul is led by grace to an intimate union with God, whom it familiarly recognizes as its Father.[13] It is lifted up "to that ineffable prayer which rises above all human consciousness, with no voice sounding, no tongue moving, no words uttered. The soul lights up with heavenly illumination and no longer employs constricted, human speech. All sensibility is gathered together and, as though from some very abundant source, the soul breaks forth richly, bursts out unspeakably to God."[14] In Conference 10, Cassian describes this prayer as "a fiery outbreak, an undescribable exaltation." The mind comes to this, he notes, "to the extent that the Lord permits."[15]

In Cassian's scheme of things the elevation to contemplation normally comes, if it comes at all, at the end of a long process of purification. In an accurate simile, Cassian compares the mind, as God created it, to a feather that floats upward on the breeze toward its creator.[16] Unfortunately, in its present unhealthy state, the mind is weighed down by moisture and dust. It can be what it was meant to be only if it recovers its buoyancy so that it can once again move spontaneously toward God.

The use of the short invocatory prayer he recommends certainly plays a role in this revitalization, but Cassian never neglects the larger picture. This is strikingly evident in the last section of Conference 10 where Cassian, after recommending the use of the short prayer to refocus the mind amidst the distractions of life, states that three things stabilize the wandering mind: vigils, meditation, and prayer. But he is careful to set even these specific exercises in the context of the monastic regime. They are useless unless the monk really accepts the normal conditions of monastic life and does what he can to be free of worldly cares. Cassian's point is that how we are before we kneel down determines our state of mind when we formally enter into prayer.[17]

We can understand him better if we remember that prayer is both a centrifugal force spiraling from the center to influence the whole of life and the focal point of the concentric circling which pulls all things together in praise. Although Cassian's recommendation that a short phrase be repeated over and over again might suggest that this prayer has a quasisacramental power to influence the whole of life, it actually functions primarily as an element in the concentric effort to make life outside of formal prayer as prayerful as possible.

Relevance for Today

How is the teaching of John Cassian relevant to life today? If we translate his teaching into terms applicable to nonmonastic Christian life in the modern world, we can say that the recollection of the biblical phrase he recommends brings us back constantly to the poverty of spirit which recognizes our inherent distractedness and our need of God's help. These frequent cries for assistance bolster the relationship to God which we foster in a more formal way by setting aside specific periods of time for daily meditation.

Cassian remarks that the "God, come to my aid" formula so effectively recalls the riches of Scripture that even the illiterate are not cut off from spiritual advancement.[18] The point could also be made that the phrase overcomes not only the handicap of those who cannot read but also the disability of those who are unable to give the Bible the attention a monk is able to give it. In the context of a life in which an individual strives to make love rather than concupiscence his or her spontaneous reaction in all circumstances, the specific verse from Scripture that Cassian recommends can be a powerful instrument against the distractions which press in on every side.

But the hard truth, when all is said and done, is that we cannot fix our mind on God as we should for the simple reason that we cannot eradicate the effects of the sin of our first parents. If we could, we would in effect save ourselves and have no need of God's grace and mercy. Therefore, the only way we can keep our mind fixed on God as things now stand is by turning our very distractions into an incentive to prayer. It may well be that, in time, grace will so increase our participation in the life of the Persons of the Trinity that we will, indeed, succeed in responding to the invitation to "pray always" in the contemplative union Cassian describes so vividly. Meanwhile, to recall in good times and bad the words "God, come to my aid; Lord, make haste to help me" can transform even our inevitable failure to love God with our "whole mind" into an act of worship.

Notes

[1] An overview of the life and thought of John Cassian is provided by Owen Chadwick in his introduction to John Cassian, *Conferences*, trans. Colm Luibheid (New York: Paulist Press, 1985), pp. 1-36. Hereafter, *Conferences*.

[2] I have dealt with the desert ideal of peace of heart and the program to attain it in *Healing the Heart: Desert Wisdom for a Busy World* (Ottawa: Novalis, 1993) and also in "John Cassian on a Delicate Subject," *Cistercian Studies Quarterly* 27 (1992): 1-12.

[3] *The Works of John Cassian*, trans. Edgar C.S. Gibson, vol. 11 of *A Select Library of Nicene and Post-Nicene Fathers of the Christian Church*, 2nd series, ed. Henry Wace and Philip Schaff (Oxford: Parker, 1894 [reprint: Grand Rapids, Michigan: Eerdmans, 1964]). Conference 14, 12, p. 441. Hereafter, *Works*.

[4] *Works*, Conference 7, 3, p. 362.

⁵ Ibid.

⁶ This free translation is an effort to capture the meaning of *contritione* in the Latin phrase "Sine ingenti cordis contritione." The term suggests the sorrow, contrition, and labor involved in the task of setting the heart straight.

⁷ Owen Chadwick, *John Cassian: A Study in Primitive Monasticism* (Cambridge: University Press, 1950), pp. 140-141.

⁸ *Works*, Conference 21, 14, p. 509.

⁹ See, e.g., the solicitude of Abba Moses for his tired visitors in *Conferences*, Conference 1, 23, p. 59, and the description of the festive meal served by Abba Serenus in *Works*, Conference 8, 1, p. 375.

¹⁰ *Works*, Conference 21, 14, p. 509.

¹¹ *Conferences*, Conference 10, 10, p. 136.

¹² John Main, *The Inner Christ* (London: Darton, Longman and Todd, 1987), p. vi. Some of Main's supporters tend to exaggerate the parallel between Main and Cassian in their eagerness to demonstrate that the mode of prayer Main advocates is authentically Christian. Consider, for example, the following statement by Paul T. Harris in "Silent Teaching: The Life of Dom John Main," Spirituality Today 40 (1988), p. 324: "What Cassian had learned from the desert fathers . . . and what St. Benedict learned from Cassian was what John Main had learned from a Hindu monk three years before becoming a Benedictine monk"; and the claim by Neil McKenty in *In the Stillness Dancing: The Journey of John Main* (London: Darton, Longman and Todd, 1986), p. 151, that "about 1,400 years ago Benedict sent his followers to John Cassian to learn to pray. Near the end of the twentieth century John Main did likewise." See John Main's own essay on John Cassian in *Inner Christ*, pp. 73-76.

¹³ *Conferences*, Conference 9, 18, p. 112.

¹⁴ *Conferences*, Conference 9, 25, p. 116.

¹⁵ *Conferences*, Conference 10, 11, p. 138.

¹⁶ *Conferences*, Conference 9, 4, p. 103.

¹⁷ *Conferences*, Conference 10, 14, pp. 139-140.

¹⁸ *Conferences*, Conference 10, 14, p. 140.

An Augustinian Way of Meditation

*M*ost people are dissatisfied with the way they pray. They moan and groan about their supposed lack of progress and treat themselves like lost causes.

> I don't know how to pray! How can I improve the way I pray? I would return to prayer if I thought I would succeed this time. Is there anyone around who can teach me how to pray?

Those who utter such cries for help must realize that they are not alone in their distress. We all tend to be concerned and to feel inadequate when it comes to prayer. We keep searching for something or someone to help us improve. We have turned to the East and to the West. Those of us who turn to the East for help may sometimes believe that Western traditions have nothing to offer; and, even among followers of Western spirituality, one of the surest and greatest sources, St. Augustine, is too often overlooked. Too many of us have forgotten that he has nourished countless people during the sixteen centuries that separate us from him. Most of the great mystics, like St. John of the Cross and St. Teresa of Avila, turned to him for help and direction. He still has the power to nourish us today. His spirit and experience can serve as both guide and model to anyone seriously determined to give prayer another try.

St. Augustine is arguably the greatest Father of the Church. He influenced all aspects of church life for hundreds of years after his death. His genius is due in large part to his keen sense of observation and wonderful power of amazement. His writings keep reminding us that he never missed a detail of anything he turned his mind to; nor was he ever a passive observer of what he saw. He marveled over everything from the fussiness of a baby to the deepest mysteries of God. These two traits helped him immensely in his life of prayer. He never tired of looking at himself, the world, and God. His intuition was that the three were meant to relate to one another in the human heart as they relate to one another in God. His whole life became a deep yearning for God above all else and for the gift to see all things as God sees them. He achieved this through the constant practice of bringing everything he experienced inward to his heart and upward toward God. Doing as he did will help us to pray as he prayed and to walk along our restless way as he walked along his, with the great desire to rest in God in trust and confidence.

The more St. Augustine advanced on his spiritual journey, the simpler his life and vision became. More and more, he saw things as God sees them and judged them as he judges them. However, as we try to understand what he did and to outline a method of meditation that emulates the one he practiced, we likely need to think of his more integrated movements in terms of the more separated ones that we tend to experience one after another until our vision becomes more focused. We do this with the Augustinian method of meditation that we present here. We distinguish three movements of heart and mind that everyone recognizes as Augustinian. They are readily understood and practiced. Remembering that for Augustine life is all that we see, hear, and experience, we come to the first movement *outward* which beckons us to live in a reflective way all of life to the fullest. The second, in response to Augustine's constant call to return to our hearts, is a movement *inward* to the core of our being and to Christ who dwells there. This return to our hearts is an effort to internalize what we experience and also to learn from the Lord who dwells there and who plays the role of the teacher within. The third movement is a movement *upward* toward God as we silently allow him to transform our limited vision through contact with his infinite wisdom.

Three Keys of Augustinian Spirituality

Before explaining each one of these movements in some detail, it will be helpful to recall three underlying principles of St. Augustine's spirituality which are the keys to our deeper understanding of what St. Augustine did and of what we are expected to do as we meditate in his way. The first is interiority, the second is rest, and the third is his constant insistence that everything outward be brought inward, and that everything of an inferior order be brought upward to a superior order.

The first key to Augustinian spirituality is interiority. For St. Augustine, this means that it is within us and not outside us that life with God becomes a reality. He takes seriously all the texts of Scripture that refer to the divine life that Christians are graced to share with God through their baptism, from St. Paul's consecrated expression of being "in Christ" and of Christ being "in us," to St. John's insistence that we abide in God as God abides in us. St. Augustine takes the promise of the inner spring of water that Jesus made to the Samaritan woman to refer to his own life in us: "The water that I shall give will become a spring of water, welling up to eternal life" (Jn 4:14). It is within us that we live in him and he in us, there that we meet him at the very core of our being. That is why St. Augustine keeps insisting that "we return to our hearts" where God is always present and ready to receive us with great love and mercy. It is there that Jesus plays the role of the "teacher within," waiting to teach us his ways. It is there also that he plays the role of physician of our souls, curing our ills and weaknesses.

> *The goal of every Christian's restless seeking is to rest in God.*

The second key to St. Augustine's spirituality is rest. He begins his *Confessions* with a wonderful summary of what the inner life means to him. "You have made us and directed us toward yourself and our heart is restless until it rests in you" (*Conf.* I, 1). The goal of every Christian's restless seeking is to rest in God. This is why human beings are created. This is their call: to rest in their Creator. Our saint contrasts rest in God to the restlessness he experienced when he searched for happiness outside of God. The more he sought happiness in worldly pleasures, in wealth, in power, and in honor, the more he realized how empty and unfulfilled he really was. The more he searched in places that did not satisfy him, the more restless he became. When he finally turned to God, he realized that God is what he had been searching for all his life. In God alone would he find happiness and fulfillment. In him alone would he find rest, the rest of being at home with God.

The third key to St. Augustine's spirituality is his understanding that everything that he experiences has to be brought to his heart to be interiorized. Everything outward must be brought inward (*ab exteriore ad interiorem*), and everything of an inferior order must be brought up to a superior order (*ab inferiore ad superiorem*).

Having recalled the three keys of Augustinian spirituality that underlie the method of meditation presented here, we can now turn our attention to its three movements. As we proceed, please note that we speak of movements rather than steps as do most methods of meditation. The reason for this is that St. Augustine sees prayer as the action of God within us. For him, prayer is something we experience rather than something we do. Prayer is mostly an inner movement that brings God into our lives in order to transform us and bring us from our limited vision to the limitless breadth of his vision, from our restlessness into his rest.

The Movement Outward

For St. Augustine, everything that God has made calls us to return to him. All of creation is meant to remind us of the Creator and to make us yearn for him. We run the risk of stopping halfway and settling for created things that do not have the power to satisfy us. Only their source and creator can do that. This is the big sin of God's people in the Old Testament. They settle for the gift and forget the Giver. In spite of the bad press that St. Augustine is often given in this matter, he does not tend to see creation as something evil. He sees it as a means and a way to God. Among many possible quotations, we present this simple one from the *Confessions*:

> Let my soul rouse itself, Lord, from weariness, lean on your creation, and hobble toward you who made it all. (*Conf.* V, 1)

What we call discursive meditation is for St. Augustine a dialogue with God and one in which God has said the first word. St. Augustine sees this as an invitation from God to turn our attention to him. The next step is ours. How are we to respond to what God tells us through his creation and through his revealed Word? He awaits our reaction. St. Augustine is a wonderful responder. He sings the praises of the God who made everything that is good and bemoans with a heavy heart everything that is bad. Though we can use any experience of God's creation in our meditation, the Scriptures are the most widely used. For this discussion we will take the Scriptures as an example. In this paper we will concentrate on how we respond to God's Word spoken to us in the Bible. In meditation we choose a particular passage of Scripture, such as the Gospel of the day, and we bring the exterior gift of its message inward to our hearts and upward toward God in order that we may be formed by a power greater than our own.

> My soul, you too must listen to the Word of God. For the Word himself calls you to return. In him is the place of peace that cannot be disturbed, and he will not withhold himself from you unless you withhold your love from him. (*Conf.* IV, 11)

The work of this first movement is largely one of observation. We take a specific passage of Scripture such as an event in the life of one of the biblical characters, a parable or a miracle account, and we make a mental effort to take in all the details that are found there. We try to stay with the story as it is, without projecting ourselves into it. Yet we do more than absorb the text as though we are trying to take a mental photograph of what we are reading. We also take note of what we see as we accept the story as it is because this is the story that has the power to work in us. We are after the Word of God, and not something of our own creation. All we bring of ourselves is our power of observation and our gift of amazement as we reflect on the Word of God and see in it a call to allow ourselves to be changed by the power of this Word. Through the passage we have focused on, we hear God's call to us today. This is the call from without that we are meant to bring within.

Another way of speaking about this first movement is to see it as an objective effort to imprint upon our memories every detail of the story as we find it on the printed page. We do this because we want to hear, in the revealed Word, God's call to respond and change. The Word of God must not be reworked into something that we think he should have said. God's Word as it stands has the power to work in us and to transform us.

The Movement Inward

We respond to the call to return to our hearts in order to learn from the teacher-within by bringing to our deepest core what we have been able to absorb from the story. We go from the text to our heart to learn from the teacher-within who is always present to us and ready to heal us and teach us whenever we return to him. It is from him that we need to hear what he would have us learn today.

Our first reading gave us a grasp of the Gospel message as we find it on the printed page. After reading with the eyes of our bodies or hearing with the ears of our bodies, we turn to listening and hearing with the eyes and ears of our hearts. It is at the very core of our being that we learn the truth of what the Gospel passage teaches. St. Augustine liked to remind those who listened to his sermons: "I fill the ears of your heads, but you have Someone within you who fills the ears of your hearts." St. Augustine expresses this truth in his reflections on Scripture in Book XI of his *Confessions*:

> Your Word made himself audible to the bodily ears of men, so that they should believe in him and, by looking for him within themselves, should find him in eternal Truth, where the one good Master teaches all who listen to him. It is there that I hear your voice, O Lord, telling me that only a master who really teaches us really speaks to us. But who is our teacher except the Truth which never changes? Even when we learn from created things, which are subject to change, we are led to the Truth which does not change. (*Conf.* XI, 8)

Nowhere does St. Augustine show more clearly than in this theme of the teacher-within that all of his spirituality is Christ-centered. From the very beginning of his description of the spiritual journey to the loftiest considerations on union with the Blessed Trinity, St. Augustine never loses his focus on Christ. This is well-expressed in his six-word summary of the spiritual journey: "*Per Christum Hominem ad Christum Deum*," Through Christ-Man to Christ-God. We meet Jesus in all the incarnational details of his earthly life and death and allow him to bring us with him to his resurrection and glorification through which we share more fully in the life of the Blessed Trinity.

As we consider the teacher-within at work in us, we need to know what kind of activity takes place in the depths of our being. St. Augustine likes to attribute to the heart a whole set of faculties all its own and similar to those of the body. The heart has ears and a mouth, for instance. He likes to say that we listen to God with "the ears of the heart." This is the kind of metaphorical approach he uses in this beautiful passage of the *Confessions*:

> I have learned to love you late, Beauty at once so ancient and so new! I have learned to love you late! You were within

> me, and I was in the world outside myself. I searched for you
> outside myself and, disfigured as I was, I fell upon the lovely
> things of your creation. You were with me, but I was not
> with you. The beautiful things of this world kept me far
> from you, and yet, if they had not been in you, they would
> have had no being at all. You called me; you cried aloud to
> me; you broke my barrier of deafness. You shone upon me;
> your radiance enveloped me; you put my blindness to flight.
> You shed your fragrance about me; I drew breath and now
> I gasp for your sweet odor. I tasted you, and now I hunger
> and thirst for you. You touched me, and I am inflamed with
> love of your peace. (*Conf.* X, 27)

All of this should alert us to the fact that communication at the
heart level is not the same as that at the head level. When we
communicate intellectually with someone, we deal with words
and ideas. Communication of the heart deals rather with symbols, attitudes, sentiments, and interior dispositions and prepares
us for God's gifts. In this second movement of our meditation,
Christ is communicating with us in terms of openness, freedom,
and peace, but also in terms of doubt, darkness, and resistance.
The process is sometimes one of pain because of the changes that
must take place before we are ready for a particular gift the Lord
has in mind for us.

Movement Upward

A rather unsatisfactory translation of the famous "*Fecisti nos ad
Te*" of Augustine is: "You have made us for yourself." The full
meaning behind his words is lost in such a translation. There is
too much left out. What Augustine wants to express is that the
soul is weighted toward God in a sort of spiritual gravitational
pull. Its proper level is divine, and it is uneasy and restless until
that level is reached. The full reality of our being is that God has
made us, oriented us, directed us, and set us in motion towards
himself. What we are doing in this third stage of our meditation
is to keep ourselves open to the full promise of these words about
our being drawn so powerfully toward God.

We must be careful in this final Movement of our meditation
not to think that in Movement II we go inward to the core of our
being where we meet Christ and in Movement III we lift our
hearts up to another place in order to find God. The reason we
went inward originally was to find Christ present in us, so it can-

not be that we are called to leave him in the following step. To have Christ is to have God. It seems safer to think in terms of allowing Christ to bring us more deeply within himself where he helps us enter more fully into the trinitarian mystery of God. It is as though we leave time to enter into the very eternity of God. Our attitude becomes one of awe, silent adoration, and praise.

If our vocabulary changes as we go from Movement I to Movement II, we must expect yet another change when we move on to Movement III. As we enter a loftier realm, everything is deeper, more silent, and more shrouded in mystery. We might not be conscious of any action on God's part and, if we are, might not comprehend its meaning. In Book IX of his *Confessions*, Augustine describes an intense moment of prayer with his mother, St. Monica. They have been wondering about the nature of heavenly bliss. Their conversation soon reflects their own desire for something of that bliss already here on earth: "The flame of love burned stronger in us and raised us higher towards the eternal God" (*Conf.* IX, 10). This finally leads them to the ultimate moment of their experience. "And while we spoke of the eternal Wisdom, longing for it and straining for it with all the strength of our hearts, for one fleeting instant we reached and touched it" (*Conf.* IX, 10).

Immediately after this ecstatic moment, St. Augustine and St. Monica reflected on what had happened. Some fifteen years later, after he became a bishop, he still carried the impression of that journey into silence, and he wrote about that blessed event to stress the importance of a silence that was heavy with God, and of a kind of speech different from that of ideas and words. What Augustine understands best is that everything created, including human thought and feelings, has to grow silent when God is contacted at his own level. Referring to the creatures of the universe, St. Augustine continues:

> Suppose, we said, that after giving us this message and bidding us listen to him who made them [the creatures of the universe], they fell silent and he alone should speak to us, not through them, but in his own voice, so that we should hear him speaking, not by any tongue of the flesh or by an angel's voice, not in the sound of thunder or in some veiled parable, but in his own voice, the voice of the one we love in all these created things; suppose that we heard him himself, with none of these things between us and him, just as in that brief moment my mother and I had reached out in

thought and touched the eternal Wisdom that abides over all things. (*Conf.* IX, 10)

It is difficult to imagine a clearer description of a human being's positive silence before God. Later on in his *Confessions*, St. Augustine addresses God as the Truth that "has walked everywhere at my side, teaching me what to seek and what to avoid, whenever I laid before you the things that I was able to see in this world below and asked you to counsel me. I heard you teaching me and I heard the commands you gave" (*Conf.* X, 40).

It is important to keep in mind that St. Augustine probably never meditated in quite this structured and organized way by going through each of these movements in a limited and specified time; such methods only came much later in the life of the church. Remember, too, that it is impossible for anyone else to speak of these different movements as richly as he does. To try to explain him as we have is necessarily to betray him. Nevertheless, it is hoped that what has been said so far will give us a feeling of the rhythm of these three movements when we try to bring them together into a structured method of meditation.

There remains an important question to consider. How can this Augustinian way of praying best be practiced today? After we have decided to meditate this way, there is the matter of time. Anywhere from thirty minutes to an hour must be set aside, preferably at the same time each day. Once that much discipline has been established, there is a lot of freedom as to the amount of time we stay with each movement. At the beginning, especially for those new at meditation, it is supposed that more time will be spent on Movement I, less on Movement II, and least on Movement III. However, either because of experience or disposition, the time a movement holds us could be reversed. The ideal is to come to the point of surrendering as long as we can to Movement III. St. Augustine himself would likely have spent whatever time he had for prayer on one or the other of these movements and would have been most pleased with his prayer when he had settled into Movement III.

The ideal for us too, of course, is to spend as much time as we can in the depth of the Trinitarian mystery. We need to ask how St. Augustine did it and to try to do the same. We find an important clue to his secret by looking at what he did when he was not at prayer. He was constantly in pursuit of God and he came to realize that God was in constant pursuit of him. St. Augustine writes this brief prayer in his *Soliloquies*: *"Noverim me! Noverim te!"* "Let me know myself that I may know thee!" This same book contains a dialogue between Augustine and Reason that is very revealing of the context of our saint's prayer life. In it we read:

> Augustine: I desire to know God and my soul.
> Reason: Nothing more?
> Augustine: Absolutely nothing. (*Sol.* II).

These brief quotations show us that St. Augustine is a wonderful model of prayer for us. The most obvious way to learn about him is to keep reading his *Confessions*, in which he praises God for all the graces he has received. The habit of reading this book a few minutes each day is a powerful incentive to devote our energies to prayer the way he did. What we find is a beautiful example of St. Augustine's own practice of the three movements of the Augustinian way. In Books I to IX, he looks at his past life and observes the details and, in particular, the ways in which he hears God calling him back to him. Book X deals with the present and with what St. Augustine knows about God and his ways now that he has returned to his heart and allowed himself to be healed by the Eternal Physician and taught by the teacher-within. Books XI to XIII look to the future and to what God the Creator has in mind for him in this life, and especially in eternity. St. Augustine has come to see his immortal life in the light of his eternity. He has understood that everything that God does is part of his creative plan as well as a revelation of the mercy out of which creation came to be. The more he came to see that God called him to a life of union with him, the more he realized that God would not keep any of the mystery of creation from him.

With St. Augustine as our guide, and with his *Confessions* in hand, we are ready to use the method of meditation that his writings suggest to us. Each day, at the time we have set aside for this exercise, we begin by reading a passage of Scripture and begin our work trusting that the Lord will do his. In a first Movement we ponder the personal call of God's Word to us. In a second Movement, we bring our reflection into our hearts and to Christ, the teacher-within. There we allow him to form us that we may become all that we are called to be. In a third and final Movement, we allow Christ to bring us to his depths, to the perfect rest of the Blessed Trinity itself, and we open ourselves up to its eternal silence and wellspring of life.

Appreciating God through Creation

"*B*lessed are you, Lord, God of all creation. Through your goodness we have this bread to offer, which earth has given and human hands have made." This familiar prayer has all the ring of a traditional Jewish prayer: blessing God for creation. In the prayer we praise God not only for the raw material of creation, "which earth has given," but also for its human transformation. Then we offer this "processed" creation to God; we gratefully acknowledge God, his creation, and our role in cocreating.

People who practice prayer through creation find that their prayer lives are enriched by their wonderment at the goodness and vastness of the creating God, who works our redemption only within his creation. If our prayer does not have an anchor in creation, we run the risk of seeing the creative initiative of the Father one-sidedly as residing in the past, not realizing that the redemption is part of God's ongoing creation. In this article I wish to draw attention to some of the deeper aspects of prayer through creation.[1]

All of us, for example, can be inspired by the mystery and beauty of a magnificent sunset or by the refined delicacy of a flower petal. Almost automatically we can be caught up into the mystery, the awesomeness and friendliness, of God. On the other hand, we readily ignore the commonplace: a stone or a weed. I enter a plea for the recognition of the commonplace. Beauty is certainly something we can praise God for, but are there other praiseworthy values as well?

It is said of St. Clare that, when asked why she had a small garden plot of roses and another one of weeds (which she equally delighted in), she replied that a weed is part of God's creation too. Unlike St. Clare we find that the unusual, like a grand sunset, is typically more apt to draw us to God than the usual. Familiarity often does lead to the proverbial contempt. What I put forward in this article is an appeal to look both at and beyond the sunset, stone, and weed and to appreciate the dignity and role that all created things, usual or unusual, ordinary or beautiful, can play in helping us pray better. With these goals in mind, I introduce three strands of an understanding of creation prayer that may help us in our own prayer, and I follow up with some observations of how the best exponent of this sort of prayer, St. Francis of Assisi, lived it.

Primitive Religiosity

Look for a moment at the religiosity of "primitive" peoples. Their culture and religion are intertwined. They do not treat created things in the compartmentalized way we treat them. They are close to nature. Life is a unity. They are very much in touch with the created world around them. For them, each object, each function has a sacramental glow: things are sacred. Everything is a manifestation of the holy, a junction point of human existence and the divine. The transcendent not only is present passively in the created world, but also works there in power. No clear distinction is drawn between the physical order and divine activity.

So deep and universal is this reverence for creation that it seems to have been built into our psyche eons ago by our Creator. It lies at the basis of all human religiosity. It strikes a chord even in city dwellers whose tempo of life is far removed from the rhythm of nature. I wonder whether we marginalize this primitive and deep reverence for creation because the rituals we associate with it, its human expressions, are judged pagan and animist and therefore unworthy of our attention in spite of our knowing that an imperfect outward expression does not necessarily invalidate the perfection of the inner reality. Nevertheless, the term *primitive* still conjures up in our minds the pejorative notions of being unformed, uncivilized, or uncultured. Perhaps there is a need for us to reexamine more finely the submerged aspects of our psyche, which are after all the driving and motivating forces of our emotions and personality and of our modes of thinking and action.

Instead of drinking from the wells of a primitive human awe of creation, we have benumbed our awe. We have "civilized" creation, trying to control it, minimize it, transform it, provide it with a new set of clothes, as Professor Higgins did for Eliza in Shaw's *Pygmalion*. But no matter how strenuously we avoid it, the primitive in all its unpredictable power lies just beneath the surface, seeking expression. We stunt our growth if we do not bring to our prayer this primitive energy, this contemplative awareness, this gift of God. We easily shy away from it because it not only beckons but threatens and that makes us afraid. We are caught up in the world of mystery, the mystery of the transcendent, powers beyond us that cannot even hope to control or understand. It affronts our sense of self-sufficiency, so we try to reject it. But mystery always demands a response. At the heart of mystery is God. Did not St. Ignatius rediscover God through gazing at the stars when he lay bedridden after being wounded in battle?

From a Hebrew Point of View

The Hebrews lived surrounded by primitive religions. They respected creation, not by making gods out of it as neighboring tribes did, but by directly linking it to the one God, the Father of all. In the Hebrew sense, creation is *spoken* by God's word (Genesis 1) and thus is not a thing but an ongoing *event*: God is still speaking his creation into existence. Creation is not the cosmic detritus of past events, as some scientific theory would have it. Creation is a carrier of God. It is a living part of God's continuing lovingkindness.

Early in church history the Christian message was adapted to Greek modes of thought—a transition that aided the remarkable growth of the church in its first few centuries in a world more at home with Greek abstract thinking than with the concrete, metaphorical, interactive thought of the Hebrews. But in switching to Greek paradigms Christians somewhat forgot their Hebrew and biblical roots. The Jewish world of the Bible seldom speaks in Greek categories like essences, logic, infinity, and concepts of being. The Jewish God whom our Lord knew and about whom we read is a God who expresses his care throughout history, and so the world, another level of the creative event, becomes an expression or instrument of God's will, love, and power.

The Hebrews knew God through their experience of his

working their salvation, especially through the historical event of the exodus from Egypt. A cursory reading of the Scriptures is sufficient to demonstrate this. So strong is this experience of God that they project the reason for the exodus (God saving his people) back to God's original creation action (God creating his people for salvation). Salvation begins with creation. God is no abstraction, some all-powerful, unchanging, remote force that sets the world in motion and then departs. God is a person deeply engrossed in the vicissitudes, trials, joys, and troubles of his people.

If Jesus is part of creation, then there must be something special about creation in God's eyes.

The creating and saving aspects of God's loving activity are assumed, for example, in Psalm 8, in which his saved people acclaim his name throughout the earth by the magnificence of his creation. The psalmist wonders at the smallness (not the insignificance) of humans, who are appointed to care for the work of God's hands. Instances of this reverential attitude towards creation abound throughout Scripture. Never is humankind or God set over against creation. Humans and inanimate creation are in solidarity. If anything, it is the human element rather than the nonhuman that blotches the beauty of creation. But then we must recall that Jesus himself belongs to the human element of creation.

Christ and Creation

If Jesus is part of creation, then there must be something special about creation in God's eyes. Jesus is truly God and truly human. Jesus shares in creation. God is not likely to join himself to something of little worth. Yet, surprisingly, created things had a poor press among the later Fathers of the Church. Often they were seen as distractions to prayer or as having an aura of moral evil about them or, predominantly, as having no moral value whatever. While there were some exceptions to this unappreciative attitude, the major turning away from it was the Franciscan renewal of the 13th and 14th centuries. Blessed John Duns Scotus, following the lead of St. Bonaventure, had an insight that put into theological terms what St. Francis and his Assisi companions had taken for granted in their experiencing of creation. Theirs was an insight that has come into its own again during this century and has influenced some of the theologies of Vatican Council II.

Scotus involved himself with this medieval hypothetical question: Would Christ have come if Adam had not sinned? Many people believed (and still believe) that, when humankind had somehow messed up God's original plan, then and only then did God resort to the drastic measure of sending his Son to save the world. Scotus, however, maintained that God the Father was not so shortsighted: God foresaw at the outset that people would sin, and so there was no need to amend his plan:

> Does the predestination of Christ depend necessarily upon the fall of human nature? . . . It is not likely that the highest good in the whole of creation is something that merely chanced to take place, and that only because of some lesser good [the redemption of humans from sin]. Nor is it probable that God predestined Adam to such a good before he predestined Christ. Yet all of this would follow, yes, and even something more absurd. If the predestination of Christ's soul was for the sole purpose of redeeming others, it would follow that, in foreordaining Adam to glory, God would have had to foresee him as having fallen into sin before he could have predestined Christ to glory. . . . I say that the incarnation of Christ was not foreseen as occasioned by sin, but was immediately foreseen from all eternity by God.[2]

Several texts of Scripture support this view: "[The Father] has let us know the mystery of his purpose, the hidden plan he so kindly made in Christ *from the beginning* . . . and it is in [Christ] that we were claimed as God's own, chosen from the beginning *under the predetermined plan* of the one who guides all things as he decides by his own will."[3] Christ, as God-become-human among us, was preordained independently of human sin right from the beginning of God's creation project, as John 1 and Colossians 1 maintain. Creation, everything that was made, was made for him. Christ is prior to sin: "[The Word] was with God in the beginning. *Through him* all things came to be, not one thing had its being except through him" (Jn 1:1-2). "[Christ] is the image of the unseen God and *the firstborn of all creation*, for in him were created all things in heaven and on earth; everything visible and invisible" (Col 1:15-26).

A ready conclusion from all this is that creation cannot be divorced from Jesus' coming into our human context. It is an integral part of it. Other theologies that admit Jesus into our world only because of human sin tend to extract Jesus from the natural world around him, so much so that creation becomes just a stage or backdrop for the real drama of human redemption to take place. Notice how easily "soul" (the spiritual side of us) replaces "human person" (the full, embodied human being) in much of the literature. In such a context creation is relegated to the sidelines and is regarded as merely neutral to salvation and expendable from the point of view of the spiritual life.[4] We even hear of misleading dichotomies like natural *versus* supernatural. Gustavo Gutiérrez sums up the more integrative (and Hebrew) viewpoint when he says creation is not prior to salvation, but salvation's first salvific event.[5]

It follows that, if creation and the salvific coming of Christ are integral and related parts of God's plan, then creation has a lot to do not only with the coming of Jesus at a particular point in history almost 2000 years ago, but also with his influence before and since. Creation is integral to his coming now, when we hear him through created persons and objects. When God created, we are told he saw that it was good. Our created bodies are temples of the Holy Spirit (1 Co 3:16). Even in the world to come, we will not be disembodied spirits. The New Creation is integral for our existence: we will have glorified bodies.[6] Our prayer becomes much more balanced if, like God, we recognize the inherent goodness and sanctifying power of creation. Creation is a worthy companion to our prayer life. Together we are a strong team.

St. Francis's "Canticle of the Creatures"

St. Francis, one of the greatest and most well known of the saints, understood clearly the role of creation in our human relationship to God and passed the message to us. We hear of his legendary kindness to animals, but perhaps have slighted the Christological core of which his kindness is the outward expression. Of his masterpiece, the "Canticle of the Creatures," a few verses are enough to suggest his Trinitarian and Christological spirituality.

> Most high, all-powerful, good Lord,
> Yours is the praise, the glory, the honor,

and all blessing . . . .
Praised be you, my Lord, with all your creatures,
especially Sir Brother Sun,
who is the day, and through whom you give us light.
And he is beautiful and radiant with great splendor;
and bears a likeness to you, Most High One.
Praised be you, my Lord, through Sister Moon and
the Stars.
In heaven you formed them clear and precious and
beautiful. . . .[7]

Francis sees a totality: God and creation together. The canticle continues using the titles of "Brother" and "Sister" in each of its praises of wind, water, fire, Mother Earth (the four elements), those who grant pardon, and bodily death. A good spirituality is one which enhances one's vision to see the entire order of things as pertaining to the Father, Son, and Spirit. Notice how Francis achieves this by the use of inclusive and personalized fraternal relationships. Elsewhere in his words and writings he applies these same highly charged, relational titles to other members of creation: rabbits, wolves, larks, doves, crickets, cicadas, pheasants, and many others. The integrating pattern is even more apparent when we realize that, for Francis, the Brother par excellence is Jesus himself.

Now what does all this imply? Obviously, Francis assumes a religious connection between the created nonhuman world and Jesus, a connection that is not just one of servant to master, artwork to artist, or stage to the actors. It is a link that is strong enough for us to think of in *family* terms. Another point to observe about the "Canticle of the Creatures" is that Francis calls on all of God's creation to join and support him in his prayer. Prayer flourishes best in an atmosphere of solidarity—with us desiring to be at one with created things (our brothers and sisters) in order to be at one with the Creator, who loves his creation dearly. This attitude is deeply scriptural and parallels the harmony of creation with God, presented to us as our goal in Genesis 1 and 2.

All God's self-communication with us is mediated through creation. Rarely if ever in the Bible or in our own experience do we find God working independently of some sort of intermediary: persons, situations, or things. Rarely does God operate absolutely. We do not know God independently of creation. Perhaps this is why Francis can say, "Praised be you, my Lord, with all your creatures," when we would not expect a reference to creation in the same breath as the praise of God. Francis does not, however, equate the Lord with creatures by saying "Praised be you, my Lord and all creation." The "with" and the "your" make the difference between God and creation quite clear while asserting the sacredness of their working unity. The fact that we humans are representatives of one party of this sacred liaison gives us plenty of wonderment for our prayer.

Yet another intriguing point to reflect on for our own prayer is that Francis does not direct his praise to the creatures themselves although it is abundantly clear that he admires them; nor is he directly praising God as the Creator of all these wonderful things. He is not thanking him here for his creation. Rather, his praise is directed towards God *through* all that he has made. This "through" is highly significant. Creation is itself a pathway to God, who is still the transcendent One ("Most high, all-powerful, good Lord"). Creation is a kind of sacrament, as we saw earlier, a sign that brings about a prayerful awareness of a provident and generous God in our hearts. Creation speaks God: God speaks creation.

Creation is a kind of sacrament, a sign that brings about a prayerful awareness of a provident and generous God in our hearts.

Moreover, this kind of prayer through creation is an unselfish one. It is rooted in our creatureliness; it is inclusive; and it focuses our attention on our God, the continuing Creator, while at the same time steeping us in a holy reverence for created things. It leaves us with a profound sense of wonder and mystery. Our experience shows we are at home in this kind of prayer. As we noted, it is rooted in a natural human religiosity that is at the base of all religion. It is a response to that deep yearning we have within us for the transcendent, which God implanted in the core of our being. This "natural" sort of prayer Francis has transformed, Christianized, and made respectable in our Catholic tradition. He centers it in the depths of the Christ event. It is a Christic prayer, an integrated prayer, a powerful prayer, a contemplative prayer, a natural prayer.

This kind of creation prayer can offset prayer that might overemphasize our sinfulness and our nonresponse to God's word. It points us, rather, to his goodness and his overall providence and to our ability to give him glory (as the second Eucharistic

Prayer encourages us to do). It makes us aware of and satisfied with our sharing in God's prolific goodness and glory.

Creating and Communing with God

Enough of the theory. Let us turn now to what others have said. St. Bonaventure talks of created things: "They are the vestiges, representations, spectacles, proposed to us and signs divinely given so that we can see God." He says, "Just as you see that a ray of light coming through a window is differently colored according to the various colors of the different parts of the window, so the divine ray shines out in individual creatures differently and in their different particularities."[8] Cousins, a modern authority on Bonaventure, can observe:

> The physical universe and the soul are seen as mirrors reflecting God as rungs in a ladder leading to God. Bonaventure expresses here, in his own way, Francis's joy in the sacrality and sacramentality of creation and, in so doing, captures an essential element in Franciscan spirituality. Basic though this element is, it would not be complete without its flowering in devotion to the humanity of Christ. There is a natural link between the Franciscan attitude toward material creation, as sacramentally manifesting God and the Franciscan devotion to the incarnation as the fullness of this manifestation.[9]

Notice that the pinnacle of creation is the incarnation. Jesus is seen not as removed from the creation process at all, but as its culmination, a culmination that receives its consummation only in the Second Coming.

Experiencing the sacramentality of creation (a sacrament is something that brings about what it signifies) is obvious to Bonaventure. He puts his case strongly: "Whoever, therefore, is not enlightened by such splendor of created things is blind; whoever is not awakened by such outcries is deaf; whoever does not praise God because of all these effects is dumb; whoever does not discover the First Principle from such clear signs is a fool."[10] He says, "It can be concluded that a creature of the world is like a certain book in which the creating Trinity shines forth."

Francis was an avid reader of this "book." In the following quotation, also from St. Bonaventure, we can taste for ourselves this form of prayer if we read it in the present tense and replace references to Francis by references to ourselves:

Francis sought occasion to love God in everything. He delighted in all the works of God's hands, and from the vision of joy on earth his mind soared aloft to the life-giving source and cause of all. In everything beautiful, he saw him who is beauty itself, and he followed his Beloved everywhere by his likeness imprinted on creation; of all creation he made a ladder by which he might mount up and embrace him who is all-desirable. By the power of his extraordinary faith, he tasted the Goodness which is the source of all in each and every created thing, as in so many rivulets. He seemed to perceive a divine harmony in the interplay of powers and faculties given by God to his creatures, and like the prophet David he exhorted them all to praise God.[11]

Thomas of Celano, one of the earliest biographers of Francis (1246), captures a little of Francis's insight:

In every work of the artist he praised the Artist; whatever he found in the things made he referred to the Maker. He rejoiced in all the works of the hands of the Lord and saw behind things pleasant to behold their life-giving reason and cause. In beautiful things he saw Beauty itself; all things were to him good. "He who made us is the best," they cried out to him. Through the Beloved's footprints impressed upon things, he followed him everywhere; he made for himself from all things a ladder by which to come even to his throne.[12]

In the next paragraph Celano gives creatures more value in their own right as distinct from being only reflections of their Maker: "He embraced all things with a rapture of unheard-of devotion, speaking to them of the Lord and admonishing them to praise him." This free feeling for creatures, at the same time sympathetic and empathetic, is often the beginning of a mystical experience for Francis, and can be so for us too.

There is a spontaneity in Francis's love of nature:

How great a gladness do you think the beauty of flowers brought to his mind when he saw the shape of their beauty and perceived the odor of their sweetness? . . . He called all creatures "brother," and in a most extraordinary manner, a manner never experienced by others, he discerned the hidden things of nature with his sensitive heart, as one who had already escaped into the freedom of the glory of the sons of God.[13]

The 13th-century "Legend of Perugia" talks of flowers which invite all people to look at them and praise God: "Every creature says and proclaims, 'God has created me for you, O man.'" The author continues: "We who lived with [Francis] saw him find great cause for interior and external joy in all creatures; he caressed and contemplated them with delight, so much so that his spirit seemed to live in heaven and not on earth."[14] A modern author expresses the same insight in a modern way: "The Franciscan world is full of magic, of reverence, of respect. It is not a dead and inanimate universe. . . . [Things] are alive and have their own personality; they have blood ties with humanity; they live in the same Father's house as humanity."[15]

Why not try prayer through creation? It introduces us to the wider world of God's own making. We see in a more balanced fashion the transcendence and the immanence of God in what he has created. Prayer through creation automatically shifts the emphasis of our prayer beyond our narrowness and sinfulness to the utter goodness of God and why he is creating. It dissolves the division between secular and the holy, for all is holy.

> Most high, all-powerful, good Lord,
> Yours is the praise, the glory, the honor,
> and all blessing. . . .
> Praised be you, my Lord, with all your creatures.

Notes

[1] Matthew Fox's *Original Blessing* (Santa Fe: Bear and Co, 1983) also looks at creation as blessing. I am surprised that he does not appear to have looked at the ongoing and widespread Franciscan spirituality as a source for his work.

[2] *Ordinatio* III, dist. 7, q. 3 (from *Joannis Duns Scoti Doctoris Mariani Theologiae Marianae Elementa*, ed. C. Balic [Sibenik, 1933]), pp. 1-16), cited by Allan B. Wolter, "John Duns Scotus on the Primacy and Personality of Christ," in Damian McElrath, ed., *Franciscan Christology* (Assisi: Tipografia Portiuncola, 1980), pp. 149-151. The last sentence is from *Ordinatio* III (suppl.), d. 19 (Assisi com. 137, fol. 161vb), p. 153.

[3] Ep 1:9 and 11; see also 1 Co 8:6; Ep 2:10; Heb 1:1-3a; Jn 1:1-3; and Rv 3:14. For further details see Joël Delobel, "Christ, the Lord of Creation," Louvain Studies (Summer 1991): 155-169.

[4] Even the term *spiritual life* hints at a hierarchy of spirit over body rather than their integration.

[5] See his "Towards a Theology of Liberation," in Alfred T. Hennelly, ed., *Liberation Theology: A Documentary History* (Maryknoll: Orbis, 1990), p. 71.

[6] See 2 Co 5:17; 2 P 3:13; and Rv 21:1-5.

[7] Regis J. Armstrong and Ignatius C. Brady, *Francis and Clare: The Complete Works*, Classics of Western Spirituality (New York: Paulist, 1982).

[8] Both quotations are from the *Hexaemeron*, quoted as Bonaventure's in Ewert Cousins, *Bonaventure: The Soul's Journey into God, The Tree of Life, The Life of St. Francis*, Classics of Western Spirituality (New York: Paulist, 1978), p. 26.

[9] Cousins, *Bonaventure*, p. 13.

[10] *Journey of the Soul into God*, 1:15, in Cousins, *Bonaventure*, p. 67.

[11] Bonaventure, *Legenda Maior*, 9:1, in Marion A. Habig, *Saint Francis of Assisi: Writings and Early Biographies: English Omnibus of the Sources for the Life of St. Francis* (Chicago: Franciscan Herald Press, 1982), p. 698. This work is usually referred to as *Omnibus*.

[12] *2 Celano*, 165 *(Omnibus*, p. 494). Note also *1 Celano*, 80 *(Omnibus*, p. 296), written in 1228, two years after the death of Francis: "For who could ever give expression to the very great affection he bore for all things that are God's? Who would be able to narrate the sweetness he enjoyed while contemplating in creatures the wisdom of their Creator, his power and his goodness?"

[13] *1 Celano*, 81 *(Omnibus*, p. 296).

[14] *Legend of Perugia*, 51 *(Omnibus*, p. 1029).

[15] Leonardo Boff, *Saint Francis: A Model for Human Liberation* (New York: Crossroad, 1985), p. 35.

Contemplation:
Similarities between St. Teresa
and St. John of the Cross

*T*he popular devotion tends to associate St. Teresa of Jesus and St. John of the Cross. This is natural, for both were Castilian and contemplative; both were mystical writers and doctors of the church; and, what is most important, both were actively involved in the 16th-century reformation of the Carmelite order in Spain.

Teresa initiated the reformation with the Discalced nuns, then helped that of the religious men; John of the Cross was one of the first and most important persons to participate in that reformation. Teresa praised the Lord at the time she first met the ascetic friar, who never disappointed her.[1] For he "is considered by everybody as a saint, and I do not think they are rating him too highly. In my opinion he is a tower of strength."[2] She writes King Philip these words: "He is so great a servant of the Lord that they have all been edified by him. . . . So people look upon him as a saint, which, in my opinion, he is and has been all his life."[3]

In spite of all these laudatory words and many others that can be adduced, the friendship between Teresa and John of the Cross—although genuine—did not go beyond certain limits. It was not as close as many may believe. They were both strong personalities, which may have made an intimate friendship difficult. Teresa was extroverted and social, John of the Cross introverted and intuitive. In Jungian language, it may be said that they were two different "types." Mother Teresa's best friend was Father Gracian, to whom the saint made a vow of obedience. John of the Cross's close friend was Anne of Jesus, a gifted and holy sister who founded the Discalced nuns in France and Belgium. At Anne of Jesus's request, John of the Cross compiled the complete commentary of the beautiful poetry of the *Spiritual Canticle*. The mystical views of Teresa and John of the Cross, however, show remarkable similarities. I intend to explore the similarities of their doctrines regarding contemplation in this article.

Contemplation and Detachment

Contemplation cannot exist without detachment, and the higher the contemplation the greater the detachment. Teresa recommends us to renounce our attachments to earthly things, to be dead to the world. A contemplative spirit does not find rest in creatures.[4] When the soul is in a state of contemplation, "He would have you keep back nothing, whether it be a little or much."[5] Even more, a single attachment is enough to disturb the soul and to hinder the road to perfect union:

> We cannot properly understand this until we have given up every thing; for if there is a single thing to which a man clings, it is a sign that he sets some value upon it, and . . . it will naturally distress him to give it up, so everything will be imperfection and loss.[6]

John of the Cross is even more radical than Teresa in demanding detachment from everything created. One expects to obtain everything from the Lord when one possesses nothing. This is pivotal to the doctrine of the famous "nadas": "To come to possess all, desire the possession of nothing. To come to the knowledge of all, desire the knowledge of nothing . . ."[7] and so forth. Absolute detachment is the prerequisite for perfect contemplation. Like Teresa's doctrine, a single attachment makes impossible the progress in perfection, even though the imperfection may be small, as he illustrates in this well known example:

> It makes little difference whether a bird is tied by a thin thread or by a cord. For even if tied by thread, the bird will be prevented from taking off just as surely as if it were by cord—that is, it will be impeded from flight as long as it does not break the thread.[8]

The ascetic saint laments that souls do not become detached from "childish things" that often God requests them to conquer out of love, but they turn back because of their small attachments.[9] This resembles Teresa's view when she exclaims: "How happy shall we be if by leaving these few, petty things we can arrive at so high a state."[10] To possess perfect contemplation the spirit must be simple, pure, and "naked" as to all natural affections.

A Passive Reception

Teresa does not use the word "passive," although her doctrine on this point is identical to St. John of the Cross's. Instead, she stresses the importance of God's action upon the contemplative spirit. In *The Way of Perfection* she compares mental prayer and contemplation, in which one does nothing: "It is his Majesty who does everything, the work is his alone and far transcends human nature."[11] In her vivid imagination she finds no better example to explain the special work of God in contemplation than the properties of the wax: "The soul does no more than the wax when a seal is impressed upon it—the wax does not impress itself . . . and it does not even soften itself so as to be prepared; it merely remains quiet and consenting."[12]

In John of the Cross, God's action in contemplation is equally important. He explains the dark night as a purgative contemplation which passively causes in the soul the negation of self and of all things:

> The reason the darkness of this contemplation frees and hides the soul from the wiles of the devil is that the contemplation experienced here is infused passively and secretly without the use of the exterior and interior faculties of the sensory part of the soul.[13]

This passivity is a most important sign to distinguish meditation from contemplation. Meditation depends upon one's free will. Contemplation, however, takes place only when it is God's wish, when one passively receives his motion.

Contemplation and Perfection

Teresa, the great mystic and "connoisseur" of human spirits, was well aware that God can enrich souls in many ways, and bring them to the Mansions by a diversity of paths.[14] She had in her Discalced convents many sisters who were not gifted with contemplation. For example, in *The Way of Perfection*, she refers to a great servant of God who for many years spent hours and hours of her time merely in vocal prayers.[15] At the time of priorities, however, she considers contemplation "the shortcut" which leads quickly to the summit.[16] There is no substitution for the loving illumination due to contemplation.

For John of the Cross, too, contemplation—especially dark contemplation—is the path for reaching the perfect union of love. His *Ascent*, for example, is a treatise which "explains how to reach divine union quickly."[17] In the beautiful stanzas he composed for the *Dark Night*, he calls attention to the "secret ladder" which is darkness, and the "narrow way to eternal life" that only a few take.[18]

Since contemplation's chief trait is passivity, God's activity upon which it depends is most important, and he is much wiser and more powerful than we are. In contrast, meditation and mental prayer depend on our activity, with power and knowledge merely human, and therefore limited. No doubt why contemplation is the best shortcut to reach the summit of divine union!

Woundings of Love

True love is always restless, and so is the love of God in a greater degree. Mother Teresa knew this; when writing on the Fifth Mansions, she considers unthinkable that souls which have arrived so far cease to grow, for "love is never idle."[19]

Hence, these souls fired by the love of God, go forward. Then things happen, namely, they are wounded. The more that love wounds the soul, the more it cures and heals. It produces grief and sweetness at the same time: "The soul is conscious of having been most delectably wounded, but cannot say why and by whom . . . and it would be glad if it were never to be healed of that wound."[20] Knowledge and love work together: the more the soul learns about the greatness of God, the more her desire for God increases.[21]

John of the Cross holds similar views: love for God is so intense that it is like a fire emitting flames:

> It is something splendid that since love is never idle, but in continual motion, it is always emitting flames, everywhere like a blazing fire, and since its duty is to wound in order to cause love and delight . . . it dispatches its wounds like most tender flares of delicate love.[22]

The mysterious phenomenon of transverberation is associated with these wounds, and it usually leads to spiritual marriage.

Teresa, in her *Life*, describes the effects of this extraordinary grace. She saw an angel in bodily form, very beautiful and all afire with a long golden spear, and at the end of the iron tip a point of fire. With this tip of fire:

> The angel seemed to pierce my heart several times so that it penetrated to my entrails. When it drew it out . . . he left me completely afire with great love for God. The pain was so sharp that it made me utter several moans; and so excessive was the sweetness caused me by the intense pain that one can never wish to lose it, not will one's soul be content with anything less than God.[23]

John of the Cross's opinion is that this phenomenon happens not only to Teresa, but to souls already in the state of spiritual espousal, and as a preparation for the spiritual marriage.[24] "It will feel that a seraphim is assaulting it by means of an arrow or dart which is all afire with love. . . . When the soul is transpierced with the dart, the flame gushes forth, vehemently and with a sudden ascent like a fire in a furnace."[25] John of the Cross who, undoubtedly like Teresa, experienced this transverberation, says that the entire universe is a sea of love in which the soul is engulfed, and that this experience is given to those whose virtue was to be diffused among their children, like the founders.[26]

The Purgative Way

The dark night of the soul is ordinarily a necessary purification that the souls must endure to attain spiritual marriage. Or, using Teresa's own words, this distress comes just before the soul's entrance into the Seventh Mansions.[27] By means of this purgation the soul becomes clean of sin and imperfection, and is ready for divine union. In her *Life*, Teresa simply describes the experience of darkness as "intolerable," but in her *Interior Castle* she is more explicit as she describes the painful darkness:

> The soul feels as if it has never known God, and never will know him. . . . The Lord makes her think herself cast off by God. . . . I do not know to what it can be compared, save to the torment of those who suffer in hell, for in this spiritual tempest no consolation is possible.[28]

This awesome experience is part of the narrow way the saints must take to reach perfect union of love with God. And among them, nobody has described it so profoundly as John of the Cross.

The second book of the *Dark Night* is almost unique in mystic spirituality. He explains in detail why this darkness is necessary even in advanced souls, and how it affects the whole personality of the mystic.

God leaves the intellect in darkness, the will in aridity, the memory in emptiness, and the affections in supreme affliction and anguish for the purpose of this union. "This privation is one of the conditions required that the spiritual form, which is the union of love, may be introduced in the spirit and united with it. The Lord works all of this in the soul by means of a pure and dark contemplation."[29]

God is infinitely pure and to be united to him the soul must also be pure. It cannot have the smallest stain of sin or imperfection. This is achieved only through dark contemplation.

Dark Contemplation and Purgatory

Teresa and John of the Cross compare the painful purification of the dark night to the purification of the souls in purgatory before entering heaven. Naturally, we cannot know the state of the "poor souls" in purgatory unless through revelation from God, since we are ignorant of the conditions of souls after death. "And it was revealed to her (Teresa) that this suffering resembles that of souls in purgatory; despite their being no longer in the body, they suffer much more than do those who are still in the body on earth."[30]

As mentioned above, no spirit can be united to God, who is infinitely pure, unless it is also totally pure. Hence, as Teresa says in the *Interior Castle*, this final distress prepares the soul to enter the spiritual marriage of perfect union of love with God, just as purgatory prepares the soul to enter heaven.[31]

It is remarkable that John of the Cross shares the same doctrine as Teresa and for the same reason: "This suffering resembles that of purgatory. Just as the spirit suffers purgation so as to be able to see God through clear vision in the next life, souls in their own way suffer purgation here on earth as to be able to be transformed in him through love in this life."[32]

Once the soul is totally pure, there is no reason for further suffering either in purgatory nor in dark contemplation. The saints accept this purification with gratitude, for as Teresa says: "The soul feels this affliction to be so precious that it fully realizes it could never deserve it."[33] This doctrine of the Spanish saints is also very similar to the well-known revelations of St. Catherine of Genoa on purgatory.

Contemplative Attraction

The majority of Christians think of contemplation as a waste of time and effort at the expense of an active apostolate. This mistaken view lies in the ignorance of the value of prayer and of a hidden life of sacrifice. Christ spent thirty years before he initiated his active mission.

Teresa, naturally, was well aware of the value of a hidden contemplative vocation. She urges her daughters to be faithful to God and avoid occasions of sin: "Because the devil sets much more store by one soul in this state than by a great number of souls to whom the Lord does not grant these favors. For those in this state attract others, and so they can do the devil great harm and may well bring great advantage to the church of God."[34] Consequently, if the devil wins one of these advanced souls he will win a whole multitude.[35]

John of the Cross describes the way that spiritual souls are tempted by devils, not directly, but with little baits, since they are strong and cannot be openly deceived. Devils are envious of all the good they see in these souls and employ all their ability to disturb them. If they are victims to these temptations, the harm done is great for, as Teresa says above, they "accomplish more through a little harm caused in these souls than by great damage affected in many others."[36]

In the state of spiritual marriage, the devil has lost his power and is much terrified by them. In the Seventh Mansions, the soul is always in tranquillity, and "it is not afraid that this sublime favor may be counterfeited by the devil."[37] This is understandable, for the lover is in such close contact with God, and the union takes place so deep, in the essence of the soul, that the devil does not dare to approach, nor can it even understand this mystery.[38]

John of the Cross, in a whole dense chapter of his *Dark Night* describes the last attempt of the devil to prevent the soul from attaining spiritual marriage. The chapter is dramatic, based both on theology and personal experience, and it poses the mysterious economy of salvation, the fight between good and evil. God permits the devil to deal with the soul in the same measure and mode that he conducts with it himself.[39] Agreeing with Teresa, John of the Cross assures the reader that once the soul has achieved the state of spiritual marriage, the devil has lost all his power. As he explains in the last stanza of the *Spiritual Canticle*: "In this place where she now dwells, she is so favored, strong, and victorious with the virtues, and with God's embrace, that the devil dare not come, but with immense fear flees and does not venture to appear."[40]

In the end, good prevails over evil, the saint over the devil.

The Mystical State of Spiritual Espousal

In order to attain perfect union with God, one has to endure first joys, trials, and sufferings beyond words. St. John of the Cross calls this spiritual espousal, because God betroths himself to souls spiritually. The souls who reach that lofty state are very much loved by God: "It is a union of love with love, and its operations are entirely pure, and so delicate and gentle that there is no way of describing them."[41]

When a man and a woman fall in love, they plan to meet for a certain period of time to prepare themselves for marriage. Something similar happens in the spiritual espousal. The lover is in love with the Beloved, and God with the lover; hence, they agree to meet again to appreciate each other better and to test if the soul is worthy of him.

The divine spirit works on the soul as the artist on the marble, and gradually carves his masterpiece, which is a soul pure and simple.

Teresa spends almost half of her *Interior Castle* describing the fascinating operations of God upon these souls. God prepares them for spiritual marriage with joys and trials whose nature is hard to describe: "Oh my God," Teresa exclaims, "how great are these trials, which the soul will suffer, both with and without, before it enters the Seventh Mansions."[42] At the end of these joys and trials the soul is totally purified and ready to attain perfect union with God in spiritual marriage.

John of the Cross emphasizes the importance of God's actions upon these saintly persons. They do not know how to please him, and, hence, he takes the initiative and shapes them to his likeness: "God communicates to the soul great things about himself, beautifies her will with grandeur and majesty, adorns her will with gifts and virtues, and clothes her with the knowledge and honor of God."[43] This seems similar to the work of a sculptor who carves the marble little by little until he produces a masterpiece. The divine spirit works on the soul as the artist on the marble, and gradually carves his masterpiece, which is a soul pure and simple, full of virtue and ready to be united to God through love.

The Spiritual Marriage

The spiritual marriage is the goal of Christian life; it consists in a perfect union of love with God. Only a few saints attain this lofty condition, which according to Teresa and John of the Cross is incomparably greater than spiritual espousal.[44] Teresa was blessed with a vision of the Trinity, and God told her that he would take her affairs upon himself. The soul shares the life of God, it is sure of its salvation and free from the risk of backsliding. These lucky saints wish only one thing: the honor and glory of God.

According to John of the Cross, the spiritual marriage is a "total transformation in the Beloved in which each surrenders the entire possession of self to the other with certain consummation of the union of love."[45] The two natures live in one spirit of love and both appear to be God. For both Teresa and John of the Cross, forgetfulness characterizes this state. [46] Everything is forgotten save the glory and honor of God. The peace and delight is incomparably more perfect than in spiritual espousal; they "live in immense tranquillity, so that it may not even with the slightest mote or noise disturb or trouble its heart where the Beloved dwells."[47]

God dwells in heaven and also in our souls because we are temples of the Trinity, as St. Paul and St. John say in Sacred Scripture. Saints describe this dwelling as the "center" of the soul. Teresa in the Fifth Mansions recommends that we enter inside ourselves, right into the center of the soul, as a preparation for the spiritual marriage which later on takes place in the "deepest center of the soul, which must be where God himself dwells."[48]

John of the Cross, in the *Living Flame*, refers to the center as the inmost recess of ourself in ways similar to Teresa:

The soul's center is God, when it has reached God with all the capacity of its being and strength of its operation and inclination, it will have attained to its final and deepest center in God, it will know, love, and enjoy God with all its might.[49]

Contemplation and the Vision of the Universe

Theology teaches that one of the gifts granted to the blessed in heaven is the vision of the universe, not in itself but in God, its Creator. Through revelation, Teresa shared with the blessed—although naturally in a modest way—the vision of the created cosmos. She describes in her *Life* how she once saw with perfect clarity how all things are seen in God, and how within himself he contains them all.[50] Later, just before she reached spiritual marriage, she had "a suspension in which the Lord communicates most sacred things to it, which it seems to see within God himself . . . a notably intellectual vision, in which is revealed to the soul how all things are seen in God, and how within himself he contains them all."[51]

Teresa received this vision in the Sixth Mansions; John of the Cross, however, ascribes this mysterious and extraordinary intellectual revelation to the Seventh Mansions, after the soul is one with God through spiritual marriage. He was conscious of how all creatures have their life in God, although naturally these things are distinct from him:

> That which it understands of God . . . is such that it knows these things better in God's being than in themselves. And here lies the remarkable delight of that awakening; the soul knows creatures through God, not God through creatures. This amounts to knowing the effects through their causes and not the cause through its effects.[52]

It is reassuring to see how mystical knowledge verifies through experience the conclusion of theology.

Gift to the Church

The lives of the saints are precious in the eyes of God, and their lives are very important in the economy of the church. Contemplatives, once in the state of perfection, pray unceasingly for the universal needs of the church, and their prayers, as well as their smallest actions, are endowed with immense value. The merit of an action depends on the degree of charity, of love, not on the mere human activity. Consequently, Teresa urges her daughters to become close to the Lord, for "if they become still better, their praises will be more pleasing to the Lord, and their prayers of great value to their neighbors . . . the love does not look so much at the magnitude of anything we do as at the love with which we do it."[53]

When the things of God are judged from a purely human viewpoint, one is often unaware of the value of a hidden contemplative life. We appreciate religious activities because of their psychological appeal. This is not John of the Cross's approach. He advises that until the soul reaches the state of union of love, it should practice love in both the active and contemplative life. Yet once the soul reaches that union, then the exterior exercises might be a hindrance to the love of God, even though the work may seem to be in great service of God:

> For a little of this pure love is more precious to God and the soul, and more beneficial to the church, even though it seems one is doing nothing, than all these other works put together.[54]

John of the Cross strongly recommends prayer for those engaged in an active apostolate, for without prayer they may do a great deal of hammering but accomplish little or even nothing.[55]

Anthropomorphism, little faith, and lack of experience all cloud our judgments. Everyone admires Mother Teresa of Calcutta because of her extraordinary work for the destitute. Only a few appreciate the hidden life of Carmelite nuns. According to Teresa, it is impossible to discern spiritual things without being spiritual. Only the spiritual person will see that which is in conformity with the Holy Spirit.[56] In the *Interior Castle* she exclaims: "How great are Thy secrets, and how different are spiritual things from any that can be seen or understood here below."[57]

John of the Cross, who combines theology and experience, observes that the individual whose spirit is purified can naturally perceive the inclinations and talents of others and what lies in the heart or interior spirit: "Just as the devil, because he is a spirit is endowed with the skill, so is the spiritual person."[58]

The spiritual, with great facility, perceives and penetrates anything earthly or heavenly presented to it. Hence the Apostle says that the spiritual penetrates all things, even the things of God (1 Co 2:10). John of the Cross explains the text of the Apostle with a profound epistemological observation: "This is character-istic of the spirit purged and annihilated of all particular knowl-edge and affection . . . it embraces all things with great preparedness."[59] Individual matter is always concrete; the spirit, however, is universal.

The Prayers of the Saints

The Lord promised to answer our prayers; it is written in the gospel. Nevertheless, it is common experience that many prayers are never answered. However, the prayers of the saints are always granted. Why? The reason is simple: The wills of the saints are so united with God's will that they only pray for the things that God wants them to pray for.

The wills of the saints are so united with God's will that they only pray for the things that God wants them to pray for.

Thus, Teresa is astonished to observe that she cannot pray for favors that the Lord knows are not good for her. Even if she tries, she is unable to beg him to grant her these favors. "However much I try to force myself to do more, I find that I cannot. Yet when it comes to other things his Majesty means to grant, I find that I can ask for these things often and with great importunity, and though I may not be specially thinking of them they seem to come to my mind."[60]

God promised Teresa that she would never ask for anything which he would not grant. We should not be surprised to read that she was granted everything in a better way than she could have planned.[61]

The same doctrine and experience is found in John of the Cross: "For God's spirit makes them know what must be known and ignore what must be ignored, remember what ought to be remembered, and forget what ought to be forgotten."[62] A person will ask for prayers and the soul will not remember to carry out this request. But if these prayers are expedient, then God will move the will, and impart a desire to do so. At times, God will give a desire to pray for others of whom the soul has never known nor heard.[63]

In other words, if God does not answer our prayers, even after years of them, it is because we are begging for favors which are not expedient for us. As a good Father, he grants us only what is good, and ignores those things not healthy for our spiritual growth.

The Death of the Saints

The death of the saints is precious in the sight of God, David says in Psalm 115. Hence, those who have reached perfect union with God cannot fear death. They are, in a sense, in a state of term; they are not in heaven yet, but their union with God resembles that of the blessed.

Teresa speaks from experience: the saints in the Seventh Mansions are no more afraid of death than they would be of a gentle rapture.[64] In her poetry she complains bitterly to God because he does not grant her death: "I live without living in myself, and in such a way I hope, I die because I do not die."[65] Teresa earnestly wanted to see God, and death was the way to achieve it.

John of the Cross, already on the top of the mountain, is expecting death as one expects a friend, for he says that the death of those in spiritual marriage is far different in its cause and mode than the death of others. The saints do not die a natural death, but by some encounter of love which, however, does not mean that they are not struck by illness. The death of such souls is very gentle and very sweet, sweeter and more gentle than was their whole spiritual life on earth. According to John of the Cross, the saints die with most sublime impetus and delightful encounters of love.[66]

John of the Cross's view is a little poetic, since saints die sometimes with great suffering; but their immense love for God transforms these sufferings into "delightful encounters of love" as he, poetically, put it above. We die as we live: a holy life is ended with a holy death, a saintly life with a saintly death.

Spiritual Directors and Contemplation

Ignorance of spiritual life is common even among those who are called to serve souls with their theology and experience. Few understand the ways and properties of spiritual life, especially contemplation. Spiritual directors should have a solid basis in doctrine, and if possible, experience. Teresa, for example, suffered much from ignorant directors:

> I am very ready to give credence to those who have great learning. For even if they have not themselves experienced these things, men of great learning have a certain instinct to prompt them . . . I have also experience of timid half-learned men whose shortcomings have cost me very dear.[67]

This is a remarkable observation, for Teresa places confidence in learning over experience, although the ideal is to possess both. She suffered the inadequacy of ignorant directors and she reacted; for her, the more learned the director, the better, particularly for a director to understand the path of prayer. The higher the state of spiritual contemplative souls, the greater their need for a solid spiritual director.

John of the Cross, if this is possible, is even more severe in his criticism of ignorant directors, who "cause great harm to a number of souls, because in not understanding the ways and properties of the spirit, they ordinarily make them lose the unction of these delicate ointments, with which the Holy Spirit prepares them for himself."[68]

The Spanish poet is severe, for in his estimation the damage made is enormous, inasmuch as spiritual directors are dealing with selected individuals and on account of their ignorance may cause almost infinite harm. In the *Prologue* of the *Ascent*, John of the Cross says that some spiritual directors are likely to do harm rather than to help these souls because they have neither enlightenment nor experience. God will be severe with them: "Those who err will not escape punishment corresponding to the harm they caused."[69] In his estimation, there is almost an infinite gain in being right and almost an infinite loss in being wrong, which is understandable if one considers that he is referring to contemplative souls called by God to great perfection.

John of the Cross lived in sixteenth-century Spain; it would be interesting to see how he would react and judge the spiritual directors of our time.

The Way of God

The common portrait of a saint resembles a person who forces himself to achieve perfection and must suffer violence, the more quickly he acquires perfection. Yet this is not God's plan.

Generosity with the grace received from God is indeed crucial in reaching holiness. But the narrow path that leads to the top of the mountain must be smooth and peaceful. This is the doctrine of the Spanish Carmelite saints.

In Teresa's words, the interior activity of contemplation is "gentle and peaceful, and to do anything painful brings us harm rather than help. By anything painful I mean anything that we try to force to do."[70] Teresa learned this doctrine by reading, by her own experience, and by observing the experience of her daughters. This is an encouraging view and shows the way God operates in our souls.

One of Teresa's spiritual directors, Gaspar Daza, tried to push her too much and too quickly, as though she was going to become a saint immediately. Consequently, she became discouraged: "For the distress which it caused me to find that I was not doing what he told me, and felt unable to do so, was sufficient to make me lose hope and give up the whole thing."[71] Daza's intention was good, but his prudential judgment wrong, for he did not realize that at that time of her life Teresa was struggling yet in her way and unable to do heroic works. The weaknesses of the saints encourage our lives and teach us precious lessons.

John of the Cross, in a famous chapter of the *Ascent*, recommends these three important principles: the first is taken from St. Paul (Rm 13:1): The works that are done by God are well ordered. The second is found in the Book of Wisdom, and says that God's wisdom disposes all things gently (Ws 7:30). The third is owed to Aquinas, who says that God moves each according to its mode.[72]

The way of God is always: (1) orderly, (2) gentle, and (3) according to our own mode. We are often in a hurry, but God is not because he sees the things from eternity and disposes everything for our own good, not in the way we expect, but in better ways— though always with joy and peace, which theology teaches are effects of charity. To become contemplatives, detachment, virtues, confidence, prayer, and many years of effort are needed. Even in the case of these extraordinary Spanish saints, it took God many years to transform them and bring them to perfect union of love with him.

Conclusion

Teresa and John of the Cross are probably the best mystical

writers in the field of contemplation, and in this field they share many doctrinal views. They also have certain differences in doctrine—a subject that lies beyond the scope of this article.

. As human beings they were different although both were very gifted. Perhaps John of the Cross did not possess the sense of humor and charm that made Teresa so attractive and popular. In a famous passage of her writings, Teresa teases her friend John of the Cross in this way:

> This Father [John of the Cross] in his reply gives some remarkable sound doctrine for those who are thinking of following the Exercises practiced in the Company of Jesus, but it is not to our purpose. It would be bad business for us if we could not seek God until we were dead to the world. . . . God deliver me from people who are so spiritual that they want to turn everything into perfect contemplation, come what may. At the same time we are grateful for having been given so good an explanation of what we had not asked about. For this reason, it is well to speak ever of God; we shall derive benefit from a place where we are least expecting to find it.[73]

Notes

[1] Saint Teresa of Jesus, *The Complete Works of Saint Teresa of Jesus*. Trans., E. Allison Peers, Vol. 3 *The Book of the Foundations*, chap. 3, p. 15 (New York, 1946).

[2] Saint Teresa of Jesus, *The Letters of Saint Teresa of Jesus*, trans. E. Allison Peers (Westminster, 1954), Vol. 2, Letter 210, p. 515.

[3] Ibid, Letter 204, Vol. 1, p. 496.

[4] Saint Teresa of Jesus, *Interior Castle*, trans. E. Allison Peers (Garden City, 1960), Fifth Mansions, chap. 2, pp. 106-107.

[5] Ibid, Fifth Mansions, chap. 1, p. 97.

[6] Saint Teresa of Jesus, *The Life of Teresa of Jesus*, trans. E. Allison Peers (Garden City, 1960), chap. 34, p. 38.

[7] St. John of the Cross, *The Collected Works of St. John of the Cross*, trans. Kieran Kavanaugh OCD and Otilio Rodriguez OCD (Washington, 1979), *The Ascent of Mount Carmel*, Book 1, chap. 13, n. 11, p. 103.

[8] Ibid, chap. 11, n. 4, p. 97.

[9] Ibid, chap. 11, n. 5, p. 97.

[10] Saint Teresa of Jesus, *The Way of Perfection*, trans. E. Allison Peers (Garden City, 1964), chap. 16, p. 121.

[11] Ibid, chap. 25, p. 171.

[12] *Interior Castle*, Fifth Mansions, chap. 2, p. 109.

[13] St. John of the Cross, *The Collected Works, The Dark Night*, Book 2,

chap. 23, n. 2, p. 382.

[14] *Interior Castle*, Fifth Mansions, chap. 3, p. 113.

[15] *Way of Perfection*, chap. 17, p. 125.

[16] *Interior Castle*, Fifth Mansions, chap. 3, p. 113.

[17] *Ascent*, Theme, p. 68.

[18] *Dark Night*, Prologue, pp. 296-297.

[19] *Interior Castle*, Fifth Mansions, chap. 4, p. 122.

[20] Ibid, Sixth Mansions, chap. 2, p. 135. See ibid, p. 126.

[21] Ibid, chap. 11, p. 197.

[22] Saint John of the Cross, *The Collected Works, The Living Flame of Love*, St. 1, n. 8, p. 582.

[23] *Life*, chap. 29, p. 274.

[24] *Interior Castle*, Sixth Mansions, chap. 2, p. 136.

[25] *Living Flame*, Sixth Mansions, chap. 1, p. 134.

[26] Ibid, nn. 10 and 12, p. 598.

[27] *Interior Castle*, Sixth Mansions, chap. 1, p. 134.

[28] Ibid, p. 131.

[29] *Dark Night*, Book 2, chap. 3, n. 3, p. 333.

[30] *Interior Castle*, Sixth Mansions, chap. 11, p. 198ff.

[31] Ibid, p. 199.

[32] *Living Flame*, St. 1, n 24, p. 589.

[33] *Interior Castle*, Sixth Mansions, chap. 11, p. 200.

[34] Ibid, Fourth Mansions, chap. 3, p. 92.

[35] Ibid, Fifth Mansions, chap. 1, p. 120.

[36] *Living Flame*, St. 3, nn 63-68, pp. 634-635.

[37] *Interior Castle*, Seventh Mansions, chap. 3, p. 222.

[38] Ibid, Fifth Mansions, chap. 1, p. 89.

[39] *Dark Night*, Book 2, chap. 23, n. 7, p. 384.

[40] St. John of the Cross, St. 40, n. 3, p. 564.

[41] *Interior Castle*, Fifth Mansions, chap. 4, p. 119.

[42] Ibid, Sixth Mansions, chap. 1, p. 126.

[43] The *Spiritual Canticle*, St. 14 and 15, n. 1, p. 463.

[44] *Interior Castle*, Seventh Mansions, chap. 3, p. 213. *Spiritual Canticle*, St. 22, nn. 2, 3, 4, 5, 6, pp. 496-498.

[45] *Spiritual Canticle*, St. 22, n. 3, p. 497.

[46] *Interior Castle*, Seventh Mansions, chap. 2, p. 219. *Spiritual Canticle*, St. 26, n. 2, p. 511.

[47] *Living Flame*, St. 4, n. 15, p. 649. See *Interior Castle*, Seventh Mansions, chap. 3, p. 224 and p. 219.

[48] *Interior Castle*, Seventh Mansions, chap. 2, p. 213.

[49] *Living Flame*, St. 1, n. 12, p. 583.

[50] *Life*, chap. 40, p. 351.

[51] *Interior Castle*, Sixth Mansions, chap. 10, p. 194.

[52] *Living Flame*, St. 4, n. 5, p. 644.

[53] *Interior Castle*, Seventh Mansions, chap. 4, p. 235.

[54] *Spiritual Canticle*, St. 29, n. 3, p. 523.

[55] Ibid, n. 3, p. 524.

[56] *Life*, chap. 34, p. 326.

[57] *Interior Castle*, Sixth Mansions, chap. 2, p. 125.

[58] *Ascent*, Book 2, chap. 26, n. 14, pp. 197-198.

[59] *Dark Night*, Book 2, chap. 8, n. 5, p. 345.

[60] *Life*, chap. 39. pp. 377-378.

[61] Ibid, chap. 375.

[62] *Ascent*, Book 3, chap. 2, n. 9, p. 217.

[63] Ibid, n. 10, p. 217.

[64] *Interior Castle*, Seventh Mansions, chap. 3, p. 221.

[65] St. Teresa of Jesus, *The Collected Works of St. Teresa of Avila*, Vol. 3, trans. Kieran Kavanaugh OCD and Otilio Rodriguez OCD p. 375. *Aspirations Towards Eternal Life, Poetry*. Trans. Adrian J. Conney.

[66] *Living Flame*, St. I, n. 30, p. 591.

[67] *Interior Castle*, Fifth Mansions, chap. 1, p. 100.

[68] *The Living Flame*, St. 3, n. 31, p. 621.

[69] Ibid, n. 56, p. 630.

[70] *Interior Castle*, Fourth Mansions, chap. 3, p. 88.

[71] *Life*, chap. 23, p. 223.

[72] *Ascent*, Book 2, chap. 17, n. 2, p. 155.

[73] *The Complete Works of Saint Teresa of Jesus*, Vol. 3, p. 267. Judgment given by St. Teresa upon various writings on the words "Seek Thyself in me."

contemplative living

Mystical Moments in Daily Life

Current interest in Catholic mystical writers is running high. Walk into any shopping-mall bookstore and the religion section will usually contain something by Teresa of Avila, John of the Cross, Julian of Norwich, or Catherine of Siena. There are anthologies of mystical writings and books devoted exclusively to techniques of mystical prayer. These mingle with works on the occult, witchcraft, and New Age religion. They give evidence of lives suffused with certitude about transcendent power and possess a fascinating appeal for people who live in an age of widespread uncertainty and doubt.

The mystical tradition has long been one of the great glories of Catholic spirituality and is enjoying a resurgence, not only in popular literature, but also in scholarly research. The scholars, however, are quick to note that mysticism is not always easy to identify as a religious experience or spiritual way. The terminology has not always been precise or commonly agreed upon, and the stages or steps of the mystical way can be complex, as Father Harvey Egan SJ explains:

> Christian mysticism is a way of life that involves the perfect fulfillment of loving God, neighbor, all God's creation, and oneself. . . . Under God's palpable initiative and direction, mystics fall in love with God—at times abruptly, at times gradually. Through God's special activity, they realize that God is in love with them, and therefore we are all, at least secretly, in love with God and each other. . . . Awakened by God to holiness, mystics are sen-

sitized to their own sinfulness and vileness. Past sins arise and torture them in a purifying way. . . . When the illuminative aspect of mysticism dominates, mystics discover a deeper sense of their enhanced, transformed self and God's intimacy. Visions, locutions, and a variety of secondary phenomena often occur. . . . The unitive life is the last stage of mystical ascent. The mystic becomes as closely united to God through God's love as God is united to his own being by nature. Mystically married to God, the mystic becomes "God by participation."[1]

Searching through anthologies and histories exposes still more surprises in this unique spiritual way of life. Genuine mystics—and this applies to all religious traditions—live with a vivid awareness of God's clear and overwhelming initiative in their life. This initiative results in a profound feeling of being loved as well as a heightened sense of their own sinfulness and need for divine mercy. Mystics respond by a gradual and painful shaping of their entire life and prayer around these intense experiences. After an arduous process of self-cleansing, there occurs the holistic merging of one's entire life with the Divine Mystery. Mystical prayer, an engaging contemporary issue in itself, accents all these qualities through a variety of visions, locutions, and intense ecstasies that eventually pass into sublime interior forms of prayer.

More than anything else, what keys the mystical way is that these heightened experiences dominate all the other aspects of the lives of mystics. The qualities and characteristics of the mystical experience flow into and shape even life's daily routines. Mystics "see" everyday events through a different lens; the smallest of passing human experiences (a greeting, a spurned look, the briefest of thoughts) is interpreted against a background of human sinfulness, divine mercy, and God's saving love.

But exalted descriptions of mysticism can also cause confusion, especially to beginning readers in spiritual literature. Despite the attention given to it, mysticism is not the primary spiritual way for most people. The Catholic tradition has continually recognized that the great majority of believers are called to pursue the "ordinary way" of the Gospels, a path of holiness acted out within the daily, regular responsibilities of social life. Ordinary gospel holiness grows through daily love and service of other people, through honesty and justice in social interactions, and through personal conversion and integrity.

There is nothing inferior about this ordinary way, for it is the way outlined by Christ himself in the Sermon on the Mount and in his parables and moral exhortations. It is the simple way that St. Paul describes excellently and frequently: "Your love must be sincere. Detest what is evil, cling to what is good. Love one another with familial affection. Anticipate each other in showing respect.... Rejoice in hope, be patient under trial, persevere in prayer.... Be generous in offering hospitality. Never repay injury with injury. See that your conduct is honorable in the eyes of all. If possible, live peaceably with everyone" (Rm 12:9-18). "Help carry one another's burdens; in that way you will fulfill the law of Christ" (Gal 6:2). "Because you are God's chosen ones, holy and beloved, clothe yourselves with heartfelt mercy, with kindness, humility, meekness, and patience. Bear with one another; forgive what grievances you have against one another. Dedicate yourselves to thankfulness" (Col 3:12-15).

The mystical way stands alongside the ordinary gospel way of conversion and love as both complement and catalyst. The path of the mystics points to the end of God's plan for all people. We might say that God's salvific plan is fast forwarded in their lives with the purpose of helping the majority keep in sight the true end of their daily efforts.

But, and this is a point often overlooked in spiritual literature, there frequently are times and events in which the two spiritualities converge. Even if most people are not mystics in the full sense of the term, many who follow the ordinary way of conversion, love, and service do experience what might be called mystical moments. A mystical moment is a brief sudden intrusion in which ordinary awareness is overwhelmed by feelings and desires that reveal a transcendent mysteriousness and often a holy presence. This sudden perception totally overturns the ordinary way of looking at things; a touch of mysticism jolts the recipient out of the usual and commonplace. Listen to this description by a young woman:

> I had an unusual experience this evening. I went to 5 p.m. Mass. About five minutes before Mass started, I was asked to fill in for an ill eucharistic minister and I agreed. Anyway, I was distributing Communion when I was suddenly struck with two distinct sensations: the first was an unnerving sense of awe, and the second was an almost overwhelming sense of unworthiness. I can't shake those feelings, nor can I understand them. The initial intensity was such that I had

difficulty (physically) picking up the hosts and placing them in people's hands. I can't explain this, but I felt something!

That is a genuine mystical moment, a sudden brief intrusion of God's awesome and grace-filled presence. They happen to many ordinary believers . . . perhaps infrequently, but they happen! Such moments people know to be radically different, "timeless" moments. The true mystic is frequently gifted with these experiences for prolonged periods. In the ordinary Christian life these mystical moments are usually fleeting and infrequent, but they can have a profound spiritual impact and should not be neglected. In *Christian Holiness*, an excellent pre-Vatican II manual of ascetical theology, Gustave Thils thoughtfully notes: "Mysticism requires, in a general way, the realization of the immediate presence of God. . . . Many of the faithful have been able to live [with this presence] at certain moments of their existence, in very brief fashion, but really: some, after they have gone to Holy Communion; others, in the course of a visit to the Blessed Sacrament; others, on the occasion of a liturgical ceremony, an ordination, a consecration; still others, in the solitude of their homes, in joy, in suffering, in mourning. If we must avoid speaking lightly of mysticism, it is also important not to underestimate certain minor transitory forms of true and authentic Christian mysticism."[2]

Mystical moments should be accepted for what they are: God's loving and overwhelming initiative in the lives of ordinary people.

For those who are unaware of this spiritual phenomenon, mystical moments may be frightening. They think that something is wrong with them or they are unsure of the source: "Am I verging on disorientation?" "Could this be an evil temptation?" The spiritual reality of mystical moments needs to be taught and more widely known in ordinary Christian teaching on the spiritual life.

Mystical moments should be accepted for what they are: God's loving and overwhelming initiative in the lives of ordinary people. They are instants when the ever present Mystery of God takes over completely and makes people see beyond their ordinary (and often dulled) perceptions. There is no human control in these moments. As St. Paul said aptly of himself, "this man—whether in or outside his body I do not know, God knows—was snatched up to Paradise to hear words which cannot be uttered" (2 Co 12:3-4). Mystical moments alert the recipient to the experiential truth of God's love. Upon understanding better the nature of her experience, the young woman mentioned earlier could profess: "This experience has given me a spiritual growth spurt. I know God loves me, not an abstract idea of belief, but a real heart and head knowledge, and I feel secure."

Mystical moments may serve to confirm people in decisions they have painfully struggled toward. A young mother, wrestling with a decision to return to graduate school, told this story:

> One night I awakened suddenly with the feeling of a presence hovering over my headboard. Since the bed was against a wall, no one could have been standing there, yet in my heart I felt so affirmed as wife, mother, and teacher that I knew from that moment on it was ok to go back to school. My nighttime realization I felt came from my Creator, whom I did not see, yet whose presence I physically sensed.

Other mystical moments call the recipients to repentance and return. Such was attested by a psychologist who had drifted away from his Catholic upbringing:

> One day I was in our bedroom packing for a business trip. My eyes happened to glance at a crucifix (an artifact of my wife's continuing devotion), and suddenly I felt overpowered by a mysterious presence that seemed just beyond my senses, but surely and absolutely there! I felt drained of all physical strength and slumped on the edge of the bed, fearful, weak, and aghast. Then a message appeared repeatedly in my mind: "Everything will be all right!" This combination of mysterious presence, weakness, and consoling message lasted only a few minutes, but it transformed my life.

It is common for mystical moments to include messages. They are not to be understood as public revelations, but as directions for this individual at this precise time. F.C. Happold describes such a moment in the life of a novelist, Winifred Holtby, when told that she might not have more than two years to live:

> Compelled by bodily weakness to give up her work, her whole being in rebellion, she was one day feeling very tired and dispirited walking up a hill and came to a trough outside a farmhouse. Its surface was frozen over and some lambs were gathered round it. She broke the ice for them with her stick, and as she did so heard a voice within her

saying, "Having nothing, yet possessing all things." It was so distinct that she looked round startled, but she was alone on the top of the hill. Suddenly, in a flash, the grief, the bitterness, the sense of frustration disappeared; all desire to possess power and glory for herself vanished and never came back. . . . That moment, she said, was the supreme spiritual experience of her life.[3]

Mystical moments are meant to guide and strengthen the ordinary way of Christian spirituality, to let us know that we are truly cared for by an awesome but loving God, to call us to the truth of our failings, to let us touch the immensity of the divine message. They proclaim forcefully that God's presence is truly with us, even if we do not always feel it in the daily and hectic routines of life. Such a moment occurred to F.C. Happold himself:

It happened in my room . . . when I was an undergraduate at Cambridge. If I say that Christ came to me I should be using conventional words which would carry no precise meaning. . . . There was no sensible vision. There was just the room, with its shabby furniture and the fire burning in the grate. But the room was filled by a Presence, which in a strange way was both about me and within me, like light or warmth. I was overwhelmingly possessed by Someone who was not myself, and yet I felt I was more myself than I had ever been before. I was filled with an intense happiness, an almost unbearable joy, such as I had never known before and have never known since. And over all was a deep sense of peace and security and serenity.[4]

In fact, after a mystical moment, much of an individual's daily routines may remain the same. Changes in life will not be nearly as drastic or all-pervasive as in full-blown mysticism, but there may be a different interior awareness. The person still knows that the ordinary Christian way must be followed, worked at, and prayed for. Daily tasks and routines (as well as personal weaknesses) remain. But a significant, fortifying experience has surely occurred.

Much more could be said about this oft-neglected aspect of spiritual teaching. Hopefully, it will receive more attention in current and future instruction. (Unfortunately, the *Catechism of the Catholic Church* has no material covering this issue.) However, the basics of these grace-filled moments can be summarized as follows: (1) Mystical moments do happen; they are the sudden awareness of an immediate and total presence of the overwhelming and awesome Divine Mystery to ourselves. (2) Mystical moments are for the benefit of the individual recipient as a sign of God's love, a call to repentance, a realization of awe, a strengthening encouragement, and so forth. (3) Mystical moments cannot be forced, and, as a rule, they occur infrequently and briefly. (4) A person should simply be thankful for them and carry their fruits into the daily gospel way of Christian life.

As Christians in today's hectic world, we must become more aware of these mystic moments on our journey with God. We must be careful not to dismiss, ignore, or fear such moments. Instead, let us truly believe that God is seeking us, reaching out and sending gifts of personal, loving attention through mystical moments. Then it shall be our gift to wait, listen, and lovingly accept.

Notes

[1] Harvey Egan SJ, *An Anthology of Christian Mysticism* (Collegeville: Liturgical Press, 1991), pp. xvi-xviii.

[2] Gustave Thils, *Christian Holiness* (Tielt, Belgium: Lannoo, 1961), pp. 543-544.

[3] F.C. Happold, *Mysticism: A Study and an Anthology* (Penguin Books, 1973), pp. 130-131.

[4] Happold, pp. 133-134.

Becoming Contemplative
Here or There

The woman sitting opposite me expressed herself with some urgency. "Can you help me, can you teach me, how to become more contemplative? I know I am being called to this; I want to respond. But I feel I don't know how." It was a request I have been hearing more often these last years and one that I welcome with all my heart. Even though I experience embarrassment mixed with humble challenge at being addressed as a "contemplative," I do acknowledge that monastic contemplatives can be expected to share with today's seekers some of their centuries-old lifestyle.

That original request and this response presuppose the truth that all of us are called to be contemplatives, that all of us will someday *be* contemplatives in the Beatific Vision when we see God face-to-face. The goal of contemplative monastic formation is identical with that of all Christian living: transformation into Christ. To grow into Christ, to become so one with him that it can truly be said, "Christ lives in me," is sufficient motivation for a whole life's striving, whether of laity, clergy, or religious, in family, parish, or religious community.

Variant lifestyles offer unique blends of the means to this transformation into Christ. Monastic formation provides one specific set of experiences aimed at helping people realize their call to contemplative living; this focus on contemplation makes the monastic lifestyle relevant for human growth anywhere. The present article shares reflections on becoming contemplative and on four major elements of monastic formation: constant prayer, silence, solitude, and life in close community.

Forming a Contemplative

How is a contemplative formed? By the overwhelming love of God evoking a free response. God's loving call is continually operative, evoking more and more freedom in human response. The initiative is always God's, not ours. This truth is basic to all contemplative living, but its practical implication usually comes slowly. Like children we protest, "Let me, let me." We want to do it ourselves. Impossible. Just how impossible we learn over and over again as our radical incapacity is made obvious by the repeated failure of our best efforts.

The only capability we have is that of being recipients. We can open our hands and our hearts to the gift that is surely being given us. We can allow ourselves to be graced. Our openness to receive, however, may wear some rather strange disguises: fear, reluctance, protest ("Why me?"), along with a whole gamut of projections. As long as these come from human weakness and not deliberate refusal, they will not stop the process but only slow it.

And process is what we are talking about. Centuries of monastic tradition place special emphasis on formation as praxis, practical process. From the beginnings, with Anthony in the desert, it was known that a person becomes a contemplative only by living contemplatively and this over days, months, years. Progression is a matter of practice, of repeated choices. What monastic life offers is a structuring of experience in ways that can contribute to contemplative response.

Experience, it has been said, is not what happens to us, but what we do with what happens to us. Events and circumstances trigger reactions, but how we respond depends on us: the past of our biology along with previous experience, all summarized in present choices. No two people see the same thing or feel the same way about anything. This is a truism we all admit. But our own everyday experience so fills the screen of reality that nothing else seems real until we stumble over another's perception of the same "fact" or come up against the hard rock of refractory reality. When this happens, we are offered the opportunity to go beyond naive subjectivism. We can open the window to let in a larger, more objective view. We are ready to learn. Since whatever lives is either growing or regressing, openness to change is crucial for realizing human potential.

Ideally, persons entering a monastery thereby make a strong statement of willingness to begin the process of contemplative formation. At least a part of them so desires. But, given the split level of the lives of most of us, this may be only surface motivation. Underneath lurk layers of unconscious resistance. When change threatens, defenses rise. Conversion seems to cost too much. Will our willingness to begin the process of formation prove stronger than the resistance? Then awareness breaks through our defenses, and decision begins to abandon them.

But the outcome is not always so hopeful. Some who begin a contemplative life never become aware of the specifics of the conversion they need. Their patterns of behavior are too deeply rooted; they change only on the surface. Others, when they feel the first cracks in their defense system, tighten their resistance, terrified that change in old patterns may lead to total breakdown. Both kinds of people interfere with the working of the process. They must be advised to leave; they have never entered into formation, no matter how long they have stayed.

What monastic life offers is a structuring of experience in ways that can contribute to contemplative response.

Those who give themselves to the process let their awareness initiate change. They are willing, if not eager, to lose their life in order to save it. They start making practical changes in the way they live. Formation begins.

But becoming a contemplative remains beyond us. We can never achieve it. Self-transcendence cannot be commandeered by any act of our will. Monastic life with its countercultural emphasis on obedience and surrender in prayer provides daily opportunities to go beyond what we can do by ourselves. While "saying prayers" can bring us satisfaction, living a life of prayer—more receptivity than accomplishment—calls for patience.

Learning to surrender has its own cheap counterfeits. Passivity it is not, nor is it clenched-teeth conformity. Authentic self-gift requires freedom's consent and leads to growth in freedom. Strain is its antithesis. When individuals try too hard, when they attempt to do more than they can, they become exhausted, anxious, or chronically irritated. What should free them enslaves them. Formation becomes deforming.

Authentic self-surrender, though not easy, is marked by a certain ease. Individuals seem relaxed, ready to continue the process which will go on for the whole of their life. A monastic novitiate stresses this continuity. What novices do, how they live, follows the same style of life as the professed. Even if it includes additional leisure for study and reflection, more opportunity for direction, less responsibility for major work, these are differences in amount rather than in kind. The content of the life is the same for all, and it lasts all their life.

Acceptance of grace, openness to conversion, self-surrender, and willingness to enter into a lifelong program characterize the interior of contemplative formation. Without these nothing happens. With them the process can proceed. It is given a certain shape and direction by the experiences life provides.

Constant Prayer

If I were to ask, "What influence has effected the most far-reaching changes in your life?" the answers would be as diverse as the people polled. But one response I would feel sure of getting: "other people." The more prolonged and deep the personal relation, the more pervasive its power.

Contemplative living raises this question and answers it by asserting that God is the most enduring and central of all relationships and so the most formative. Of course, God is so necessary, so attractive, so powerful, so close to us that this relationship should transform all others. But we know that in practice this is often not the case. What individuals experience of God's relation to them ranges from vague ineffectiveness and disinterested distance to consistent control and punishment. In between these extremes lie relations in which God is kept at the safe distance of Sunday propriety.

In providing a situation where individuals will have to "live on" or "live out of" personal relationship with God, monastic formation uncovers the weaknesses as well as the strengths in this most personal of relationships. More importantly, it makes possible a growth that will be life-sustaining.

Most of us get along well enough with the relative whom we never see, the person we only hear from at Christmastime. Absence succeeds in making the heart grow fonder. Keeping God at a distance makes for interpersonal "safety." We may not even realize this until God begins to move in. Then everything changes. We come to recognize that we have filled in the blanks of our experience of God with projections from our past. We may be angry at God as we work through the unfinished rebellion of our adolescence. We may be filled with fear, expecting punishment from a God who is disgusted with our moral lapses. We may dread an exacting God who expects continual perfection. The way we relate to ourselves often enough gives rise to distortions that cripple all our relationships, especially the one with the divine.

We may not know any of this until we begin to give God more room in our lives. What changes is not God but ourselves. We have said yes with the practical language of time and space. We have opened the door just a crack, and divine revelation streams through. Now we are faced with a choice, as we are in any relationship; we can settle for where we are or go deeper. We can even slam shut the door, preferring darkness to light.

Resisting truth's revelation remains a possibility in any lifestyle. Human ingenuity can choose pleasure, power, possessions in the most austere of circumstances. Monastic life is designed to make these deceptions less satisfying. As one experienced religious told me, "There are escape hatches in the monastery, but they are rather small." Deliberately so.

In contemplative life, relationship with God becomes an urgent priority because community living deliberately limits hours of work and time for interpersonal relationships and also builds in a certain paucity of possessions in order to provide more opportunity for prayer. Such freeing of the heart at least *can* happen. Daily listening to God in Scripture, liturgy, and reflective reading should challenge complacency while the example of others gives encouragement and the practical wisdom that flows from experience.

Relation with God is strengthened and deepened by daily periods of prolonged prayer. The Holy Spirit teaches prayer to those who are desirous of learning. The lessons are simple, even though learning them is not easy: taking time and making the effort without expecting to "produce" prayer; turning away from distractions without becoming discouraged by them; realizing that nothing, absolutely nothing, can separate us from a loving relationship with God save only willful refusal. The contemplative in formation learns to be satisfied with daily bread of dry prayer, knowing that relationship with God is growing even when emotions are on short rations. Experiences of light and strength are received with gratitude, but are neither demanded nor used as criteria of "successful" prayer. God is at work in prayer, as in life, emptying our hearts. Ours to be there, not fussing nor focusing unduly on the process, allowing the Spirit to pray in us "with unutterable groanings." These practices form the prayer of the contemplative. Fidelity to them deepens relationship with God till it becomes a person's raison d'être. There is no other.

Silence

Since the word of God is the source and the goal of contemplative life, silence to hear and solitude to seek are no longer luxuries but necessities. Silence, the quieting of external noise and the stilling of a distracted heart, makes listening possible. It forms an essential discipline of monastic life.

If silence of speech, gestures, and actions helps to quiet the heart, the reverse is also true. A silent heart makes for external silence. Spirit and body reinforce each other. But the heart has priority; otherwise silence risks sterility. Yet external silence has its own unique importance since its practice concretizes our intentions. So the process of contemplative formation includes a certain commitment to turning off unnecessary noise, the assault of television and tapes, the distraction of purely curious reading, the waste of unnecessary comment.

Since actions speak even louder than words, they too need to be stilled. Emotions have their say in the heavy walk, the package ripped open, the door banged too hard. Moderating this body language creates an atmosphere of peace, slowing and stilling the interior—but only if such practices of external silence are without the strain that would but add to the confusion and din.

At first the practice of external silence may seem to increase the decibels of internal sound. But whatever appears as we become more quiet has always been there: the repetitious patterns of self-justification, the anxious review of what "she said" and what "I said," the censuring of others' conduct, the circling of anger back over some presumed injustice. Something in us must enjoy sucking on the sour ball of our misery; at least it distracts from the question of personal responsibility.

How to still these destructive voices? That is the work of a lifetime. But we can begin by hearing the conflicting voices clamoring for our attention, listening to what they say, and accepting responsibility for answering appropriately. Slowly, over the years, the contemplative grows more quiet. Conflicting desires no longer play tug-of-war; "one thing only" is enough. Motivation is less apt to bend back on itself in devious forms of selfishness. God holds fast the center, and everything else can be tested against this truth.

"There is a time to speak and a time to refrain from speaking." A stilled heart grows in the charity that smoothly balances silence and speech. It is better able to discern the appropriate word and grows freer to say it. It remains at peace no matter how others respond. Its speech is more effective because less contaminated by vanity and self-seeking. Speaking in charity does not break silence, no matter how numerous the words. A silent heart remains at peace in the Lord.

Solitude

Internal and external silences learn to speak in solitude; there union with God grows deeper and more pervasive; there the solitary heart discovers everyone and everything in their reality in God. Just as silence stills noise, making possible a more intense form of listening, solitude focuses us on the place of God and others in our life.

True solitude needs to be distinguished from escapism, depressive withdrawal, or selfish isolationism. All of these put self on center stage, narrowing our world to the immediate and the problematic. Authentic solitude moves inward only for the sake of moving outward. Diving deep into the mystery of our essential neediness and dependence on God and others gives promise of the treasure of more selfless involvement.

The solitary displaces self in order to find a God "large enough" to fill one's whole universe of meaning. Obviously, God is big enough to do so; but, until we deliberately place ourselves in a situation where there is nothing else, we may not experience this largesse. Before solitude can bear such fruit, we must go apart and be brought face-to-face with God and ourselves. Alone. Only then can solitude hollow out our heart, emptying it so it can be filled. The process is painful; the positive aspects are at first imperceptible. Temptation suggests filling in the space with anything available, and human ingenuity is creative in discovering projects and errands and people that "simply must" be completed and run and contacted. Anything would be better than what feels like nothing.

Becoming comfortable with solitude can be learned only through patient experience. Short spaces of time by oneself can gradually be lengthened. Freedom to choose the when and where of these initial experiences helps to dissipate some of the almost-terror that may overtake someone contemplating the prospect of being alone. But finally the contemplative must confront the aloneness barrier in the hope of seeing what is discoverable on the other side.

What is discovered is God and self and everything else besides. The solitary's apartness becomes rich in the realization that we are never really apart, but rather are always a part of a greater whole. Periods of solitude are now treasured as opportunities, nourishing unity and union. They are sought out and prolonged when this is possible. They open out into ever greater inclusiveness. The reality of this expansiveness is evident as judgment grows more compassionate, detached concern for one's neighbor becomes more practical, and the poor, whoever they may be, become special favorites.

Just as silence prepares one to speak, solitude forms one for some kind of caring. Then physical apartness may become less important. Though a certain amount of it remains necessary, the heart stays solitary even in the midst of a crowd. Being by oneself has fostered a sense of uniqueness, the aloneness that is true identity. More secure in self, the solitary is present in that Reality which unifies all being, independent of space or time. The heart of the true solitary experiences that everything is one in Christ Jesus.

Community

Just as love of God requires love of neighbor, so too a life of prayer, silence, and solitude must be verified in community. Life together challenges, purifies, and sustains contemplation on its "way" toward completion in the communion of saints.

Contemplation begins in love and leads to growth in love. Why contemplate? Because one loves and wants to see more of the beloved, and then the long look of love increases desire in a process of continual renewal. This expresses the secret of contemplative living: Love leads to looking, and the seeing of the contemplative enkindles still greater desire for loving union.

Where is community in all of this? Right at the heart. Love

that looks at God sees everyone and everything else with new vision. Love of God and love of others are not two loves, but two expressions of the same love. Any union with God that would bypass the immediacy of one's neighbor is deceived. How can we love a God whom we do not see if we do not love our neighbor whom we do see? This basic question asked of every Christian distinguishes authentic contemplation from techniques designed to produce a spiritual experience through altering brain waves or promoting relaxation. Whether induced by hypnotism or by mood-altering drugs, such "contemplation" is unrelated to charity.

Life in community forms the solid rock on which to build a life of sacrificial love. This is true at the beginning of contemplative formation and true at its end. Those who come to the monastery usually expect long hours of prayer and the disciplines of silence and solitude. They may not anticipate the implications of close living with a whole group of others who are also "on the way"—but in their own way.

One of the first surprises of the neophyte in a contemplative community is the wild variety of persons called; God's tastes are certainly eclectic—something for which each of us has reason to be grateful. As persons mature in a contemplative community, they often grow still more individual. Experiencing the divine love, they are freed to become the "beloved" of God that they are called to be. They are themselves. ∅

Unfortunately, our tastes may not be as catholic as God's. We would prefer others to be more like us; that way it would be easier to find them likable, but at the risk of reducing reality to the narrowness of our preferences. Formation in a contemplative community stretches us and, in doing so, opens us to the all-embracing love that is God's.

Contemplative charity will have to work through layers of negativity before it grows into acceptance and hopefully comes to joy in the creative power of love. The process is long and costly, one that is unlikely ever to be completed. That is part of its capacity for purification. Humility grows deeper as one is brought face-to-face with repeated failure. One is always a beginner in the ways of love, and this, not in easy theory, but in daily practice.

The closeness of a contemplative community makes these demands very real. Opportunities to serve others abound: finishing a job that someone else has begun, volunteering to help when one is already tired, listening to the repetition of a too familiar story, stilling the quick retort that could cut, forgetting a past hurt to allow someone a new beginning. Sacrifices so small seem unworthy of mention. This is part of their value; they leave little room for that self-glorification which destroys true contemplation.

The heightened awareness, however, that the silence and solitude of contemplative life foster can find itself focusing on the defects of others. One's neighbor is so immediate, right next door, morning, noon, and night. Small wonder that minding one's own business becomes an important element in contemplative formation. Phrased more positively, belief in the good intentions of others, trust in their deepest desires, leads to a love that is truly compassionate. Then the weakness of others calls forth understanding support. If we perceive what might occasion the sin of another, we sacrifice to avoid it. Instead of taking scandal at another's failure, we try to provide encouragement by living more faithfully what we ourselves are called to. In this way community calls us forth to "build each other up in love."

It is the consistency of these practices of love which makes them so formative. Love deepens love. Competition, comparison, criticism grow less possible. The kindly deed, the charitable judgment, the supportive stance become almost instinctive. Practiced over the years, contemplative charity seems second nature. Such charity is not self-conscious. It simply does what needs to be done and goes on. Always ready to help, it does not need to do so. Awareness of the needs of others is balanced with sensitivity to their privacy. Warm and affectionate, it remains detached, ready to serve another's freedom by letting go.

Long before love has matured into this kind of tried and true virtue, it has begun to bear other fruits. Life in close community is a tremendous source of encouragement. Underneath the obvious differences in personality and ways of doing things, there lies a great commonality of purpose. Why have we come here? In whatever accents the response may be phrased, what is said is the same: "Love of God and of neighbor, realized in the prayer and silence and solitude of this community." This is what keeps all going in the same direction. This purpose becomes a love that grows stronger with the years of living closely together; a love that knows another's poverty, not to take advantage of it, but to supply for it; a love that appreciates another's richness, but does not abuse it by overreliance, much less dependence. Mature love is secure enough to admit a mistake without undue embarrassment, accept an apology even when unspoken. Like God's love for us, true charity for our neighbor is given so freely that it creates freedom in the recipient.

Love formed in a contemplative community is expressive even if its language is somewhat muted by the demands of silence and solitude. It speaks in the wordlessness of an understanding glance, a gesture of genuine compassion. It supports another's burden without seeming burdened. Such love is blessed with a kindly sense of humor that laughs with others, not at them. It is quick to appreciate and commend, very slow to criticize, unable to condemn. Real charity has learned concrete ways of preferring others to oneself. It is sacrificial and thus sanctifying.

Contemplation Here or There

Constant prayer, attentive silence, and fruitful solitude, all lived in the realism of close community—these are basic to contemplative formation. Practicing them is central to monastic discipline, but those who are not monks are not excluded. All the monastery does is highlight the elements that are formative in every Christian life. Anyone who desires to live more contemplatively needs to incorporate these disciplines into daily living, and each one who is called to life in a monastery needs to reaffirm his or her lifelong commitment to them with the fresh observance appropriate to the reality of today's religious life.

Mysticism as Flight

Someone asked recently if mysticism is an escape. Yes, it is—from the "unreal to the Real." Yes, mysticism is a flight, not so much from the world as we know it, but to the world for which we have been created, which for the most part we do not know. The breakthrough to the mystical, to the Transcendent, is the true goal of our lives.

Not long before his death, a saintly octogenarian monk in South India gave an overview of how he saw life.[1] He loosely divided life into three stages: From birth until one is twenty years of age, the body, the physical aspect of a person, is being developed and one is eventually brought to the threshold of maturity; from twenty to forty, then, the psychic realm develops more fully, and a person usually marries, reaches his or her peak in sports and the arts, specializes and trains in certain job interests, develops various talents, and enhances the mind in many ways. Many people today believe that this is all there is to life and that we are "over the hill" from there on. But this is far from the truth. At forty we are usually ready for a breakthrough to the Transcendent; the mystical dimension awakens in us, and our whole personality begins to flower. We are not fully developed human beings until this comes to be. It is for this final stage that all the rest has prepared us, but few are aware of this and try desperately to cleave to the first two stages. Is this breakthrough to the mystical, to the contemplative level of life, escapism? Yes, if you truly let go and let God be God in you. "Be still and know that I am God" (Ps 46:10). You will be escaping the prison of the first two stages of development into that reality for which you have been created. This breakthrough can happen before a person turns forty years of age, but ordinarily it happens at about that time.

Detachment

Is detachment necessary for the Christian at this stage? Yes, but surely there has been for various reasons some detachment along the way in the first two stages—probably, however, with much self-interest mixed in. The kind of detachment needed in the mystical flight calls for a pure heart. Jesus implies in one of the beatitudes that it takes a pure heart to see God. Meister Eckhart describes a pure heart as one that is unworried, unattached, and uncommitted and wants its own way in nothing except to be submerged in the divine will. There must be detachment from the ego, the false self that seeks to be first, best, and greatest. The breakthrough to the mystical is a breakup of the selfish self, a surrender to the Divine Self so that one is overwhelmed with divine love. While all of creation can help us to God, without detachment from outward multiplicity there can be no arrival at inward unity. Asked why many good persons miss this mystical breakthrough, Ruusbroec (1293-1381) says it is because

> they do not respond to God's movement with a renunciation of themselves and therefore do not stand in God's presence with living fervor. They are not careful in the way they interiorly observe themselves and accordingly remain always turned more to outward multiplicity than to interior simplicity. They perform their works more out of good custom than out of interior experience and pay more attention to particular methods and the greatness and multiplicity of good works than to having their intention and love directed to God. They therefore remain caught up in the exterior multiple concerns of the heart and are not aware of how God lives within them in the fullness of his grace.[2]

In another of his writings, Ruusbroec insists that God's work in the emptiness of our soul is eternal. He is constantly begetting Jesus in us, but we are unaware that we are so loved. If only we would pause more often and "fan the fire"!

The desert monks have much to say about detachment. They refer to it as death in relation to every person or thing. This, they say, is what produces the very desire for God.[3] Without this we kill either ourselves or others by our overattachment. Detachment, they claim, is the "mark of a perfect soul, whereas it is characteristic of an imperfect soul to be worn down with anxiety about material things." The perfect soul is called a "lily among thorns" (Song of Songs); "it lives with detachment in the midst of those who are troubled by such anxiety."[4] Indeed, God has made us "little less than the angels" (Ps 8). We are neither animals nor angels, yet participate in both realms and are pulled by both poles.

Dynamic Yearning

The desert monks have much to say about people who live at either pole or extreme. The mystic journey, contemplative life, takes us beyond rational thought, beyond concepts and images. It is prayer, which is a state of presence, a dynamic, yearning, loving presence. This "craving for Absolute Truth is the whole meaning of our life," according to Evelyn Underhill.[5] She encourages us to give ourselves to this divine and intimate life in which we are immersed. In fact, the longing for completeness has been called the "starting point" of the devotional, mystical way.

Lama Govinda calls this dynamic, yearning, loving way of being present "feminine passivity," the most active stance one can have because it involves total receptivity. "Be still and know. . . ." He refers to masculine passivity as laziness. There is a danger, when we desire detachment and surrender, of falling into a false inertia, supposedly the "angelic life." We must be aware of such dangers and be able to discern, to sort out what spirit is at work in us.

> Because Ruusbroec lived before the official condemnation of Quietism, he never mentions the word, but he describes it in no uncertain terms, condemning it as strongly as he can: "When a person wants to rest in a state of emptiness without interior yearning for God and devotion to God, such a one is liable to all kinds of error, for such has turned away from God and toward himself with a natural love, seeking and desiring consolation, sweetness, and whatever else pleases this one. . . . A person who lives like this in a state of natural love is constantly closed in upon himself through his self-seeking and lack of detachment."[6]

Ruusbroec saw this as completely contrary to charity because, as we know, charity is that bond of love which lifts us up above ourselves and through which we renounce ourselves and become united with God and one another. Jesus begs us to remain in his love and promises to come and manifest himself to us (Jn 15:10 and 16:16ff). This is the divine life in which we are immersed. This breakthrough to the Transcendent for which we have been created is God's greatest desire for us, and he gives us all the grace and help possible to awaken us to it. Once we awaken, detachment loses its sting. To lovers nothing is too much.

Our Beloved is ever present. Even the falling away of the body, as time and aging take their toll, is all part of the process onward beyond time and space. Like the snake losing its skin, so we eventually go beyond. Yet that body has been a great blessing and will be reunited to us again, sharing our eternal joy with our incarnate God who came to lead us, to show us the way, and to be our strength on it.

Jesus the Way

Jesus—the way, the truth, and the life for the Christian—gave us many glimpses of that divine and intimate life in which he was immersed. Early in childhood he was "about my Father's business" (Lk 2:49), and throughout his public life he frequently spoke to and of the Father from the depths of his heart: "I know that you always hear me" (Jn 11:41). "I am not alone; the one who sent me is with me" (Jn 8:16). "The Father is in me and I am in the Father" (Jn 10:38 and 14:11). "I came from the Father and . . . go to the Father" (Jn 16:28; see also 14:28). He even let us in on his in-depth experience of being called by the Father "my Beloved" (Lk 3:22).

A contemplative lifestyle is one in which simplicity and stillness of heart are enhanced by one's surroundings and choices.

During his passion and death agony, Jesus was aware that the cup he was to drink was the cup that the Father has given him (Jn 18:11), and he told Pilate, "You would have no power over me if it had not been given you from above" (Jn 19:11). Again, after the resurrection Jesus said to his disciples, "I am ascending to my Father and your Father, to my God and your God" (Jn 20:17). Never unmindful of the Father, in commissioning his apostles Jesus said, "As the Father sent me, so I am sending you" (Jn 20:21).

His craving for Absolute Truth knew no bounds and was indeed the meaning of his whole life and ours. His dying wish, his heart's desire for each and all of us to the end, was directed to his Father: "May they be one in us, as you are in me and I am in you" (Jn 17:21). It is for this that he came; as John's Gospel puts it, "No one has ever seen God; it is the only Son, who is nearest to the Father's heart, who has made him known" (Jn 1:18). Jesus pleads with us: "Make your home in me as I make mine in you" (Jn 15:4).

Readiness

On the mystical path, one is usually gifted with contemplative prayer. There is a difference between contemplative prayer, contemplative life, and contemplative lifestyle. One may be living an in-depth contemplative life without necessarily being graced with a contemplative lifestyle. A contemplative lifestyle is one in which simplicity and stillness of heart are enhanced by one's surroundings and choices. Thomas Keating OCSO and other spiritual writers use the words interchangeably: The mystic life is the contemplative life. This is not something one achieves or "turns on," but is pure gift of God for which we can prepare ourselves.

"My heart is ready, O God, my heart is ready" (Ps 57:7). Contemplative life and contemplative prayer go hand in hand, heart in heart. Awaiting, yearning for God's gift, one can choose among many helpful methods to prepare for the gift. Evelyn Underhill says the business and method of mysticism is love. She often quotes Eckhart and others who refer to God's "spark" of love aflame in each of us. Our part is to fan the flame insofar as we are able. Some helpful practices are:

> • mantras and ejaculatory prayers to keep us mindful of God's presence throughout the day, mindful of who God is, who our neighbor is, and who we are. We need to put in our mind what we want there instead of letting our mind run rampant.

> • good reading, such as well-chosen portions of Scripture. "The word is a two-edged sword" (see Heb 4:12). "Make my word your home" (Jn 8:31). Spiritual books written by those who have traveled the path can be very helpful.

> • keeping company with those who love God and are seeking to surrender to him. Many parishes have small faith-sharing groups. Form your own. Hindus have a wonderful ancient practice called *satsang*: keeping company with the saints or those who love the Lord and want to hear stories about his deeds and his words. They believe great blessings come to those who seek out such company regularly.

- good motivations. A daily practice of discernment of spirits is very helpful in checking on our intentions. The Dalai Lama says he checks his intentions both morning and evening and that this has been a longtime practice of his which he finds most fruitful.

- some form of devotion, for a healthy balance. Remember that "the business and method of mysticism is love," and so find ways to bring spiritual gifts to the Beloved during the day and night and pause to recognize the gifts coming from the Beloved. A great way to "fan the fire."

- regular practice of meditation. Whether one chooses centering prayer, Christian Zen, or another method for going beyond concept, thought, and image and just being in the Presence, it is important to give regular and prime time to such "preparation" for the mystical encounter, remembering that the mystic knows God by communion.

Is the mystical life a flight from the world? Yes, to the world of divine and intimate life in which we are immersed. In Ruusbroec's words, "When the vessel is ready, the precious liquid is poured in. There is no more precious vessel than a loving soul, and no more beneficial drink than the grace of God."[7]

Notes

[1] Bede Griffiths OSB. A Briton, he lived many years in South India, in Shantivanam Ashram. Audio tape of a talk given at Osage Monastery, Sand Springs, Oklahoma, in July 1992.

[2] *John Ruusbroec: The Spiritual Espousals, the Sparkling Stones, and Other Works*, intro. and trans. James A. Wiseman OSB (Mahwah: Paulist Press, 1985), p. 259.

[3] St. Isaiah the Solitary, *The Philokalia*, vol. 1, p. 27.

[4] St. Neilos the Ascetic, *The Philokalia*, vol. 1, p. 244.

[5] Evelyn Underhill, *Mysticism* (New York: E.P. Dutton and Co., 1961).

[6] *John Ruusbroec*, p. 137.

[7] *John Ruusbroec*, p. 74.

Unceasing Prayer:
Romancing the Divine

A mystic poem from India suggests, "If you make love with the divine now, in the next life you will have the face of satisfied desire" (Robert Bly, *The Kabir Book*, Beacon Press, 1977). Anyone who has been in love or has experienced friendship with a soul mate knows something about praying without ceasing. In such relationships one's heart is in constant, unceasing communication with the beloved or the friend. The dynamics of such experience can open a window into relationship with God. This article invites you to peer through this window and see how natural it can be to pray without ceasing.

God as Lover and Soul Mate

If prayer is a process of relating to God, romancing the Divine can become a profound and powerful image for shaping this relationship. Human beings are created for intimacy with the Holy as well as intimacy with the human. It makes sense, given that God has created us to be lovers, to approach intimacy with God as a lover approaches the beloved, to make ourselves accessible to God as the beloved makes herself or himself accessible to the lover.

One of the most intriguing pieces of literature in the Bible is the Song of Solomon, a love poem depicting the intimate relationship between a lover-God and his beloved people.

> I am my beloved's, and his desire is for me. Come, my beloved, let us go forth into the fields, and lodge in the villages; let us go out early to the vineyards, and see whether

the vines have budded, whether the grape blossoms have opened and the pomegranates are in bloom. There I will give you my love. (Sg 7:10-12, *NRSV*)

Another part of this love poem to God asks, "What is your beloved more than another beloved?" The answer: "This is my beloved and this is my friend" (Sg 5:9,16, *NRSV*). God is Lover *and* Soul Mate. The poem offers us the model of lover and soul mate as an aid to prayer without ceasing.

Communion of Lover and Soul Mate

Lovemaking and unceasing prayer, surprisingly, are closely akin to each other. It is natural for prayer, like true human lovemaking, to be unceasing communion, not merely occasional acts, when it is experienced as romancing the Divine.

To be in love is to have the lover alive in one's heart all the time. It is no chore (as praying can be) to find this presence within. She can come in memory and hope at any moment, whether beckoned or unbidden, asserting the gentle pressure of her presence on the beloved's heart, softening it and making it receptive to her loving desire, shedding her light in the beloved's soul. He can be within your mind and within your soul, quickening your awareness with a sense of promise, a word of wisdom, a life not your own yet accessible to your desire, whether bodily you are near or far apart.

Making love, in its truest and deepest sense, involves intimate exchanges between souls, not just bodies.

The lover reveals things to you that come not just from her heart but from your own as well, extracted by her keen understanding of your depths, or teased out of hiding by her tenderly inquisitive interest in the mystery of you. His mind is in you and yours in him in ways that stimulate each other with the sweet challenges of love.

It is similar with a soul mate, though this relationship does not have the romance that being in love does. A soul mate can evoke within us qualities of being that were not previously evident. He can inspire a courage to be, to risk, to venture, to blossom in ways that never before seemed possible. She can ignite the fires of a passion for living well, creatively, with a deep and abiding care for justice, compassion, peace.

A soul mate can awaken new consciousness of deep self-knowing that is trustworthy. She can open sources of well-being that are deep within you and are not dependent on external conditions, not even on relationship with her. A new sense of self can emerge in a soul mate relationship and, while it bears more brightly its own light, it also reflects the light of the other. The two lights joined together offer the world something that could not have existed without their meeting, and the world is blessed.

When one has fallen in love, or when the love relationship is with a soul mate, making love becomes an unceasing, life-encompassing process, not just something one does occasionally when the mood strikes. This is because making love in such a relationship includes thoughts, feelings, desires, purposes, hopes, plans, goals—all joyously related to the lover and infusing everything one does throughout the day and even in sleep's dreams. It is also because, in such a relationship, making love is an action of the heart, the soul, the feelings, the conscious and unconscious mind, the "guts," the spirit, as well as the body. Lovemaking, in some form, is going on in some dimension of the lover's being at all times.

Making Love with the Divine

How does one engage in romancing or making love with the Divine? First, scrap the idea that making love is primarily about bodies touching in intimate ways. Making love, in its truest and deepest sense, involves intimate exchanges between souls, not just bodies. Making love with the Divine is an act of the soul that is just as real as making love with another human being. Therefore, anyone who has made love with another human being at the level of soul knows something already about how to pray without ceasing.

Second, make use of the electrically charged atmosphere of passionate romance in experiencing communion with God. Let yourself feel the eagerness of a lover, the readiness, the longing, the joy that comes with each sighting of the beloved. Hold yourself open as to a lover, open to receive, open to reveal. Let yourself experience the safety and security that characterize a strong and deep bond between lovers. Recall a time when you have failed, or disappointed, or even betrayed a human lover and have been loved in spite of your transgression. Let the spontaneous thanksgiving for such a relationship well up in you and spill over into expression, perhaps in poetry, or song, or dance, or in a love letter to God.

Third, pray the Scripture. A prayer from the 1st-century church lends itself well to unceasing prayer as making love with the Divine:

> Let the same mind be in you that was in Christ Jesus, who, though he was in the form of God, did not regard equality with God as something to be exploited, but emptied himself, taking the form of a slave, being born in human likeness. And being found in human form, he humbled himself and became obedient to the point of death—even death on a cross. Therefore God also highly exalted him and has given him the name that is above every name, so that at the name of Jesus every knee should bend, in heaven and on earth and under the earth, and every tongue should confess that Jesus Christ is Lord, to the glory of God the Father. (Ph 2:5-12, *NRSV*)

This prayer is so rich that this article will be able to treat only the first phrase, "Let the same mind be in you that was in Christ Jesus." A slight change in pronoun from "you" to "me" (or "us," for a group) can personalize the prayer: "Let the same mind be in me (us) that was in Christ Jesus."

What is this "mind" that we invite to enter our being, to come alive in us, to ignite the Christic presence within us? Scripture uses various metaphors to picture this "mind." "Servant" is a prominent image in the prayer itself. It connects us with the image of the Suffering Servant. This is a valid image, but a word of caution is in order. It is possible to become so caught up in the Suffering Servant image that this "mind" comes to be associated only with hardship, burden, and suffering. We may create an imbalance that will sooner or later render this "mind" unwelcome.

Jesus was Suffering Servant, indeed, but he was Suffering Servant *because* he experienced the incredibly generative power of being beloved by God and giving God great delight. This metaphor of "the Beloved" broke into Jesus' self-awareness at his baptism when the voice of God addressed him with this very personal message: "You are my son, the Beloved; with you I am well pleased" (Lk 3:22, *NRSV*). This breakthrough affirmation energized his unceasing communion with God. The assurance of being God's Beloved was reinforced in him at his transfiguration: "This is my Son, my Beloved; listen to him!" (Lk 9:35, *NRSV*).

How different is this sense of self as Beloved and as source of divine Delight from the sense of obligation and responsibility that goes with being Suffering Servant. We would do well to reflect on the following questions:

> • If the self-awareness of being God's beloved and of giving God delight dominated our heart, how would this alter our sense of self, our experience of the day, our presence in relationships, our communion with God?

> • What if we were to experience God, as Jesus did at his baptism and again at his transfiguration, coming to us for no other reason, at least some of the time, than that he is delighted to be with his beloved and to bless us for our own sake?

> • Is this not the primary orientation of a lover, the desire to be with the beloved for mutual blessing, whether any service to others gets done at a given moment or not?

Make no mistake, where there is a deep sense of blessing and of being beloved, one will spontaneously desire and creatively fashion ways of serving the lover's will. To concentrate on experiencing belovedness is not to shirk service. On the contrary, it will inspire and empower service of the highest, most creative, most energetic and faithful kind.

The Self-Awareness of One Beloved

We have now made a subtle but fundamental shift in how we think of this "mind." Mind is a state of self-awareness as much as it is a mental activity. Using the image of the Beloved, the prayer becomes "Let this self-awareness of being God's Beloved be in me." In light of this, we can consider these questions for reflection:

> • What is the state of self-awareness with which I most habitually operate?

> • Is it dominated by a sense of blessed being or by a gnawing feeling of unworthiness toward God that causes me to shrink from intimacy or to expect little from God?

> • Is it dominated by trust or by distrust in my God-given powers of knowing, of being, of doing?

> • Is it dominated by pride in certain God-given abilities upon which I depend to the neglect of other less visible but equally important gifts?

> • Is it dominated by unhealed wounds that cause me to shrink from fuller engagement with God and with others out of anxious self-protectiveness?

- Is it dominated by anxiety from family conditioning that has taught me that all love, including God's, is conditional and hinges on quality of performance?

Whatever may be the dominant kinds of self-awareness in us toward God and others, they can be transformed and healed by our ever more earnest desire that the self-awareness of Christ come to us and dominate our inner atmosphere. One way of doing this is to enter through imagination into Jesus' baptismal and transfiguration experiences and feel what it is like to hear the voice of God saying to us personally, "You are my beloved; I take great delight in you!" Expanding the term "mind" (of Christ) from intellectual mindset to conscious self-awareness opens a new realm of experience for us in praying without ceasing that "this self-awareness of the Beloved be in me." With this expansion another subtle but decisive shift in metaphor offers itself here: "Let the heart of Christ the Beloved be in me."

Let This Heart Be in Me

For this "heart," the energy of this prayer, to grow in us as a dynamic daily presence and an unceasing communion with the mind and heart of God, some diligent work will bear good fruit.

- First, becoming more and more deeply acquainted with the "mind of Christ" through regular Bible study will help immensely.
- Second, deepening this acquaintance by entering through imagination into the consciousness of this mind in different kinds of real situations, both biblical and contemporary, will bring new insight.
- Third, simply praying the prayer in some form regularly enough will permit the Guest it invites to become a resounding presence in us somewhat in the way that a song heard on the radio keeps recurring in our consciousness. Yes, this means memorizing the prayer; then it is accessible at all times.

Through these efforts, especially when undertaken with a lover's heart toward the Beloved, we will soon find that the prayer is praying itself within us. More accurately, we will find that the "mind of Christ" is living itself in us and through us, the heart of Christ beating its rhythms of love at levels of our being of which we are not even consciously aware. We will be praying without ceasing much as a lover interacts unceasingly with the beloved within.

The most critical move toward unceasing prayer comes in the first word of the prayer from Philippians: "Let." "*Let be* in me this mind, this heart, this self-awareness of being God's Beloved." It comes down to a matter of yielding, of surrender, to God who strongly desires to live in us as eternal and supreme Soul Mate. It is also a matter of yielding to our own deepest desire, for we are created with the inescapable inner yearning to love and enjoy God forever. This yearning is at the heart of our being human, even when it is not recognized and acknowledged, or is misdirected.

Poet Mary Oliver puts it succinctly: "You do not have to walk on your knees / for a hundred miles through the desert, repenting. / You only have to *let* the soft animal of your body love what it loves" ("Wild Geese," in *New and Selected Poems*, Beacon Press, 1992, p. 110, emphasis mine). What the soft animal of our body loves, at the heart of all its desire and above everything else that seeks to claim this love, is God and the magnificent works of God in others and in our self. Here, at the depths, the heart of the self beloved is joined with the heart of Christ the Beloved in unceasing communion with God the Lover. Therefore, "let be in us the heart of Christ the Beloved." This prayer can only be offered in the first place as a response, not as an absolutely self-generated initiative, to the God who has already begun romancing us, creating in us the desire to pursue our romancing the Divine.

The Struggle with Prayer

darkness

Having given retreats to priests, religious, and the laity, I have become aware of how much people struggle with their prayer life. It comes up in confession, spiritual direction, and informal conversation. It is not uncommon to hear people say that they do not take time to pray. Some say that they do not believe that they have a good prayer life. I can hear the disappointment in their voices. It is not that they do not believe in praying, it is just that they find it a real struggle. They will quickly say that it is important to pray, but they cannot seem to find the time. They wish that they would pray more. They find that the renewed interest in the Church in praying does not seem to help them. After spending many hours listening to people share their spiritual journey with me, I have come to realize that the issue is more complicated than just not taking time to pray. When people say that they do not have time to pray, they often mean something else. It is this something else that I would like to consider in this article.

For some people the issue is really not wanting to pray. They would be embarrassed to be that blunt about it, but it is nonetheless true. Prayer is a burden for them. It always has been. They often have an image of God which has God nagging them to do more with their prayer life. They have learned to dread this image of God, and find that any effort they make in their prayer life never seems enough. Soon, overwhelmed with guilt, they use avoidance techniques to resist the pain. That is why they do not want to pray. Any praying they do just brings more guilt and pain. They would rather keep this demanding God at a distance. They do not understand when other people speak about the joy associated with prayer because there has never been any joy around prayer for them.

All that they hear when they go to prayer is "you should." They would like to experience a relationship with Jesus that tells them to come to him when they are heavily burdened and they will find comfort. Such a relationship seems to elude them.

There are other people who do not want to pray because they have experienced a recent trauma. The pain of a lost loved one can cause a person to question God's love. If a person is going through the stages of a terminal illness, his or her prayer life may suffer. As anger or denial surfaces, any desire to pray may wane for a period of time. With some people there is a tendency to reject a friend or end a relationship before they get hurt. If I think that God is no longer interested in continuing a friendship with me because I believe that God is the reason for the recent trauma, then I may decide to quit praying and thus do the rejecting first so that the pain will not be so great.

It is important to encourage these people who do not want to pray. It is helpful to suggest that they simply say, "Lord, help me to want to want to pray." In this way, the communication never stops. The very fact that a person says to God "I want to want to pray" is pleasing to God. It does not sound like much, but one is showing some openness to God, and that is all God needs to begin the transformation in one's life. It is important to say to God, "I want to want to pray, but I am scared, so you will have to work powerfully in my life to help me move beyond my fears." If one can say that much without running away, then the fears can be addressed and a new image of God can begin to surface. Saying "I want to want to pray" establishes a relationship with God and allows one to face the ultimate temptation in life, a temptation to despair of ever pleasing God. It creates a hope that something can still happen in communicating with God. It is a very tentative yes to God. It may not seem like much, but God is able to do with our initial yes more than we can possibly imagine. Whoever prays this simple prayer is continuing to proclaim an allegiance to God. After saying it over and over, one finds that prayer has been going on at a deeper level of consciousness. It is the kind of prayer that the Holy Spirit does in someone without the person recognizing it. St. Paul says in Romans 8 that the Spirit will pray in us when we are weak and unable to pray. As Paul promised, the Spirit of God has made contact with the spirit of the person. A dialogue takes place without the person recognizing it. As the person struggles with the temptation to give up, the deeper dialogue that is happening serves as a supply line that keeps feeding the person just enough energy to continue the struggle. The person is not left an orphan. With each passing day the spark that has been kept alive by the desire to pray begins to grow until it becomes a desire to pray always and not lose heart.

Taking time to pray even when we do not feel like it is an act of faith.

Sometimes a person says "I don't have time to pray," but really means "I don't feel like praying." Such a person lives by feelings and gauges the quality of prayer by how he or she feels while praying. If one has experienced a period of dryness in prayer, one may not feel like praying and may be tempted to wait for the "right" mood. Such waiting does not help a prayer life to mature. This is especially true if one is a beginner and has recently experienced a great deal of emotional consolation when praying. It is common for God to grant emotional consolations to beginners and after a while to withdraw them. God wants a person to pray in good times and in bad, whether one feels like it or not. When the emotional consolations are withdrawn, one can then determine whether one has prayed chiefly in order to feel a certain way. If one prays for that reason, one readily shies away from certain issues, perhaps embarrassing ones, that need to be brought to prayer for healing and forgiveness.

One cannot measure the quality of one's prayer life by the intensity of a particular emotion. Mere feelings cannot do justice to the way God works through prayer. God asks a person to pray not in order to feel good, but to remain faithful. By praying we give God a definite place in our lives. We affirm that God loves us unconditionally no matter how we feel. It is not that we must ignore feelings; rather, we must simply recognize that feelings are not always facts. Feelings are dependent on so many variables in our life that they cannot be used as a barometer to determine how good our prayer life is. The lives of many saints reveal long periods of dryness, yet they continued to pray no matter how they felt.

Taking time to pray even when we do not feel like it is an act of faith. It is a way of saying that there is more to life with God than how I feel. It allows God to be a mystery and myself to become sensitive to the many movements of God. Like the great men and women of Scripture, one says to God: "I will follow you wherever you lead me. If you choose to be present to me as a cloud by day or a fire by night, I will be attentive to you. However, if you choose to leave me in the desert for a period of purification, then this is where I will pitch my tent and wait upon you with hope." As one's prayer life becomes this flexible, then it no longer is a matter of feeling this way or that; rather, one becomes free to pray with a heart that experiences all of the seasons of life.

When people say that they do not have time to pray, they sometimes mean that nothing seems to come from their prayer. They do not see many results. They question the value of prayer. In a world full of so much pain, they wonder why they should bother praying when the problems do not seem to go away. These people need to realize that, when they quit praying, hope slowly dies in their lives. When there is no hope, either people become concerned only about themselves or they become violent. Praying allows a person to stay in touch with the larger world without being overwhelmed by its problems. As a person prays, conversion of heart is possible. Eradicating injustice always begins and ends with individual conversion of heart. When people say that nothing seems to be accomplished by praying, they miss the most significant result of prayer. Transformation of the human heart is what God wants when we pray. Prayer changes people so that people can turn war into peace, hatred into love, and vengeance into forgiveness. Asking God to change other people without asking for the grace to have a conversion of heart myself ignores the real problem. God does not need to be reminded that other people need a change of heart since God has been working on them for a long time. The real issue is whether or not I will allow God to work on my heart. By praying I extend the invitation to God to put the finishing touches on the spiritual heart transplant he has been working on. I pray not so much to change God's mind as to change my heart.

Some people want instant conversion of the world's population, and they become very disappointed with God when it does not happen. They question why they should continue to pray. They do not keep in mind that God gives individual attention to everyone in the world. It is the classic case of thinking of the world in terms of the masses instead of individuals. Each individual needs to be healed of selfishness, greed, jealousy, pride, and lust. As each individual receives a new heart, only then will the world become full of justice and peace. This is a hard lesson to learn because we become impatient with the way God gives us individual attention. Some people become irritated with God for giving the human race free will; they begin to blame God for the problems in the world. When this happens, they soon stop praying. They say that there is no use praying because the world cannot possibly change. They say that one person cannot do much anyway.

At this point their prayer life faces cardiac arrest. That kind of despair can be dealt with only by massive doses of prayer. Yet this very remedy is what they question. They say that they feel trapped. They feel that God is teasing them. On the one hand God tells them not to quit praying, and on the other hand they do not see what difference it makes. They keep thinking about their prayer. Now they have to decide whether they will pray even though part of them does not see any value in praying. Once the analysis is over, a person of faith can begin to pray in a way that brings hope. God does not mind if we agonize over the world's problems. In fact, God wants us to use all of the talents that we have been given to address these problems. However, when it comes to prayer, God is looking for us to let go so that we can pray with trust. As people struggle with problems that are bigger than they are, there comes a time when they must hand them over to God and rest in God's love. To deprive themselves of time to pray in quiet trust is to risk genuine burnout. Burnout does not happen because people have too much work to do. Burnout happens because people face enormous problems without the prayer support they need. When a person challenges societal injustice and attempts to be prophetic, the opposition will respond with tremendous power. No one dares to face the power of evil without constant prayer.

Jesus knew this lesson and prayed as if his whole life depended on prayer. Even on the cross when he cried "My God, my God, why have you forsaken me?" he turned that cry into a prayer. Every crucial step Jesus took towards Calvary was accompanied by prayer. When he faced the power of evil in the desert at the beginning of his ministry, it was in a setting of prayer. When the attack became ferocious in the garden of Gethsemane, it was met in the context of prayer. Luke's gospel reveals Jesus as a man of constant prayer. Out of that prayer flowed his outreach to the needy and his preaching of a gospel of justice and peace. If a person wants to identify with Jesus' message of justice and peace, then prayer is a nonnegotiable when deciding how to spend one's time.

Prayer will always be a struggle for us humans. Since our prayer flows from our experiences, we will struggle with it as we try to make sense out of the nonsense we often experience. There will always be the temptation to quit praying. If we succumb to the temptation, our hearts will dry up and wither. We will find ourselves imprisoned in a very small world bordered on every side by only ourselves. Without prayer a person can quickly give in to cynicism. However, if we "pray always and never lose heart," then a new power will be released in us that will renew the face of the earth.

Spiritual Dryness:
Some Practical Guidelines

The Lord, your God, will circumcise your hearts . . . that
you may love the Lord, your God, with all your heart and
all your soul, and so may live. (Dt 30:6)
   Blessed is the person who can call the darkness holy,
who can desire its purification, who can rest in its presence.
Such a person will grow rapidly because the process of
purification is facilitated by generosity. (source unknown)

*E*very praying person sooner or later experiences what is
called *dryness* in prayer. In spiritual dryness we have no *felt
sense* of God's presence. We may even think we have lost our
Beloved or feel abandoned by him. In the school of prayer, few
things are more important to understand than the nature and role
of spiritual dryness. I intend to deal with this important dimension of the spiritual life by responding to five important questions that one can ask about prayer in the desert.

*Question 1: What is it that praying people experience during the
desert periods of the spiritual journey?* The actual desert experience
of praying persons will vary depending on the level of faith and
spiritual maturity. For example, for the beginner in prayer spiritual dryness frequently means not just the absence of a *felt sense* of
the presence of God but also feelings of what Saint Ignatius calls
desolation—that is, feelings of anxiousness, sadness, or loss of peace
flowing from the thought, "I have lost God," or "God has abandoned me." On the other hand for the person who is more mature
in faith and advanced in the ways of prayer, spiritual dryness may
not be an experience of desolation. The experience will be one
which lacks a felt sense of God's presence but may be accompa-

nied by the conviction: "Even though I can't feel his presence (at least on the external level), I do believe he is close and active in my life. Even though I cannot feel his presence (that is, spiritual dryness), I don't feel anxious, sad, or abandoned (that is, desolation). In fact, I feel peaceful."[1] To believe that God is present and active despite his apparent absence can be considered one of the greatest blessings of the spiritual life. For most of us, particularly in the early years of prayer, spiritual dryness usually includes the experience of desolation ("I have lost God; God has abandoned me"). Usually it is a time of spiritual suffering. We think we are getting the "silent treatment" from God. We "call out to him all day long, but he never answers" (Ps 22:3).[2] Spiritual dryness is like journeying in the desert with no water in sight. Prayer is no longer exciting; rather, it is a weary struggle. Spiritual exercises that once nourished us now are empty, and we have little or no desire to do them.

Another dimension of the desert experience may be a feeling of discouragement as we become keenly aware of our own sinfulness. (We may not yet know that one of the surest signs of growth in the interior life is a growing awareness of our own sinfulness.) We may begin to think we are regressing rather than progressing. We may begin to experience one of the great paradoxes of the spiritual life: the closer we come to God the further *it seems to us* that we are away from him. As we get closer to the all-piercing Light of God, the more our own darkness shows itself. Our lives will appear to be hollow and mediocre. The Scottish priest the late Father John Dalrymple writes: "It is as if I were to bring the sleeve of my coat toward the window of the room, and as I move into the light, the dust and dandruff on the sleeve become more obvious. It is not that as I moved the coat got dirtier, but that the light got brighter."[3] All in all, the thing that scares us most and even hurts us is the thought, "I have lost my Beloved; he has abandoned me" (See Song of Songs, chapter 3). This thought or feeling is the experience of desolation described above.

To sum up, we can say that while the actual experience of the desert will be different for different people, for all of us it will mean a *felt sense* of the absence of God. And for those of us whose faith in God is still fragile, it will frequently involve the experience of desolation (the "I have lost God" feeling).

In reading the above description of spiritual dryness, one may think that it is something only experienced by monks, religious, and the exceptional lay person. Yet spiritual directors tell us that this experience is quite common in the lives of many average, prayerful people who discover somewhere in the midst of their spiritual journeys that spiritual exercises that once nourished them spiritually now do nothing for them.

Question 2: Why is an understanding of this dimension of prayer so important? There are at least three reasons why some understanding of spiritual dryness is important. First, if we do not know the role of the times of dryness, we may think that we have "lost God" and that our prior, positive feelings in prayer were not a gift from God but the creation of our own imaginations. This frequently happens. Many people who have a genuine conversion and get all excited about prayer quit when the well runs dry. This is sad because it is now that God wants to do his real work in such persons. Second, lack of knowledge about the purpose of spiritual dryness may cause us to continue praying in a way that, at *this particular stage* in our spiritual journey, may be more of an obstacle than a help to our spiritual growth. Many people are unaware that at some stage in the spiritual journey God calls us to become *less active* in prayer so that he can be more active in our spiritual transformation. Third, the experience of spiritual dryness may be something caused by ourselves or something permitted by God. When it is permitted by God, it is meant to purify us and bring us closer to him. Such dryness is a gift to be accepted and embraced. When spiritual dryness is our doing, we need to work at removing the causes of such dryness. Lack of knowledge about the nature and role of spiritual dryness may lead us to believe that a particular experience of dryness in prayer is authentic and God-given when in fact it is something brought on by our own infidelities.

When spiritual dryness is our doing, we need to work at removing the causes of such dryness.

So the time of spiritual dryness is a critical time in the spiritual journey. How we respond to it will determine whether we move forward spiritually or stagnate.

Question 3: Why does God permit us to experience desert periods in the spiritual journey?

> So I will allure her
> I will lead her into the desert
> and speak to her heart. (Ho 2:16)

God permits us to experience spiritual desert periods in order to purify us of those things that hinder our spiritual transformation and to teach us some important lessons about the spiritual life and how it works. In our answer to this question we will look at some specific purifications that God works in us and lessons that he teaches us in the desert.

Purifications of the Desert

In the desert God will want to *purify us of any excessive attachment we may have to consolation in prayer*. If in prayer God blesses us with a lot of consolations (or "spiritual highs" as we often say today), there is a danger that we may seek and love "the consolations of our God more than the God of our consolations" (Saint Teresa of Avila). In time of spiritual consolation it is easy to pray. The challenge is to remain faithful to prayer when we experience little or no *felt* sense of God's presence or action in our lives. During such dry periods God is asking us to love him for himself and not just for the spiritual highs or consolations he offers us in prayer. He is asking us to show that we are not just *fair*-weather friends but *all*-weather friends. And he is teaching us the important lesson that he is to be found more deeply in the desert than in the garden of superficial delights.

Secondly, in the desert God *purifies us of spiritual vanity*. John Dalrymple explains spiritual vanity in this way:

> Someone taking to religion in all zeal, becoming caught up in a campaign of prayer, fasting, spiritual reading, liturgical practice, and retreat weekends might be indulging unawares in one big ego-trip. Conversion of the soul from a worldly life to a spiritual life is at first superficial only. The convert has been given new, spiritual goals; but the conversion is only external. In itself the soul is as full as it ever was of unregenerate tendencies to vanity, arrogance, acquisitiveness, the only difference being that after conversion these tendencies are now attached to spiritual instead of worldly objects. . . . The zeal of such a person is infectious, but it is, as yet, chiefly the expression of the person's vanity or self-centeredness, dressed up in Christian clothes.[4]

For God to do his work of spiritual transformation in us, he must purify us of such spiritual vanity. God often brings about this purification in us by bringing to naught our best efforts to change ourselves and everything and everyone around us. As we sit on the ruins of our self-made temples and projects, we are purified of spiritual vanity and arrogance, and we learn the meaning of spiritual poverty, which is realizing our complete dependence and need for God to bring about any spiritual growth in others or in ourselves.

In the desert, God's intention is not to punish us but to purify us. In the journey of life we consciously or unconsciously become overly-attached to persons or things—so much so that they become idols (that is, more important to us than God). This happened to Israel after she lived in the Promised Land for some time. She became so enamored with the blessings of the land that she forgot the One who gave her the land. To purify her of this idolatry God led Israel into the desert for a second time where she would be free of all her attachments and free to listen anew to the Word of God (See Hosea, chapter 2).

Lessons to Be Learned in the Desert

Now let us briefly look at some of the lessons that God wishes to teach us in the desert.

When God takes away consolation in prayer (that is, the *felt sense* of his presence), he wants to teach us the important lesson that *he can be encountered at a deeper level than our emotions*. He wants to teach us that we are no longer dependent on emotional returns to know we have encountered him. As we grow in our relationship with God, the more we will "learn to be at home in the dark because we are sure, in faith, that the potter is truly shaping the clay, even though the clay sees nothing of what is happening."[5]

An example about eating food might help to illustrate this point more clearly. Sometimes we may immensely enjoy eating a delicious meal. We may savor every morsel of the food. All in all, it is a delightful experience. On another occasion we may not enjoy at all another type of delicious meal. We may not be feeling well, or the food may not appeal to us. Yet, from a nutrition point of view, both meals are equally good. Our lack of enjoyment of the second meal in no way diminishes its nutritious value.

The same principle is at work when it comes to prayer. Sometimes when we pray we really feel and savor God's presence and love. At other times the prayer is empty and dull. Who are we, though, to say that the latter time is of no benefit to our spiritual growth or is less pleasing in God's sight?

A second lesson God teaches us in the desert is that *spiritual consolation is his pure gift to us* and not something we can earn by being good or by praying in a particular way. In prayer God teaches us this important lesson by "dropping in" on us when we least expect him and by "failing to show" when we very much want to experience his presence.

A third lesson that God wishes to teach us in the desert is that *spiritual growth is totally dependent on his work in us* and not on anything we do. Our task is simply to be flexible and cooperative with the movement of his Spirit. In the spiritual life, "working at it" often means "being still," "just being there" and exercising discipline over our doing and achieving self which so often wants to run the show. This is a difficult lesson for us because so much of our training for the outer journey of life has told us to be "take-charge" and self-sufficient persons. It is not easy for us to switch gears in the inner journey.

In the spiritual life God is the Chief Actor; we are the acted-upon. Mary, at the Annunciation (Lk 1:26-38), is our perfect model. When God mysteriously breaks into Mary's life and invites her to become the mother of Jesus, she does not respond, "Sure, Lord, *I'll do it!*" Rather, she says, "I am your maidservant; work in and through me as you want." Mary's response was "Fiat, be it done unto me," not "I'll do it." This attitude is one of *active receptivity*, and it is the secret of Christian spirituality and spiritual growth. Active receptivity is characterized by the effort to place our energy, will, and freedom at the disposal of God, so that he can do with us and in us what he wills.

Finally, when God our Father allows our prayer to run dry, *he is inviting us to participate in the cross of Jesus.* In times of dryness we are experiencing the thirst of Jesus on the cross. If the cross was Jesus' way to the Father, then surely we, the disciples of Jesus, cannot expect to travel the scenic route free of all pain and hardship. When we experience darkness in prayer or in the marketplace, we are being invited to identify with Jesus in his suffering, in his experience of feeling abandoned by the Father. Also in the desert we are being invited and challenged to trust that our God will not abandon us but will come to rescue us and redeem us (See Exodus, Chapter 16).

Question 4: How can I tell when a particular desert experience is caused by my own infidelity or is something permitted by God to help me to grow in my relationship with him? When dryness occurs in prayer, particularly in the early stages when God is giving alternative periods of dryness and consolation, we may tend to blame ourselves for dryness. We may wonder what latest infidelity we committed to bring about this dryness. The fact may be that we have done nothing wrong to occasion the dryness. God may be allowing us to experience the dryness because he wants to teach us some lesson and/or purify some aspect of our relationship with him. On the other hand, we may think the dryness is from God when in fact it is caused by our own laxity and sinfulness. Therefore, it is important that we be able to discern the true cause of the dryness because our response to it will differ, depending on whether the dryness is permitted by God or is something brought on by ourselves.

Let us now identify several ways that we can bring about our own spiritual desert.

(1) *Indifference to a Sinful Pattern of Behavior*: If we are indifferent to some sinful pattern of behavior in our lives, then we can expect difficulty in prayer. In a human friendship a negative pattern of behavior (for example, a critical or lying spirit), which we make no effort to change, will have a destructive effect on the whole relationship. Likewise, if in our relationship with God, we are deliberately ignoring a sinful pattern of behavior (for example, involvement in an illicit relationship, unforgiveness, unethical business practices), then we can rightfully expect tension in our relationship with God. When we do the above, we are deliberately excluding the Lord and his influence from some area of our lives. In such a situation we should not be surprised that we do not feel God's presence very much in prayer. Here it is important to note that I am not referring to a sinful pattern of behavior that we are *trying to change* and that we are bringing before the Lord in prayer. In this case we are recognizing sin and struggling with it. Instead of keeping us from God, our struggle with a particular sin or weakness may be the very means that God will use to allow us to experience his love, mercy, and power. (See 2 Co 12:7-10 for Paul's famous example of how his thorn in the flesh became the very means of God's power.) In the former case, we are not even confronting our sin or seeking God's help with it. Instead we are deliberately ignoring its existence or trying to rationalize its okayness. In the latter case, our sin grieves

In the spiritual life, "working at it" often means "being still."

us and we are doing what we can to remove it from our lives.

(2) *Repressed Anger at God*: Two highly-respected spiritual directors, Fathers William Connolly and William Barry, write in a co-authored book: "When prayer flattens out, or appears to be facing an iron wall, the director must always suspect the presence of unexpressed anger."[6] To add to this problem, many of us were raised in a culture where appropriate expression of anger was socially unacceptable. "Hence resentments, holding a grudge or subdued rage, when they are present, are all likely to be given other names like indifference and rational analysis."[7] When someone hurts us, our relationship with that person will diminish, even if we decide to present an affable, friendly front; but in reality we will distance ourselves emotionally from the person. In a similar way, if we become angry with God about something, we may continue to be faithful to our prayer time, but on an emotional level we can be fairly sure we have distanced ourselves from him. (It is important for us to be aware that if life is handing us a raw deal, we may well be unconsciously blaming God, the Source of all things, for our lousy situation.)

(3) *Separation of Prayer and Life*: The spiritual life is *all* of life and not just one segment of it. The Lord refuses to be a compartmentalized God; he wants to be a part and parcel of our whole life. When we try to keep God in church or in our prayer closet and not allow him to guide all the activities of our day, we can be sure that we are setting ourselves up for dryness in prayer. If we exclude God from the activities of our day, then we should not be surprised if he is missing from our prayer time. Even on a human level, no one likes to be a "tag-along" in someone else's life.

(4) *Overwork*: When our prayer life dries up, it is good for us to ask if we are pushing ourselves too much on the vital and functional dimensions of life. "Am I overworked? Am I over-tired? Am I coming down with the flu? Am I neglecting physical exercise? Do I have a tendency to make leisure time work? Or do I have leisure time—period?" These are important questions to ask. These things affect our prayer life. If we fail to care properly for our bodies, then we are neglecting a dimension of ourselves that we depend on to help us to pray. When we are very tired and overworked, prayer may well be seen as just another duty or thing to do.

(5) *Lack of Honesty in Prayer*: Just as shallow or dishonest sharing dulls human relationships, it also dulls the Divine-human relationship. If our prayer is no more than "sweet talk" to "sweet

Jesus," we should not expect Jesus to be too interested in our conversation. We must learn to talk to the Lord about the real stuff in our lives.

(6) *Halfhearted Efforts at Prayer*: On a human level two friends may fail to really connect with each other because their conversations are "just words," words that fail to express what they are truly thinking and feeling. The problem may be that deep down they do not want to or are scared to encounter each other in a deep way. When a relationship is characterized by this type of communication, then we should expect it to be empty and unfulfilling. In a similar vein, when our prayer time mainly consists of the rote recitation of certain prayers or of inattentive spiritual reading—if beneath the "saying of prayers" and the acts of piety there is no real desire to encounter God and grow in relationship with him—then we should expect little or no satisfaction in prayer. In fact, our spiritual exercises may become a substitute for a real relationship with God.

If we discern that we are the cause of our spiritual dryness, we should do all we can to remove the particular obstacle. For example, if the problem or obstacle is that we are holding onto a grudge and doing nothing to let it go, then we may need to pray for forgiveness for that person and/or we may need to have an open chat with the person with whom we are having a problem. If we discern that our experience of spiritual dryness is due to our tendency to separate prayer and life (see obstacle number three above), then our solution will be to work at allowing the Lord to walk with us in all the activities of our day. In short, when we discern that we are the cause of the spiritual dryness, then we ought to do something to remove the obstacle. It is the experience of most, if not all, disciples of the Lord that once they begin to struggle with an obstacle, prayer again becomes alive and they experience a new closeness to God. Finally, it should be noted that in trying to discern the cause of our spiritual dryness we would be well advised to seek the counsel of a good spiritual director. When we experience spiritual dryness most of us have a tendency to think that it is due to some infidelity on our part. The truth may be that *God* is permitting us to experience the desert so that he can continue his purifying work in us.

This brings us to the second part of our response to Question 4: "How might we know that it is God and not us who is calling us into a spiritual desert?" While we can never be absolutely sure—

since we live by faith and not by clear vision—when spiritual dryness is being permitted by God, we can say that the following are good indicators that the dryness is the purifying work of God:

- If during the time of dryness we remain faithful to prayer.
- If our prayer is honest and flowing from the real stuff of our lives.
- If we are trying to integrate prayer and life.
- If we are trying to live a life of charity; if our prayer is helping us to be more loving.
- If we are genuinely trying to avoid sin and live our lives according to God's Word.
- If we thirst for God as we walk in the desert. (It is crucial that we, remember that *our desire* for God is in itself a tangible sign of his presence in our lives. We couldn't even desire God if he didn't place that desire in our hearts.)

You will notice that the above signs are pretty much the opposite of the ways that we ourselves bring about our own spiritual desert.

Prayer, like so many other things in life, is a series of "arrivals" and "starting points." We arrive at a point where we feel good. We experience the grace of consolation. But that only lasts a little while and then a certain discontent (a kind of desert) sets in—a discontent that may be caused by ourselves or permitted by God. Then we are faced with the challenge of discerning who is causing the discontent: "Is it God or me?" The purpose of the discontent caused by him is to create in us a longing for more, to create in us a desire to move closer to God. In the spiritual journey God brings us to a particular point or state; he lets us rest there and enjoy that plateau for a little while, and then he says, "O.K. Let's move ahead and seek for more" (see Ex 40:36-37). Of course, it is not easy to move when we are not sure where he is leading us. All he says is, "Move and trust that I'll take you to a new and better place."

Finally, if we are in doubt about the cause of our discontent or dryness, then we should talk to a spiritual guide or, if that is not possible, simply say a prayer like this: "Lord, if this dryness I am experiencing is due to some failing of mine, please reveal it to me. Until you do I am going to assume that I am not the cause of the dryness."

Question 5: What are some resources available to us to sustain us in the desert? Four resources that will sustain us in the desert are:

- a wise spiritual director;
- a strong faith;
- fidelity to prayer;
- the support of fellow pilgrims.

Our first help is a wise *spiritual director*. By wise I mean one who understands the role of the desert in the spiritual life and hopefully one who has experienced and grown through the desert in his or her own spiritual journey. Many people whom God led into the desert for purification have suffered much at the hands of well-intentioned but misinformed spiritual guides. Saint John of the Cross reserves some of his harshest words for such misinformed guides.[8] For example, a misinformed guide may insist that a directee continue to meditate and do a lot of spiritual reading when God is calling her to the prayer of contemplation. In the desert a good spiritual director will be a source of guidance, encouragement, and inspiration. When we are in a spiritual desert, it is important that we learn to place our trust in a good spiritual director. But, as most of us know, wise spiritual directors are nearly as scarce as palm trees in the northern states of America. The truth is that the road to authenticity is dangerous, hard, and narrow, and few decide to travel it. In the absence of a wise spiritual director (and there is really no substitute for such a person), one may receive some guidance from books that are written or recommended by people who are recognized guides of the inner journey.

A second important resource is a *strong faith*—a faith that enables us:

- to believe that God knows what he is doing when he allows us to experience the desert (Rm 11:33-36);
- to believe that in the desert God is not punishing us but is purifying us (Dt 30:6);
- to believe that God works in us while we rest in him (Mk 4:26-29);
- to believe that in the struggles of life God is on our side fighting our battles (Ex 14:13-14 and Dt 1:30-33);
- to believe that in the desert God's *seeming* absence is just a different type of presence, one that we may not as yet have recognized (Ex 16);
- to be secure with insecurity (Rm 8:28);
- above all, to generously abandon ourselves to the purifying work of God (Lk 23:46).

A third important resource as we struggle in the desert is fidelity to prayer. In the desert, prayer is usually dry and therefore all the more difficult to remain faithful to. When it comes to praying in the desert, spiritual guides counsel us to avoid two extremes or temptations. The first temptation is to quit prayer, thinking that our best efforts are leading us nowhere. The second temptation is to "junk up" our prayer time with extra prayers, rosaries, Scripture reading, and so forth, thinking that if we only try harder maybe we will feel the presence of God. This second temptation needs to be resisted not only because it blocks what God is about in the desert but also because it is (usually unconsciously) our attempt to stay in or get back into the driver's seat.

In general, prayer in the desert will become much less active, more passive—less us, more God. The challenge will be to learn to sit quietly in the presence of God, trusting that he is at work in us while we rest in him. Learning to "waste time doing nothing" in prayer is, without a doubt, one of the most difficult lessons we have to learn in the school of prayer. Unfortunately, most of us never learn to waste time gracefully in the presence of God. Such a practice goes completely against our western, work-ethic nature that is usually driven to do, to achieve, and to produce—that likes to see tangible results for its efforts. Because of this need in us, most of us fill the vacuum that we feel in the desert with reading or prayers of some sort. For those of us who are willing to try and do less (that is, to be less active) in prayer so that God may do more in us, the following suggestions might be helpful.

- Spend some time just "being there" with the Lord, aware that as "we rest in him he is at work in us." We put aside all effort to achieve because now we are learning that achievement (growth) is God's work. By periodically spending some time "doing nothing" in the presence of the Lord, we are expressing our faith in an important spiritual dictum: "God's activity in prayer is more important than my activity."
- Spend some time slowly repeating prayers like: "Incline my heart to your will, O Lord." Make me want you, O Lord, more than anyone or anything in my life.
- Take a phrase of Scripture like "You are my beloved Son" and dwell on it.
- Simply take one word like "Jesus" or "love" and repeat it gently and slowly, letting God work in us, leading us beyond

conceptual thoughts, images, or feelings to wordless depths.

- Image and be present to Mary in the Temple after she lost Jesus (Lk 2:41-50) and at the foot of the cross (Jn 19:25-27) which must have been a real dark night of the spirit for her. Ask Mary to intercede for you so that you may have something of the faith which she had when she thought she had lost Jesus.

- Finally, you may want to read something on spiritual dryness. By simply reading and rereading portions of a book like *When the Well Runs Dry*, I am encouraged to persevere in the desert. Personally, I need to hear over and over again the teaching and encouragement that a book like Father Green's offers.

In prayer our role is to be faithful in coming aside, to be at God's disposal. What actually happens in prayer is God's business. For me this piece of wisdom has always been very consoling. It helped to free me from thinking that it was up to me to make things happen in prayer. Now I am more relaxed, knowing that my role is to be faithful in coming aside, to do what I can to eliminate distractions from within and without, and to pray as I feel led. ("Pray as you can, not as you can't.") The rest is in God's hands. If he chooses to bless me with a deep sense of his presence, I am indeed very grateful. If he chooses to bless me

Most of us never learn to waste time gracefully in the presence of God.

with his seeming absence (God is always only seemingly absent), then I try to be grateful for that, also believing that God knows what will best help me to grow. "Our prayer is good when our hearts are fixed on God, even if it is filled with boring aridity or passionate turmoil."[9]

A fourth resource in the desert is the prayer and personal *support of fellow pilgrims*. While each person's inner journey is very personal and unique, still we can learn much from the journeys of co-pilgrims. Only the foolish try to travel the inner journey alone. In the desert we are all beggars sharing morsels of bread with each other. Also, if we are blessed enough to be a part of a small, faith-sharing group, then we have available to us an excellent resource for the dry times. In the dry times the prayers of fellow pilgrims are usually a big help.

I would like to conclude our discussion on spiritual dryness with a prayer that I have found to be a source of great encouragement during times of spiritual desolation.

> Dear Lord, in the midst of much inner turmoil and restlessness, there is a consoling thought: maybe you are working in me in a way I cannot yet feel, experience, or understand. My mind is not able to concentrate on you, my heart is not able to remain centered, and it seems as if you are absent and have left me alone. But in faith I cling to you. I believe that your Spirit reaches deeper and further than my mind or heart, and that profound movements are not the first to be noticed.
>
> Therefore, Lord, I promise I will not run away, not give up, not stop praying, even when it all seems useless, pointless, and a waste of time and effort. If want to let you know that I love you even though I do not feel loved by you, and that I hope in you even though I often experience despair. Let this be a little dying I can do with you and for you as a way of experiencing some solidarity with the millions in this world who suffer far more than I do. Amen.[10]

Notes

[1] See Thomas H. Green SJ, *Weeds among the Wheat* (Notre Dame, Indiana, 1984), chapters 6 and 7. Also see Thomas H. Green SJ, *When the Well Runs Dry* (Notre Dame, Indiana, 1979), p. 92.

[2] Some other Psalms that reflect darkness in the prayer of the psalmist are Psalms 60, 69, 74, and 88.

[3] Father John Dalrymple, *Simple Prayer* (Wilmington, Delaware, 1984), p. 69.

[4] Ibid, p. 93.

[5] Thomas H. Green SJ, *When the Well Runs Dry* (Notre Dame, Indiana, 1979), p. 119.

[6] Fathers William Barry and William Connolly, *The Practice of Spiritual Direction* (New York, 1982), p. 73.

[7] Ibid.

[8] Saint John of the Cross, *The Collected Works of John of the Cross*, translated by Kieran Kavanaugh OCD and Otilio Rodriguez OCD (Washington, D.C., 1979), pp. 620-634.

[9] Father John Dalrymple, *Simple Prayer* (Wilmington, Delaware, 1984), p. 66.

[10] Henri J. M. Nouwen, *A Cry for Mercy: Prayers from the Genesee* (Garden City, New York, 1983), p. 102.

Feeling and Pain and Prayer

Like many Christians, as a child I was taught that church was a place in which to keep quiet. Pinching my younger sister was not allowed; neither was incessant wiggling, waving at my friends, or climbing over the pews. Although these rules no doubt ensured a relatively peaceful worship experience for the adults, they served to reinforce my general impression that God liked people who were well-behaved, obedient, and quiet. When I was five or six years old, I wrote a message to God and threw it out my bedroom window so that it would get to heaven. My mother retrieved the letter and kept it for some years in her file cabinet. Not surprisingly, the letter to God was a plea that I be good. For a child who longed for contact with the divine, the only way that I could imagine God was as a giant version of my parents: someone who loved me best when I was "good." And so I tried to pray accordingly: I dressed up in my Sunday best. I offered God my good and holy thoughts. I showed God my warm and loving feelings. I put my best foot forward: here was my nicest, kindest, loveliest self, the self that it seemed my parents liked best, the self that I liked best, the self that surely God liked best, too.

As grace would have it, God would not settle for this, and my journey in prayer has moved over the years from the desire to be good to the desire to be real. When we are driven by what Thomas Hart calls the "pseudo ideal" of prayer as a place to express only our "good" self, how much of ourselves we then shut off from God![1] Hidden away are exasperation and anger, shame and sorrow, frustration and fear, and our relationship with God takes on a rather formal, predictable quality. We offer to God a false self, a partial self, and then we wonder why our prayer life seems unbearably boring and dry.

But what if God is longing to encounter not only our best selves, but our whole selves? What if God yearns to know and to enter not only our warm and loving feelings, but the depth of our anger and sadness and fear and doubt? What if God not only tolerates, but actually welcomes, the expression in prayer of our true selves, including those feelings that we tend to hide away and repudiate and despise?

C.S. Lewis once observed that "the prayer preceding all prayers is 'May it be the real I who speaks. May it be the real Thou that I speak to.'" If this is so, then our intention in prayer is to be our real selves and to encounter the real God. As Hart pointedly puts it, "The first principle of prayer is to be yourself. Prayer is being yourself before God."[2] It is as if God were whispering in our ears as we begin our prayer, "Get real."

The question is whether we are willing to let God in on the depth of our anger and sorrow and anxiety and shame. Are we willing to disclose these parts of ourselves to God?

Getting real involves opening to the truth of what we feel. When we are out of touch with our feelings, we are not fully present, not fully available to ourselves, to one another, or to God. Part of us is shut away. The question is whether we are willing to let God in on the depth of our anger and sorrow and anxiety and shame. Are we willing to disclose these parts of ourselves to God? Are we willing not only to name these feelings, to gesture vaguely toward them as if we were standing at a respectable distance from them ("Well, God, the other day I got kind of angry . . ."), but actually to feel them in God's presence, actually to experience and express them in prayer, in all their vividness and urgency? How we answer these questions will profoundly affect our sense of intimacy with God. Unless we begin to risk disclosing and expressing these parts of ourselves to God, we will keep God at arm's length. We will think that we have to keep up appearances with God, to keep smiling or achieving or earning approval, or doing whatever it was that we learned as children we had to do in order to please our parents or the other important people in our life. "A friend is a person with whom you can afford to be yourself," writes Thomas Hart.

Just yourself, nothing more or less. That is enough. There are plenty of people in the world with whom you cannot afford to be quite yourself. You have to present the proper face, make the right impression. For them you have to make something beautiful, or attempt to. With them you need to be strong and have yourself together; at least you would like to appear that way. With a friend, none of this is necessary. When you meet others, you need to have some energy, to be 'up for it.' With a friend you do not really need that. You can open the door to a friend even when you are a wreck and could not turn on the charm if you wanted to.[3]

Do we consider God to be a friend, with whom we can afford to be ourselves? "Just as I can choose to disclose myself to my friends, so I can also choose to disclose myself to God. . . . Setting out to disclose ourselves . . . if only for a moment, promotes our relationship with God."[4] I am sure that God welcomes our attempts to reveal our deeper feelings, however fumbling these attempts may be, for it is only in risking such self-disclosure that our relationship with God can finally become authentic. In prayer as in other forms of communication, "we often reveal more of ourselves as we are at a given moment by expressing to God the feelings we are experiencing than we would if we described our thoughts for an hour."[5] As Evagrius Ponticus, one of the 4th-century desert fathers, reminds us, "A single word in intimacy is worth more than a thousand at a distance." If we hope to develop a conscious relationship with the loving Mystery who dwells within and among us, then we must grow in the willingness, the commitment, and the capacity to share with God whatever is stirring within us, including the feelings that we tend to hide from the world and even from ourselves.

Great, you may say, this is all very well and good, but many of us do not find it easy to express our feelings frankly, either to one another or to God. "How are you doing?" a colleague asks us. "Fine!" we answer merrily, swallowing the grief or rage or loneliness that was rising in our throat. Even in our close relationships, we may not do much better than this. Growing up in my family, for instance, I rarely witnessed any direct expression of anger. With clenched jaw and burning eyes, someone might go so far as to say, "I am cross with you." The only words more alarming than these were the dreaded sentences, spoken with averted gaze, "It's not that I am angry with you. I am just *disappointed*." In families like mine, where certain feelings are apparently so dangerous, so potent, or so evil that they cannot be freely admitted and directly expressed, it is unlikely that anyone will feel particularly encouraged—much less eager—to reveal honest feelings to God.

For those of us trained by upbringing or culture to temper the expression of our feelings and to be less than frank with one another and with God, it is probably worth reflecting on what we tend to do with our feelings when we pray. The following questions may stimulate personal insight. As you read through them slowly, are there one or two that have some energy, some "juice," for you?

Do you consider God a friend, with whom you can afford to be yourself?

Do you seek to express to God the full range of your feelings, the "negative" as well as the "positive"?

Do you consider prayer a place to express mainly warm and loving feelings?

Do you consider prayer a place to be "peaceful," a place where you no longer feel anything at all?

What feelings are easy for you to express to God?

What feelings do you tend to shut down, block, or shy away from in prayer?

What are the tears that you need to shed?

Are there areas of your life that you have shut away from God?

What is the grief or anger or secret that you need to express to yourself, to God, or to someone else before you can open to new life?

Are you willing to let your anger, or mourning, or secrets become a place of encounter with God?

Are there losses that you need to grieve? Is there something or someone that you need to mourn and to let go so that God can draw you into an even deeper love?

Is there an image of God that frees you to know that you are safe, free to be real, free to tell the truth? (For example, you might imagine Jesus gazing upon you with tenderness and respect, holding your hand, embracing you, or weeping beside you. You might imagine God as mother or as friend.)

What happens as you reflect on these questions in the presence of God? What spontaneous prayers arise within you?

Until we come to the inner stillness of contemplative prayer, when all thoughts, images, and movements of the heart are stilled and there is nothing to do but to breathe in the presence of God's silent love, our feelings will be the language of our prayer, as surely as sounds are the language of music. Until and unless we are called by God to silence, can we learn in prayer to give our feelings full play? Can we let the song that is singing through us discover its place in the symphony of creation? As Alan Ecclestone writes, "Our business is not to invent a peculiar song of our own or make do with a hotch-potch of scraps got from others, but to discover . . . our part in the song of the earth, the music of the spheres, the Lord's song, and the hymn of creation . . . and give it utterance."[6]

Praying with Feeling

For many of us, it is in learning to pray the whole range of our feelings that we encounter most fully the tenderness of Christ. After my daughter died three years ago, I was filled with both grief and rage and, for many weeks thereafter, spent long stretches of prayer time simply sobbing and pounding as the waves of feeling passed through me. There was no other way for me to be real in prayer. It was here or nowhere that I would find God and that God would find me. One afternoon, when I was boiling with anger, I imagined myself hurling my fists against a wall. After a while the image changed, and I found that I was beating my fists, not against a wall, but against Jesus' chest. I was raging and pounding within his embrace.

The anger was still there, as was the fierce need to express it, but everything had changed: I was feeling it now within the embrace of love. Like a canopy, love enclosed and embraced all that was within me. All that I felt, all that I needed so urgently to communicate—all this was received, accepted, understood, and blessed. I was still angry, yes, but now I was also amazed, surprised, and grateful, as well. Love had found me in my anger. The part of me that had been most raw and most violent, even to the depths of despair, had been met and held and touched by Love. Healing had begun. Healing was here.

For those seeking to be real with God, one simple way to begin prayer is to ask ourselves, "What am I feeling right now?" and "How would a person with this feeling pray?" If the reality is that we feel stuck and blocked and bored, then that is the prayer that we have been given to pray, at least for the time being. Rather than instantly trying to pep ourselves up—counting our blessings, perhaps, or turning at once to a psalm of praise—what would happen if instead we gently opened to the sense of being bored and stuck? Is it possible that here, in the very place where we least sense God's quickening presence, God might have a gift to give us?

How quick we generally are to label our feelings, to pass judgment upon them, and, when we deem it appropriate, to hustle them off out of sight! When a flicker of anger arises within us, do we immediately tamp it down, accusing ourselves of being "judgmental"? When the wind of sorrow blows through, do we slam the windows shut and berate ourselves for "self-pity"? Aren't these rapid-fire self-condemnations a way of maintaining tight control? What would happen if we came to prayer with the intention of loosening that control just a bit and allowing the repressed parts of ourselves a gentler, more generous hearing? What if we sought to pray with an attitude of interest and respect toward our inner selves? Isn't it possible that such an attitude is more akin to God's than the relentlessly self-critical gaze that so many of us turn upon ourselves?

For many of us, it is in learning to pray the whole range of our feelings that we encounter most fully the tenderness of Christ.

One way of praying with feelings is to experience them in God's presence and to express them to God as simply and directly as possible:

> Spend some moments settling down. Take several slow, deep breaths, taking care to exhale completely. Use whatever ways you have learned to center yourself. Adopt the posture you find comfortable so that you can be both relaxed and alert.
>
> Open yourself to God's presence. Entrust this time to God.
>
> Allow your awareness to settle in the center of your body, noticing how you feel inside. . . . Gradually allow this inside awareness to extend to the rest of your body, noting whatever might be there. . . . What are you aware of feeling right now? . . . Whatever you are feeling is fine. . . . Where do you feel it in your body? . . . How big is it? . . . If it had a color, what color would it be?

Check for a moment: Is it OK to be with this for a few moments, to give it a friendly hearing, to let it tell something of its story?

Open yourself to the feeling, while remaining aware that you are in the presence of God. Try to be with whatever you are feeling in a gentle, caring way. (If you are feeling something painful, you might see if you can hold and feel it in the same way that you might hold a little child who has come to you for comfort. You might put your arm around it or seat it beside you—whatever makes it easier for you to let yourself feel what you are caring inside.)

Gently open to the emotion while remaining steadily in the presence of God. Let arise within you whatever images, thoughts, and feelings spontaneously arise, but continue to be open and receptive to the presence of God. Express to God whatever is within you as simply and directly as you can. Let your feelings—and the images that may arise with them—flow as freely as possible.

If you get overly caught up in the images, thoughts, and feelings and lose contact with the sense of God's presence, return for a while to the simple awareness of God's presence.

Weave gently back and forth between exploring your feelings in the presence of God and returning to a simple awareness of God's presence.[7]

The purpose of this way of prayer is to explore and express our true selves while remaining conscious of the presence of God. It is one thing to tell ourselves how angry or sad we may be; it is quite another to express these feelings to God. The former may leave us self-absorbed, spinning in a web of our own self-talk. The latter opens us to personal relationship with God. After praying in this way, it is often helpful to reflect, perhaps in writing, in a journal: What happened during this prayer time? What was it like to disclose these feelings to God? When did I feel that God was closest to me? most distant? Was there any sense of God listening to me? responding to me? Were there any surprises? How did praying with these feelings affect my relationship with God?

Only I Suffer

The degree to which we are present to the woundedness and brokenness in ourselves is the degree to which we are present to the woundedness and brokenness of the world. Only by exploring our own woundedness to the depths can we respond to the woundedness of the world.[8] Nevertheless, many of us feel blocked from entering or expressing our pain because of a myriad of inner voices: "Nice girls don't get angry!" "Big boys don't cry!" "You should be over this by now!" "You're wallowing in self-pity!" "It can't be that bad!" All these voices, and more, may clamor within us, urging us to silence, to secrecy, to denial. One particularly insidious voice for spiritual seekers is the one that argues, "Your suffering is insignificant compared to the suffering of the poor, the homeless, the war-stricken, the hungry." One way of avoiding, minimizing, and denying our own pain is to compare it with someone else's and to conclude—with either relief or disappointment—that ours is not real and does not count. As a result, we never dare to explore our own pain, and we never learn what it has to teach us.

Sound familiar? If during our prayer we find ourselves trying to talk ourselves out of what we are feeling by comparing our pitiful, unimportant suffering to the much more worthy and interesting suffering of someone else, perhaps it is time to explore the following way of prayer:

> Listen to the pain with respectful attention. Honor it. Trust it. Try not to minimize or deny it. Your pain is real. Your pain has a gift to give to you, if only you are willing to let it be felt.
>
> Gently open to the feelings, while remaining aware of the presence of God. You are not alone with these feelings: you are feeling them in the presence of God.
>
> Now imagine that you are the only person who has ever suffered in this way. You are the only person who knows the exact degree and shape of your suffering. You are the only one who knows the particular meaning of this pain. In this sense, you are alone in your suffering.
>
> Let God know exactly how this suffering feels. Your suffering is the only suffering in the world. You have God's complete and compassionate attention. No one else matters but you. No suffering matters except yours.
>
> Allow yourself to enter the depth of your pain. God is here.

We All Suffer

As in the exercise above, when we are in pain, sometimes the way to open to God's love is fearlessly to enter the pain and to experience it as if there were no pain in the world except our own. Sometimes we have no choice: in the extremity of suffering, all our energies may be absorbed in dealing with our own pain, and we may be unable to notice or to respond to the pain of others. In times of great shock, this response is natural.

However, when we are in pain, sometimes the way to open to an awareness of God is to open our awareness to the suffering of others. If pain is isolating us so that we feel cut off from God and from the rest of the human race, can we find a way of prayer that will connect us again, perhaps even at a new depth? Can our own particular pain lead us beyond ourselves to the pain of others? Can our own suffering teach us empathy and nurture in us the holy compassion that connects us with all living souls? In discovering the pain that we share, will we also discover our human connectedness and the divine love that flows through us all?

In times of great suffering, you may be led to try this prayer:

> Open yourself to feel your suffering in the presence of God. Feel its particular shape and weight. Breathe with the suffering.
>
> Let your breath bring you an image of someone else who is suffering. It may be a person that you know. It may be a person whose picture you have seen in the newspapers or on television. Perhaps she (or he) lives in the same town or perhaps somewhere far away. Imagine what she is doing. Imagine what she is feeling—the anger, pain, grief, confusion, fear, distress.
>
> Open your heart in compassion to that person. Let your pain mingle with hers, and her pain with yours. You may have never met her, but that does not matter: you are close to one another. You are sharing the same pain.
>
> Let your breath bring you images of other people who feel what you feel. . . . Imagine them, one by one, in their distress.
>
> Open your heart in compassion to them, too, one by one. How many of you there are who share this pain, this suffering! Feel your suffering in solidarity with theirs. Let your suffering be a window into the human suffering that fills the earth. Let your cry of pain include their pain as well. You are giving voice to their prayer as well as to your own.

Grounding in the Cross

As we grow in sharing our true selves with God, including our deeper and more painful feelings, we will probably find that we are becoming more, rather than less, aware of the suffering that lies within us and around us. God is leading us beyond the pretense that neither suffering nor death is real, and we may come to feel overwhelmed by our own pain or the pain of the world. Famine, war, environmental disaster, innocent suffering, violent deaths—how can we take all this in without being defeated by despair or going numb with horror? How can we open to such suffering and respond to it without falling apart?

As we grow in awareness of suffering, we may need to take hold of our prayer life with a fervor that we have never felt before, for it is in the face of enormous suffering that we must admit our complete dependence upon the mercy of God. It is here that we bow before the cross of Christ and offer him our pain—the pain and grief shared by all human beings, the pain that none of us can "fix," the pain that none of us can "solve." The cross of Christ is the place where all the suffering and evil of this world are met by God's infinite compassion and mercy. Because there is no suffering or evil we can experience that is not met by the cross of Christ, we need not succumb to hopelessness, apathy, or despair. Because the cross is planted before us, we are free to open to the reality of suffering and evil: *here* all suffering and evil are touched by Love. We can let pain and evil pass through us into the cross of Christ. The cross of Christ is like a lightning rod that draws to itself all suffering and evil and "grounds" them in Love. The cross of Christ bears all pain, endures all pain, and transforms all pain into love.

> *As we grow in awareness of suffering, we may need to take hold of our prayer life with a fervor that we have never felt before, for it is in the face of enormous suffering that we must admit our complete dependence upon the mercy of God.*

The following form of prayer is inspired by Joanna Rogers Macy's adaptation of an ancient Tibetan meditation for the development of compassion.[9] As Macy observes, "We will never perceive the full beauty of life if we close our eyes and ears to its suffering."[10] Or as novelist Franz Kafka once put it, "You can hold yourself back from the sufferings of the world, this is something you are free to do and is in accord with your nature, but perhaps precisely this holding back is the only suffering that you might be able to avoid."

    Spend some moments settling down. Take several slow, deep breaths, taking care to exhale completely. Use whatever ways you have learned to center yourself. Adopt the posture you find comfortable so that you can be both relaxed and alert.

Open yourself to God's presence. Entrust this time to God.

Let your breath bring you an image of the cross of Christ. . . . Perhaps it is in front of you, or behind you. . . . Sense its weight, its placement deep in the ground. . . . Its roots go deep into the earth, deep into all the muck and mess and pain of human life. . . . Its top lifts high into the sky. It stretches far above you. . . . Sense the presence of Christ upon the cross. . . . Here is the place where heaven and earth are joined. . . . Here is the place where every suffering and evil is lifted up, and met by the love of God. . . . Sense the holy power that is before you or behind you.

Relax. Center on your breathing. . . . Visualize your breath as a stream flowing up through your nose, down through windpipe, lungs. Take it down through your lungs and, picturing an opening in the bottom of your heart, visualize the breath stream passing through your heart and out through that opening to pass into the cross of Christ.

Now open your awareness to the suffering that is present in the world. Drop for now all defenses and open to your knowledge of that suffering. . . . Let it come as concretely as you can . . . concrete images of your fellow beings in pain and need, in fear and isolation, in prisons, hospitals, tenements, refugee camps. . . . No need to strain for these images, they are present in you by virtue of our interconnectedness. Relax and just let them surface, breathe them in, breathe them through to the cross of Christ . . . the numberless hardships of our fellow humans and of our animal brothers and sisters, too, as they swim the seas and fly through the air of this ailing planet. . . . Breathe in that pain like a dark stream, up through your nose, down through your lungs and heart, and out again into the cross of Christ. . . . You are asked to do nothing for now but let it pass through your heart. . . . Keep breathing. . . . Be sure that stream flows through and *out* again, do not hang on to the pain. Surrender it for now to the healing power of Christ. . . . Christ can bear it all. . . . The love of God is larger and more enduring than suffering, pain, or death. . . . Breathe in all the suffering of the world, and breathe it out into the cross of Christ. . . .

With Shantideva, the Buddhist saint, we can say, "Let all sorrows ripen in me." We help them ripen by passing them through our hearts . . . making good compost out of all that grief . . . so we can learn from it, enhancing our larger, collective knowing.

> If you experience an ache in the chest, a pressure within the rib cage, that is all right. . . . When our heart breaks open to the sufferings of the world, we are entering into the heart of Christ. . . . The heart that breaks open can contain the whole universe. Your heart—Christ's heart—is that large. Trust it. Keep breathing.

The Passionate God

This essay has sketched four ways of prayer to deepen our intimacy with God and our capacity for full responsiveness to the pain and joy and being alive: praying the full range of our feelings (Praying with Feeling), honoring in prayer our own particular pain (Only I Suffer), perceiving our solidarity with all human pain (We All Suffer), and entrusting all our suffering to the transforming love of Christ (Grounding in the Cross). None of the steps in these prayer exercises should be taken as rigid rules, but rather as suggestions for helping us to listen more attentively for how the Holy Spirit seeks to pray through us. Prayer is inherently unpredictable, and these guidelines are intended not to inhibit or force our prayer, but rather to encourage some possibilities for prayer that may free us for a new depth of intimacy with God.

Daring to pray our honest feelings opens us to encounter the passionate God, a God revealed in Christ who seeks to offer us abundant life (Jn 10:10). According to the testimony of the Gospels, Jesus freely felt and expressed the whole range of human emotion—anguish and anger, joy and grief, gratitude and tenderness—and all within the context of loving intimacy with the Father. Jesus himself sought to elicit a response from those around him: time and again he questioned his listeners, challenged and provoked them, as he tried to stimulate thought and awaken emotional response. Clearly he felt frustrated when he was greeted with indifference: "But to what will I compare this generation? It is like children sitting in the marketplace and calling to one another, 'We played the flute for you, and you would not dance; we wailed, and you did not mourn'" (Mt 11:16-17, NRSV).

The God we meet in Christ is One who galvanizes us to engage fully with life and to join in the dance. And if we do so, we will be changed. To pray is to invite God into our depths—or, more accurately, to begin to realize that God is already there—and we cannot encounter God without being changed. The person who learns to pray the whole range of feelings may notice any number of changes over time. For example, we may find our-selves less numb, less emotionally inhibited and withdrawn, for we have begun to connect with the One who welcomes us as we are and who listens attentively to our sadness and hope and anger. Our feelings have found their voice, and in God's loving pres-ence we are safe to express them fully. We may find ourselves less scattered and more serene, for now our various emotional impulses have begun to connect with the heart of reality that holds all things together. Now it becomes possible to experience equanimity, to stay steady even while the whole range of feeling washes through us. We may find ourselves less hopeless and passive, for in praying our anger and sorrow we discover the One who not only consoles our suffering, but also strengthens us to hope and empowers us to act. We may find ourselves less self-centered and more compassionate as we begin to realize that, through intimacy with God, we have touched our solidar-ity with all people, indeed, with all living beings. More than one person of prayer has discovered that, in praying with others in their suffering, it is possible not only to empower the sufferer to bear the pain, but even to relieve it. As a Hasid woman, Rifka, concludes in a poignant story recounted by psychologist Robert Kegan, "I cry tonight now this mother vit her idiot vhat is so beautiful vhat is life, tomorrow she vill cry less." [11]

To pray is to invite God into our depths—or, more accurately, to begin to realize that God is already there—and we cannot encounter God without being changed.

To pray our feelings is to express who we are, to be a real self in search of the real God. In praying our feelings we become more fully human. And we discover the passionate God who draws our full humanity into the divine life so that Christ's joy may be in us and our joy may be complete (Jn 15:11). As Irenaeus wrote in the 2nd century of the church, "The glory of God is a person who is fully human, fully alive."

Notes

[1] Thomas N. Hart, *The Art of Christian Listening* (New York: Paulist Press), p. 53.

[2] Hart, p. 52.

[3] Hart, p. 56.

[4] Madeline Birmingham RC and William J. Connolly SJ, "Talking to God," Human Development 10, no. 3 (Fall 1989): 44.

[5] "Talking to God," p. 44.

[6] Alan Ecclestone, *Yes to God* (London: Darton, Longman, and Todd, 1975), p. 124.

[7] For an excellent presentation and theological reflection on a non-verbal, body-centered way of prayer based on Focusing as taught by Dr. Eugene Gendlin, see Peter A. Campbell PhD and Edwin M. McMahon PhD, *Biospirituality: Focusing as a Way to Grow* (Chicago: Loyola University Press, 1985). This suggestion for prayer is loosely adapted from their approach, esp. pp. 122-130.

[8] Michael Dwinell, *Fire Bearer: Evoking a Priestly Humanity* (Liguori, Missouri: Triumph Books, 1993), p. 82.

[9] Joanna Rogers Macy, "Despair and Empowerment Work," in *Living with Apocalypse: Spiritual Resources for Social Compassion*, ed. Tilden H. Edwards (San Francisco: Harper and Row, 1984), pp. 117-133. The last three steps in this prayer are drawn—with the addition of Christian imagery—directly from the words of Macy.

[10] Macy, p. 126.

[11] Robert Kegan, *The Evolving Self: Problem and Process in Human Development* (Cambridge: Harvard University Press, 1982), p. 21.

The Fragile Connection between Prayer and Suffering

*T*his article has a very personal history. It represents an effort to integrate into a learned, structured spirituality a series of shattering experiences which did not immediately fit into that neat order. In late adolescence and early adulthood, I received a thorough formation in the established spiritual patterns of a Benedictine monastery. That formation was positive and solid and provided an effective guidance within the mostly enclosed life and work of the religious community. I delighted in the richness of that Benedictine tradition and absorbed its spirituality whole-heartedly. Yet future events were to present a much more diver-sified and challenging experience of life and spirituality.

The key transition was from religious community life and seminary teaching to ordinary parish ministry. For several years it was my privilege to serve two parishes as an associate pastor. I count those years to be as formative of my current spiritual views as were the years of early religious community formation. I found much love and satisfaction in being a part of a parish commu-nity—living, learning, and worshiping together. These were ordi-nary parishes, no different from most in the United States; they certainly possessed their fair share of problems.

One of the most moving aspects of that parish ministry was responding to the many moments of excruciating sadness in peo-ple's lives: tragic accidents, sudden deaths, painful illnesses, angry divorces, sufferings of poverty and failures, and the despair of trapped lives. In those moments of sadness, in sharing the tragedies and the failures of life, I was taught something of the gritty real-ity of prayer and its place in Christian spirituality. In parish life prayer gets to be intimately woven with the experience of suffering, and the pattern of the weave is not always easy to discern.

One who ministers within that complex web gets drawn inevitably into this mix of suffering and prayer. I can honestly say I do not think I have ever prayed more earnestly or powerfully than on my way to the hospital to meet "who knows what." Yet the impact of such moments on the minister goes well beyond pushing one to pray for assistance. Questions are raised about human life and its hopes, about faith and its depth in people's lives. Eventually the questioning spills over into all of a person's previous spiritual formation with enough power to significantly revamp that earlier formation. This happened in my own life and spirituality, and I wish to share the experience with readers. This experience remains "in process," and my current thoughts represent but a pause in that ongoing journey. I am convinced, however, that any truly human and Christian spirituality must be able to negotiate the alternation of peaks, plateaus, and pits. In suffering and prayer one looks into a deep pit.

The Many Moods of Prayer

Prayer possesses an almost endless variety of structures and attitudes when explored through the lens of academic religious study.[1] The religions of the world offer a splendid array of prayer forms: from the trance-like meditation of the Buddhist monk to the vigorous dance of the American Indians; from the lovemaking of the Hindu tantras to the choral recitation of the Benedictine monk. One may find almost any aspect of human life brought into the dynamic of how human beings have expressed their connections to the God, gods, or spirits they believe in.

Perhaps the incredible variety simply shows the urgent need of human beings to affirm their basic attachment to the Mystery they believe in, the Beyond which has touched their lives. It is a truism to say that one's whole life can become prayer, that any experience can be brought into the dynamic of an attachment to the Mystery of God.

Suffering is one of those common human experiences that often become associated with prayer. For Christians who pray the Psalms, the evidence of suffering-provoked prayer lies daily before their eyes. In the daily recitation of the Liturgy of the Hours, such verses as these often cross our lips: "Lord, heal me, my body is racked; my soul is racked with pain" (Ps 6:3-4); "A band of the wicked beset me. They tear holes in my hands and feet" (Ps 21:17); "Through your anger all my body is sick . . . my wounds are foul and festering" (Ps 37:4-6).

But human suffering has also been profoundly ambivalent in its connection with prayer. My parish experiences proved that repeatedly. On the one hand, I met many people who easily connected suffering with prayer, as do the Psalms. In their pain they cried to God for help, deliverance, or at least the strength to bear the suffering. But, on the other hand, suffering can render prayer problematic. My parish experience provided many instances of that, especially when suffering was prolonged or many fervent prayers seemed unanswered. I remember the real anger of a young woman whose brother had suffered for years a crippling disease. She did not even want to pray and "give God the satisfaction of my obedience." Or again, when the suffering comes unexpectedly, like the death of a child, it can arouse a resisting anger just as easily as a prayerful cry for assistance.

The Real Questions

More than anything else, it is this ambivalent connection between prayer and suffering that I want to reflect on in this article. Is there anything which can be learned for Christian spirituality as a whole about the duality noticed there? Are there some guidelines to help us understand what really happens in people's lives who face some great suffering? Can we discover a few more hints on how a Christian ministry to the suffering can be more understanding and compassionate? How can this fragile yet universal connection between suffering and prayer fit into the spirituality of an ordered religious community? The last question pertains not just to my Benedictine tradition, but also to the past and future history of many other religious orders. It should make spiritual directors and formation personnel take a long hard look at their teaching and practice of prayer. ❂

While all these questions have importance for contemporary spirituality, I wish to give most attention to the last: integrating prayer and suffering into the ordered spirituality of religious communities. I also hope to provide a few insights into the question of the implications for Christian spirituality in general.

After my return from the parish to the routine of my religious community, it struck me how little our regular forms of prayer and spirituality allude to human suffering. In my initial monastic community formation and in the ongoing formation given to the entire community, prayer is generally understood as choral prayer (the Opus Dei, Liturgy of the Hours), forms of contemplative prayer, and lectio divina or spiritual reading. Personal prayer is surely encouraged, but usually in the latter two forms. From my years of formation I cannot recall any emphasis or even serious discussion on how human suffering and prayer are linked together. We pray the Psalms regularly—and they express lots of suffering—but the pace of praying in common makes them more like "official prayers" which are hardly reflected on deeply. The Prayers of the Faithful at the Eucharist regularly make reference to the many sufferings of people throughout the world, but they generate little of the urgency felt in the immediate pains of parish situations.

Suffering can render prayer problematic.

Perhaps the reason for this "unawareness" of suffering and its intrusions into prayer lay in the *ideal* that religious life must be a calm, ordered rhythm of Christian community. That certainly describes the routine which the Rule of Benedict proposes and the way the Rule has in fact been taught through the centuries. I recall reading a synopsis written by the abbot of one monastery which described the sick of the community as an "unavoidable detail" in the sacred rhythm of community life. The goal of monastic spirituality was often summarized in the traditional *apatheia*—not to be swayed by any emotions or passions. Many other religious communities through the centuries have followed variations of that spiritual path.

Yet there is a great deal of human suffering in any religious community, as much as in many parishes. We have our sicknesses: arthritis, heart disease, cancer, and deteriorating bodies. We have people in mental hospitals, in houses for emotional and alcoholic rehabilitation, burdened with all the pain and suffering that attends those failures. Religious community members have their own natural families, too, and share their pains. And there are the untold heartaches that seldom get treated in hospitals or therapy: community injustices, loneliness, betrayed promises, spiritual doubts, and so on. We may also count the sufferings of others whom our ministries bring us into contact with. I have not forgotten the sufferings of those I knew years ago; they live as permanent fixtures of my spiritual world. In the past twenty-five years, I have given enough retreats to communities of men and women, both contemplative and apostolic, to get a pretty good feeling of the pain in the lives of many who live behind "religious walls": those tortured by memories of sexual abuse, neglect, or unwantedness; those spiritually deformed by ludicrous religious training and wrenched by guilt and scrupulosity; those injured by personal betrayals and unjust actions of superiors or others. The list goes on and on.

Our examination of this issue will have an eclectic character about it, yet will move towards a synthesis. We will first look at the Jesus stories of the Gospels, since these have long been considered a privileged source of Christian spirituality. In fact, these stories will provide some paradigmatic experiences of the relation between suffering and prayer. Then we will try to integrate these insights in a more orderly manner, using a phenomenological method that moves from personal to social to universalized experiences.

Suffering and Prayer in the Gospel Stories

Every great world religion enshrines and embeds its major symbols in master images.[2] For Christians those images are preeminently contained in the four Gospels of the New Testament. The life patterns of Jesus depicted therein provide for Christians their model of a "true life of faith." I will suggest four points taken from the Jesus stories that focus on the interface of prayer and suffering to see what insights they might provide for meditation and reflection.

The first is a theme which appears frequently: Jesus' great personal concern for human suffering. How many Gospel stories capture the immediate attention Jesus gives to people who are blind, lame, crippled, emotionally disturbed, epileptic, hemorrhaging, or deaf! As Jesus comes from the Decapolis, they bring a deaf and dumb man before him. Immediately Jesus takes him off by himself, puts his fingers in the man's ears, touches his tongue with saliva. Then Jesus groans and says, "Open" (Mk 7:31-37). Embedded in this story is the fact that Jesus actively participates in the suffering of the man, as shown by his groaning. His concern is so great that he identifies with and shares in the suffering which the man is enduring.

When we read Jesus stories like the healing of the deaf and dumb man, the centurion whose child has died, the widow of Naim, or the many lepers Jesus cured, a principle emerges: Jesus has great understanding of and kindness towards those whose pain is profound, and his example is a mandate to all his followers: Recognize human suffering. See it, respond to it; realize it as a dominant fact in people's lives and their relationship with God. It cannot be avoided because it does not fit into an orderly spiritual pattern. Jesus' perspective is similar to that of the Buddha: suffering is life and life is suffering.[3] This perception is a pillar of any authentic Christian spirituality.

There is nothing shameful in fearing pain.

A second major aspect of prayer and suffering may be seen in Jesus' prayer in the Garden of Gethsemane (Mk 14:32-36). Here we witness an example of prayer joined to the suffering of fear and distress. Scriptural exegetes note that the Greek word Mark uses in verse 37 denotes a shuddering horror, a terror, and the threat of boundless suffering.[4] In Luke's account (22:44) the presence of bloody sweat shows the physical reaction of his body to the threat of pain. This is mental and spiritual suffering overflowing into his body. The fullness of Jesus' human condition expresses itself. He does not want to suffer or experience pain; that desire becomes a part of his prayer itself. "Father, if you are willing, remove this cup from me; yet not my will but yours be done" (Lk 22:42). This story carries a signal message for Christian spirituality, one that touches directly on the connection between prayer and suffering: It is all right to want to avoid suffering. It is all right to fear the operation, to worry about the medical treatment, to be a bit anxious about the regular trip to the dentist. There is nothing shameful in fearing pain. And that applies to the members of any religious community, who will face their own share of physical, psychological, and spiritual sufferings.

I recall an older priest once commenting that religion should make people suffer. He believed that is how faith is learned and that people nevertheless avoid it if they can. But the Gospel stories contain nothing of that attitude. Manufacturing suffering has no place in the spiritual dynamics of the Gospel; it knows that life brings suffering enough.

A third relevant point can be discerned in the very structure of the passion narratives. Everything is connected to pain of some kind: the humiliation before Pilate, the mocking by the soldiers, the betrayal by Jesus' closest friends, the realized separation from loving family members, the scourging, the way of the cross, the nailing, the hours of agony while his body is being torn apart. The passion accounts might simply be seen as multivalent symbols of the many types of pain which we human beings must undergo in our lives. Perhaps we should take more notice of how large a part of the Gospels the passion narratives occupy.

While official religious community spiritualities may not have been formed along the lines of this Christian perspective, the piety of ordinary Christians has been. Above all it has been ritually enshrined in the Stations of the Cross. They have retained a long-lasting popularity because people can identify with the sufferings depicted there. The acceptance of suffering as part of our humanity and a way to salvation touches the deepest part of Christian spirituality. This is the burden of accepting our created humanity—the very Mystery of Humanity, as impenetrable as the Mystery of God.

The last point and perhaps the most perplexing moment of the Jesus stories is that cry of desperation on the cross, "My God, my God, why have you forsaken me?" (Mk 15:34). His body torn apart by human cruelty, Jesus knows he is about to die. He is frightened to the core of his being. Here is a human being humiliated and degraded—hardly a just end for one who was so compassionate to all he met. And, as his sensitivity is so acute, the more sharply does he feel the suffering. He can no longer stand it and cries out in words that jumble a despair (an answerless void) with prayer (that basic affirming connection with God).

This passage functions as a balancing force to any facile assimilation of prayer and suffering. It tells us there is no easy response to the challenge of acute suffering. Towards prayer, suffering remains ambivalent. Suffering can at times mute our positive relation with God and can even blot out our religious desires. That possibility must never be forgotten. It was admirably remembered by John Henry Newman writing his mystical poem on the experience of dying:

> 'Tis this new feeling, never felt before, . . .
> That I am going, that I am no more.
> 'Tis this strange innermost abandonment, . . .
> This emptying out of each constituent

And natural force, by which I come to be.
Pray for me, O my friends; a visitant
Is knocking his dire summons at my door,
The like of whom, to scare me and to daunt,
Has never, never come to me before. . . .
So pray for me, my friends, who have not strength to pray.[5]

In the life of every one of us there may come that moment of terror, of facing the unknown void, and who knows how we will respond? Perhaps, as in Newman's poem, our own prayers fail us and we must rely on the prayer of others. Such moments certainly face members of organized religious communities.

We need to appreciate and interiorize much better the insight that the Letter to the Hebrews gives us about Jesus: "Jesus in his life on earth offered prayers and entreaties, crying aloud with tears. . . . And, although he was a Son, he learned to obey through what he suffered" (Heb 5:7-8). The distinctive aspect of Jesus' prayer here is the wide range of expression: it is a groan in suffering solidarity with others, a cry of desperation, an acknowledging of anxiety and fear, all directed toward God. These are also root metaphors for the prayer of all followers of Jesus.

Prayer and Suffering as Spiritual Moments

We need now to take the lessons from the Jesus stories and put them into a more systematic exposition. I propose to do so by positing three progressively larger concentric circles. The first is prayer when suffering occurs in our own self, the second is how we perceive and pray for other people who face suffering, and the third is a realization that suffering and prayer form a lens through which the whole of the Christian life may be viewed.

In the innermost circle are those events of personal pain which touch our own bodies, minds, and hearts. Pain and suffering are universal human phenomena; everyone knows them in some fashion. Children come forth from the womb screaming and crying. From the beginning, something about life hurts. That perception stays with us: from scraped fingers to serious disease to agonizing heartbreaks. We all know suffering and it frightens us. A young priest, entering the hospital for exploratory heart tests, said, "I'm not afraid of dying, but I'm scared to death of what they will do to me in the hospital." When I repeated that remark to a parish group, somone blurted out, "Ain't that the truth?" We know personal pain and it affects us deeply.

The Jesus stories tell us that prayer in such moments of pain can sometimes be only a groan. That principle comes from Jesus' own life and example: the sweating of blood and the wrenching cry, "My God, my God. . . ." Prayer in these moments is not elegantly phrased words or positive feelings; it is just an awkward expression that unites our suffering with that of Jesus Christ. Sometimes it is only the barest indication of that unity: a glance at a cross, a rosary clutched a little tighter, or a handclasp with a little more pleading in it. But we should realize that moment of expressiveness as a prayer, a joining of our lives to the mystery of Jesus' sacrificial death. It occurs in a moment of deepest weakness.

The Jesus stories tell us that prayer in such moments of pain can sometimes be only a groan.

This first moment of prayer and suffering joined in our own bodies needs to be acknowledged in all Christian spiritual traditions, for it is the universal human condition. The sick in religious communities should be aware that their pains and sufferings are a unity with the passion of Christ and the suffering of the world. They need continually be reminded of this in a consoling and compassionate way. And somewhere in their formation they should have learned about the barest simplicity of that prayer.

From that innermost circle we move outward to a wider perspective which recognizes the suffering of life as a learning moment of prayer. Commonly suffering is thought of as an occasion for prayer, a time for turning to God. But, through most Christian traditions of spirituality, the very activity of praying has its own unique element of suffering; prayer itself is the cause of some suffering. How so? Because the activity of attending to God and the presence of God day after day can be tedious and even painful. Anyone who has tried to practice formal prayer on a daily, continuing basis learns how hard such perseverance is.

Christian spiritual traditions have often asserted that prayer itself is a form of purification, because the learning of an attentiveness to God is truly a discipline. The discipline dimension of prayer was strongly affirmed by early monks. They knew that prayer cannot always be a joyful, overflowing, emotional experience; it can be tedious and seem useless. One suffers a sense of futility. It is hard to attend to the Mystery of God when one is angry, bored, or disappointed. But regular prayer builds the courage and inner strength to continue one's life commitment. There is, however, suffering involved.

This connection between prayer and suffering also links us to the sufferings of Jesus, through our sharing in his patient perseverance. Thus we prepare ourselves to recognize the sufferings of others and respond to them while strengthening ourselves for when severe suffering touches us. The Rule of Benedict says, "Faithfully observing his teaching in the monastery until death, we shall through patience share in the sufferings of Christ that we may deserve to share in his kingdom" (Prologue, 50). This point needs to be taught anew. While well known in past ages, it has slipped to the side in an age of charismatic, creation-centered, and joyful styles of praying. Religious communities should teach their members the need to persevere in prayer as a discipline with its own suffering.

If we have interiorized the close connection of suffering and prayer in our own selves and practiced the discipline of regular prayer, then we can move to the larger circle of a prayerful solidarity with others who are suffering. All Christians have regular times where this joining of prayer and suffering comes naturally. When our father, mother, brother, sister, relative, friend, or work associate must endure difficulties and pain, we pray for them; we suffer with them, gladly. Prayer and suffering are linked by the natural bond we feel with these people. This type of prayer often fills the lists of Prayers of the Faithful at the Eucharist and the Liturgy of the Hours. But the example of Jesus goes further. His perspective goes beyond natural bonds of blood relationship and communal interests. He also feels the suffering of those of different ideas, religions, and races. The Gospel stories and the example of Jesus call all Christians to truly join in a suffering solidarity with those who struggle for the necessities of life, who suffer the ravages of famine or disease, who are oppressed by unjust powers in this world. A practiced awareness of the intimate relation of suffering and prayer should unite all Jesus' followers with any human suffering in this world.

A powerful artistic representation of this vision may be seen at Thomas Merton's abbey (Gethsemani, Kentucky). Some distance from the monastery in a wooded grove are several bronze statues erected in memory of Jonathan Daniels, the Episcopalian seminarian murdered in Mississippi for promoting civil rights. The disciples sleep near the figure of Jesus kneeling upright yet looking overwhelmed, feeling the pain of the world and praying for that world. It is an eloquent memorial of the place that prayerful solidarity with the suffering of the world should have in the consciousness of even a contemplative religious community. Such solidarity belongs in the hearts of all religious communities and in their daily prayer. Prayer formation should foster it. People in formation should be encouraged to keep in touch, by letter or visit, with some who directly contact the suffering of the world. They can then fast and pray for them and with them, as early Christians prayed for and waited with those who visited (or were) martyrs in prison.

The final concentric circle of our expanding awareness of the interplay of suffering and prayer is to recognize that suffering is an intrinsic principle of our very relationship with God. This means that, if we are to enter fully into union with Christ, we must experience some of the suffering he endured. We too must take up the cross and follow him. St. Paul was of this mind when he viewed the entire creation as "groaning in labor pains" (Rm 8:22).

Suffering is an intrinsic principle of our very relationship with God.

In the last twenty-five years the theme of the paschal mystery has become primary in Christian spirituality, and rightly so. But too often the emphasis seems almost exclusively on the resurrection and on new life. The passion and death— also parts of the paschal mystery—are downplayed; but they happen first. All people, no matter what their state in the church or their success in life, will come to know the passion and death in their own selves. Such moments of suffering are surely a part of our configuration to the pattern of Christ. We hope that the trial will not be too intense, and so the phrase of the Lord's Prayer "Lead us not into temptation" takes on a powerful meaning.

In conclusion, I hope I have shown some of the systematic linkages between suffering and prayer in Christian life, with particular reference to religious communities and their formation in prayer. (These reflections have come a long way since those drives to the hospital to minister to accident victims.) Religious communities regularly instruct new members in the prayer of the Hours, kinds of personal prayer (including some forms of contemplation), and lectio divina. It would be well to integrate a component that connects prayer to the many kinds of human suffering that we all experience. Then we may all glimpse the religious power within Paul's words: "I make up in my own body the sufferings that are lacking in Christ Jesus" (Col 1:24).

Notes

[1] For example, see Alfonso di Nola (comp.), *The Prayers of Man: From Primitive Peoples to Present Times* (New York: Ivan Obolensky, 1961); F. Heiler, *Prayer: A Study in the History and Psychology of Religion* (New York: Oxford University Press, 1958); Vladimir Lindenberg, *Meditation and Mankind* (London: Rider and Co., 1959).

[2] For a good treatment of the concept of "master images" in religious traditions, see Ray Hart, *Unfinished Man and the Imagination* (New York: Herder and Herder, 1969), pp. 281-305.

[3] For the place of suffering in the religious vision of Buddhism, see Robert Lester, *Buddhism* (San Francisco: Harper and Row, 1987), pp. 75-80; Peter Harvey, *An Introduction to Buddhism* (New York: Cambridge University Press, 1990), pp. 47-60.

[4] J. Dunn, *Jesus and the Spirit* (Philadelphia: Westminister Press, 1975), p. 19.

[5] Cardinal John Henry Newman, *The Dream of Gerontius*, part 1.

ANTHONY H. OSTINI

Four Types of Prayer

prayer forms

Four major types of prayer have developed and flourished throughout the church's long tradition of spirituality. They may be called prayerful reading, meditation, prayer of the heart, and contemplation. Each type can be used separately, or each can be regarded as a "moment of prayer" and all four used within a given period of prayer. The tradition is rich and quite flexible according to one's needs. An awareness of that tradition can be helpful in developing a life of prayer. Let me attempt to describe how to pray using each of the four types.

Prayerful reading consists, very simply, in reading Scripture, or any other written text, in an attentive, prayerful manner. Scripture is the unique word of God, the presence of Jesus, God's Word among us. Reading Scripture with attention, seeking God's Word, is itself prayer.

To pray in this way, begin by reverently taking up the Bible and asking for a sense of God's presence. Then choose a text from Scripture, one that is not too long. Read the text slowly, with attention, simply listening and not being overly concerned at first with its meaning. If you are alone and will not distract anyone, read the selection aloud so that you are listening with both the inner and the outer ear. Reread the text two, three, or more times. It is prayer simply to listen with reverence to God's Word. As you listen over and over, some word, phrase, sentence, image, or idea will probably stand out and become the focus of your attention. This is God's Word speaking to you in your own particular circumstances at that time. Reverently repeat several times the idea, image, sentence, phrase, or word which draws your attention. Listen to it; get the feel of it. Let it rest with you. After some time you will occasionally want to know why this particular word or phrase has attracted your attention and what it might mean for you. At that point you are ready to move to the second moment of prayer. Do not, however, be anxious or too quick to move out of this first moment. God's word spoken this way is always a privileged moment of prayer that nourishes the spirit and refreshes the soul.

Meditation is prayerful consideration of the meaning of the text which has attracted and held your attention. It involves discovering the meaning or importance of the text *for you*. Meditation does not "study" the text but raises the question: What is God's Word saying to me? This type of prayer is sometimes called "discursive." The word discursive comes from the Latin verb *discurrere*, which means to run about from place to place. It graphically describes the mental activity of meditation during which your mind jumps about from one possible meaning to another and explores the various reasons the text attracts you. Meditating on the word of God is something like wrestling with it, like probing it deeply, pondering its parts, and seeking its application to your own life and especially to your unique relationship with God.

These first two moments of prayer, reading and meditation, involve the action of receiving, of taking in God's word. Reading involves both your body and your senses. You reverently place yourself in God's presence. You take up the Bible, hold it, read its words, listen to their sound. You reverence the book and its contents. You take in and receive from God what is God's. Meditation engages your mind, which makes the word your own. Thus prayer moves from the exterior to the interior; from the written and spoken word to interiorizing and personalizing that word.

At some time in your process of centering on the meaning and application of God's word, there is likely to come a moment of realizing "this means something to me!" This "aha!" moment touches you where you live. You are moved deeply by God's word; you experience profound feelings and are ready to respond. At that point you are ready to move on to the third moment of prayer. Again, however, you should not be anxious to move beyond the mental prayer, the wrestling with the meaning and application of God's word. Let its meaning soak in and challenge you. To move on quickly might indicate a reluctance to allow God's word to get too close or probe too deeply.

Prayer of the heart happens when prayer moves from the mind to the heart. When Scripture and the various prayer traditions of the church speak of the heart along with its feelings, they point to something much deeper than mere surface emotions. The "feelings of the heart" are the movements that affect you deeply, something closer to what we would today call "gut feelings."

When you become aware that the insights from the meditation are moving you deeply, let those feelings themselves become your prayer. This moves prayer from the head to the heart. As you were meditating, and arrived at an "aha!" moment, your deeper affections, in response to your meditation, could have been joy, sadness, thankfulness, contrition, love, anger, peace, or any other of the many feelings which we humans experience. Stay with that feeling or those feelings. Try less to understand them than to let them simply be your response. You might understand the feelings, or you might not. Allow your attention to focus on God and away from yourself. Let the feelings themselves express what you want to make known to God. This is the language of the heart, the language of love. Often a *mantra* (a word or several words repeated to hold one's attention) will help to keep your attention centered on the deeper feelings. Sometimes you might feel inclined to put your feelings into words addressed to God. What is most important is that the feelings themselves, along with your attention, be focused outward—on God—since this moment of prayer is one of response.

When you begin to feel restless or to feel that you have adequately expressed the feelings of your heart, then you are likely ready to move on to the fourth moment. Once again, do not move on too quickly. We sometimes shy away from our deepest feelings when we most need to express them to God.

Contemplation is the deepest moment of prayer, the simplest, most silent. Contemplation has been described as "a simple, loving gaze." Once the prayer of the heart has expressed itself, you can be drawn to "silent presence." This fourth moment of prayer might be somewhat brief, and it should not be hurried. In this moment of prayer you are simply, silently alone with God. The prayer has moved as deeply within as possible. You have employed your mind and heart to express yourself, and now you are quiet; you are just with God. You have moved through and beyond words and feelings. Do not hurry the stillness; just remain quietly in this moment of union. Your attention is now focused outward from self and entirely on God.

The prayer has moved from receiving, to appropriating, to response, to union.

These four moments may fill up the entire time of your prayer, or you might find yourself repeating the cycle of four moments several times during a time of prayer. Generally you will find that you can use all four moments only during longer periods of prayer. For shorter times of prayer, you might use only one or two of these moments.

The traditional Latin names for the four moments I have described are "lectio" or "lectio divina" for prayerful reading, "meditatio" for meditation, "oratio" (the Latin word meaning prayer) for prayer of the heart, and "contemplatio" for contemplation.

Liturgy of the Hours:
Path to Integration

*P*ilar Feliu STJ, former superior general of the Teresian Sisters, once described the Liturgy of the Hours as the frame that encloses our day. Like the frame of a painting, our common prayer time can radically change the way we perceive the day as we look forward to it at Lauds, and back on it at Vespers. Bringing our lives to prayer through the Hours can effect far more than bringing a new perspective or adding a rosy tone to our view. It can also be the channel for the powerful working of the word of God, which is "living and effective, sharper than any two-edged sword" (Hb 4:12). Encountering in a prayerful setting the psalms and other scripture texts again and again through the cycle of the seasons, allows them to work on us, "penetrating even between soul and spirit, joints and marrow, . . . to discern reflections and thoughts of the heart." Perhaps the image of a loom is more appropriate than a simple frame, for through the Hours run the threads of the word and the threads of our lives, which can be woven together into a fabric both beautiful and whole. The Liturgy of the Hours is the frame on which we can discover unity and wholeness, helping us to integrate our lives.

The first task at Lauds is to become engaged in the act of prayer. For some of us this may not be an automatic event. At times I have found myself physically present at Lauds, perhaps even mentally present, but somehow not engaged. I have not tuned in to the act of prayer, the fundamental attitude of worship. It is as if I were racing the engine, but in neutral. With the clutch disengaged, the highest octane gas is not going to produce one foot of forward motion. And so it seems with prayer when we are not engaged—nothing happens, in spite of all the proper rituals and words. For me it is often something from without that calls me into prayer—a word of introduction, a song, or perhaps a line from a psalm engages me and leads me into prayer. When this happens, I am integrated into prayer, into the moment, and into relationship with my Creator. My focus changes as once again I realize the simple truth that I am creature entering into praise of my Creator. This shift in focus is the narrow doorway through which I can encounter the divine.

The Liturgy of the Hours also provides a way of bringing us a deeper awareness of the passage of time, not just in a chronological sense, but as sacred time: time as participation, together with the universe, in God's plan of salvation. The cycle of the Hours, praying Lauds at sunrise, Vespers at sunset, helps to integrate us with the rhythm of the *day*. We find our place in the diurnal cycle. The day begins at Lauds, and in a sense the whole day becomes present as we look towards it. This is the proper moment to consecrate the day to God, to invoke the Spirit, to ask for a blessing on all that we will do, to form within our hearts the intention to serve God well this day. At Vespers the day is again present—in memory—and is gathered together in thanksgiving. Whether we have succeeded or failed, found joy or sorrow, there is thankfulness that God has brought us through the day, never abandoning us. Vespers joyfully remembers, gives thanks, celebrates, and offers the day back to God, with a sense of completion.

Through the celebration of the seasons, we also find our place in the liturgical *year*. Advent, Christmas, Lent, Easter, Pentecost, ordinary time, and special community feasts all give us reference points within the flow of time. The simple act of becoming aware of the season in a prayerful setting helps us to become more integrated in time. Just as the priest puts on vestments to celebrate the Eucharist, so do we put on the season through the Hours. The mood and nuances of the season become our own. Participating in the season in this way heightens our own sense of wholeness and of being at one with the world we dwell in. This is especially meaningful in a society which anticipates seasons for commercial purposes, discarding them as soon as their monetary potential has expired. In many ways, as we have become insulated from natural surroundings, we have lost much of our connection with seasons, and the Liturgy of the Hours helps to mend this separation.

At times we commemorate special moments of our lives in

the Liturgy of the Hours: personal milestones, community feasts, civil occasions. This too helps bring unity to our lives, putting the milestones in Christian perspective, forging new bonds as we each celebrate our unique heritage, and making connections with the stream of civilian life.

In a different sense we may find a new integration in time through the repetition of the psalms themselves. I may be struck for the first time with an application of a psalm to some event of the past. Suddenly both the psalm and the event become fresh for me and acquire new meaning. The psalm becomes my own (integrating my life with Scripture), and the past is integrated with the present as it is reinterpreted in the context of the whole. This process is like weaving, going back to pick up the old threads of our lives and weaving them together with the new. The fabric of my life becomes a little more whole; time itself is being redeemed. The past is not lost forever, but brought back, cleansed a little, purified a little, healed a little, as it is brought to prayer and we discover God moving within those bygone events.

Our physical presence at community prayer enfleshes and symbolizes our commitment to be one, a commitment that will demand a little dying from us each day.

The very act of praying together with the community has aspects of integration. The community chooses an hour for prayer, often one that few actually find optimal. Nevertheless, we commit ourselves to this time, integrating our desires and needs as community. Our physical presence at community prayer enfleshes and symbolizes our commitment to be one, a commitment that will demand a little dying from us each day.

The intercessions that we offer also provide an opportunity for further integration within the community. To the extent that we are willing to bring our petitions to God before our brothers and sisters, to the extent that we are willing to hear their intercessions and hold them in our hearts, to the extent that we are willing to pray earnestly for one another, making one another's burdens our own, we deepen our community life. Here is a wonderful opportunity to risk loving one another in community by sharing our concerns, our needs, our failures; by accepting the concerns, needs, and failures of others.

Our union with the entire Body of Christ is also strengthened as we pray the church's own prayer. We join with all the church in praying the psalms, in celebrating feasts and seasons, in lifting up our hearts to praise God for the resurrection, in thanking God for the day. In daily intercession we pray with and for the church, just as we do for our own needs and for those of the community. We expand our horizons to the whole church, indeed, to all of humanity, through prayer. We can give a voice to the voiceless as we offer prayers of praise and petition on behalf of all those who cannot pray, those who do not know how to pray, those whose hearts are hardened against prayer. When we speak to the Lord on behalf of others, we share their burdens and find communion with them. This communion, the fruit of prayer, is a grace for us, a gift that brings us to our rightful relationship with our brothers and sisters, a relationship that allows us to become more whole, more human.

Our prayer with and on behalf of others is not limited to our fellow Christians, nor even to all humanity, but includes all of God's creation. We are voice for the whole universe, awaiting redemption: "Creation awaits with eager expectation the revelation of the children of God; for creation was made subject to futility, not of its own accord but because of the one who subjected it, in hope that creation itself would be set free from slavery to corruption and share in the glorious freedom of the children of God. We know that all creation is groaning in labor pains even until now" (Rm 8:19-22). All creation is groaning, crying out for redemption. The universe itself suffers the wounds of sin and alienation and yearns for healing. We can become voice for all creatures, for all creation, in our prayer. When we lift our voices in praise or petition to the Creator, we offer praise and petition on behalf of all creatures, all creation: birds and fish, trees and rocks. The same psalms that we recite proclaim the praise of God's silent ones:

> Let the rivers clap their hands,
> the mountains shout with them for joy. (Ps 98:8)

> Let the plains be joyful and all that is in them.
> Then let all the trees of the forest rejoice. (Ps 96:12)

> You mountains and all hills,
> fruit trees and all cedars;
> You animals wild and tame,
> you creatures that crawl and fly;

You kings of the earth and all peoples,
princes and all who govern on earth;
young men and women too,
old and young alike.
Let them all praise the LORD's name,
for his name alone is exalted,
majestic above earth and heaven. (Ps 148:9-13)

The untilled meadows also drip;
the hills are robed with joy.
The pastures are clothed with flocks,
the valleys blanketed with grain;
they cheer and sing for joy. (Ps 65:13)

In becoming voice for the speechless, we find union with creation, and in that union we also find our creaturehood, so that we can become more the persons we are called to be: creatures, redeemed, proclaiming God's goodness. There is a wholeness and unity suggested here, a sense of peace deriving from this kind of connectedness to the whole of God's world. To make that connection, even for a few moments of prayer, spins another thread that can help bind the wounds of separation for ourselves, for our communities, for our world. Indeed, the hour we spend praying the Liturgy of the Hours offers us a path toward wholeness.

The Examen of Particulars

*T*he examen of conscience belongs to many traditions. It has been a cherished exercise of desert fathers and mothers, Stoic philosophers, Zen masters, and mystic and monastic ascetics. Over the centuries Jesuits have kept recalling, as a dictum of St. Ignatius, that even if one is too sick to meditate one does not omit the daily examen of conscience. The early Jesuits expected, and so wrote in the official Directory of the Spiritual Exercises in 1599, that all who made the Exercises would continue making the examen of conscience for the rest of their lives.

Down through the ages the examen has been practiced in many different ways, from the meticulously methodical to special kinds of self-awareness. It has been practiced for various purposes, too, from self-regarding to self-emptying and from sin-centered to a focus on self-transcendence. In the Ignatian tradition it has been thought of as the five-point General Examen proposed in the *Spiritual Exercises* (§43). That precise exercise shaped the prayer of Jesuits and others who have followed Ignatian spirituality over the years and right on into the 20th century. But, by the middle of this century, the five-point examen had taken on the aspect of behaviorism or voluntarism, and one writer after another complained that it no longer helped prayer.

During the past few decades, the practice of the examen has become more current. It became the "examination of consciousness" when George Aschenbrenner, in his landmark 1972 article, introduced insights from depth psychology into the exercise and indicated how tightly the Ignatian examen related to the movement of spirits. Aschenbrenner acted on a principle enunciated by Dominic Maruca. The five-point examen given in the *Spiritual*

Exercises is meant for beginners, that is, for those going through the *ejercicios leves*, the brief simple exercises of Annotation 18. The examen of those who are more practiced, Aschenbrenner proposed, reached into the discernment of spirits. After that development the examen as an exercise continued to expand. Anthony DeMello designed some Gestalt practices to help self-examination. John English, in the "awareness examen," accommodated the examen to the way people currently perceive the self.

Recent Developments

Two developments during the past twenty-five years encourage continued attention to the examen and have motivated this article. The first is the swift spread of the individually directed Spiritual Exercises. In both eight-day retreats and retreats in daily life (also called 19th-annotation retreats), the Exercises are now offered to people who have no intention of making an election or even a serious decision, but who want only deeper peace and better order in their lives and who look for it in deeper relationship with God in prayer. Historically, such exercises are what Iñigo called *ejercicios leves*, simpler exercises. He described them in the first part of Annotation 18 and in the lengthy material on the General and Particular Examen.

Iñigo used these simpler exercises to help souls to a method (five points) of self-examination and a system (approach for general and particular examen) for doing it continually. But, as far as my information goes, few directors of the Exercises today really urge the importance of the examen of conscience. Some do, indeed, promote some similar practices such as journaling, one of the favorite ways of self-examination (or, better, of self-appreciation) in the New Age. And yet those who direct the Exercises in daily life and those who preach the Exercises to men and women are giving help to Christians in much the same spiritual condition as those Iñigo helped. In Oregon, Dublin, Seoul, St. Louis, and Naples, Jesuits and their colleagues are helping people who have no great decision to make, but who want a deeper interiorized faith-life, to have a more vibrant relationship with God and find more meaning in their lives.

People like this once found everything they needed in Divine Providence and the church's vibrant practices of sacrament and sacramental. They no longer find there what they need, and their loss must be carefully appraised by spiritual directors. For the loss and the consequent spiritual search does not mean that they have been invited by the Holy Spirit to the kind of interior life practiced by privileged religious and the theologically educated. They remain ordinary faithful in the core of the church. For every four women who go to Central America and face martyrdom, four hundred thousand stay home. For every man given by God the privilege of an hour of quiet every single day, there are a hundred thousand who have to fight to find ten minutes of quiet in an ordinary day. We know that these women are *politically* invisible; are they, perhaps, also invisible *spiritually?* And what about their husbands? As we have moved the Spiritual Exercises further into feeling and concreteness, have we left the males without masculine formats?

These people form the vast majority of Catholic Christians. They are not called to centering prayer or contemplation in any particular form, or to make retreats annually. Rather, they relate to God our Lord mainly by meeting obligation and keeping the commandments (one way Iñigo described them). When they pray, they usually seek to know the law that the Spirit has written on their own hearts. But they need adult catechesis, by which I mean instruction in the interior life. We teach children the faith; we teach adults how they do interiorize or might interiorize the faith they know.

For most Christians, religion—creed, code, cult—is their way of experiencing God, and directors are mistaken to take it upon themselves to force them away from that into the direct experience of God called spirituality. For them God is not dead and never has been. They still do pray for rain (unless the more advanced have taught them not to) and for help in rearing their children and sanctifying their marriages. They will never suffer a Dark Night except in the most tenuous analogous sense, and that framework will not help them to deeper meaning and relationship with God. They need other kinds of frameworks and other kinds of direction. These are the people Cardinal Bernardin was referring to when he said that millions do not want to be drawn into a hostile stance toward their church. They do not and cannot live on any brink, and they are not able to join joyfully in prophesying structural change in priesthood or marriage or medical care or social security. For them, directors exercise the ministry of reconciliation. These are the people that Iñigo and his first companions, and a great number of the founders of other congregations, reached out to when they helped souls.

Vatican Council II, it is important to recall at this juncture, called them to ongoing *metanoia*. They are not the church *semper reformanda*—a mandate to papacy, episcopacy, and parish priests. They are the church *semper renovanda*. Hence, for them the examen of conscience ought to supply a means and a method for ongoing metanoia, that is, of continually growing in their graced self-awareness and steadily purifying their sinfulness. This article addresses the issue of how they might do that.

This brings me to the second reason to attend to the examen at this time: developments in psychology that offer help in self-examination. I refer here particularly to recent focuses on the positive development of the ego and of the self. In particular I draw from the cognitive behavioral theories and practices of authorities such as Dr. Aaron Beck and Dr. David Burns. These psychological processes allow one to connect one's actual everyday thoughts, feelings, desires, and behaviors with deep character traits and conscious commitments. Obviously, these theories and practices promise to be helpful in spiritual self-examination. I am sure that the cognitive behavioral materials can be applied in more than one way. I have been using them for some time, and I will propose one possible way that has proven helpful to exercitants and directees.

We teach children the faith; we teach adults how they do interiorize or might interiorize the faith they know.

Before turning to what might be called an "examen of particulars," we need to explore three of the things entailed by the examen in the Ignatian tradition. First of all, this examen shares several important characteristics with all prayer in the Ignatian tradition, even with such set frames of prayer as the Contemplation for Love. Second, since the examen deals directly with sin and sinfulness, the Ignatian examen implies a characteristic Ignatian understanding of sin that includes shame as well as guilt and focuses on sin as failure. However, third, Ignatius connects sin with ingratitude in various ways throughout the Spiritual Exercises. He once stated explicitly that all sin is at root ingratitude, the failure or refusal to give thanks to God for his gifts.

Hence, the Ignatian examen shares with all Ignatian prayer an emphasis on the concrete existential gifts and graces of God.

Each of these points about the Ignatian examen of conscience—characteristics of Ignatian prayer, sin as failure, and an emphasis on divine gifts—calls for careful reflection. So I will take the three in turn. Taken together, these three points of reflection suggest why a particular variation on the five points given in the Spiritual Exercises is proving useful at the dawn of the 21st century.

I might usefully point out here that the connection between the Particular Examen and the General Examen is not clear in the *Spiritual Exercises.* Does one make them both together? Is the more general examen to prepare for the sacrament of reconciliation, and the particular exam to help in daily life? Not even later Jesuit legislation by general congregations clarified that. I tend to believe that people practiced in the interior life ordinarily use a general examen for the sacrament of reconciliation and that the form suggested at the end might serve them for the particular examen. I can testify that it has been serving some of us very well.

◢ Some Characteristics of Ignatian Prayer

To begin with, Ignatian prayer grows from and flourishes in story, a point not irrelevant to the examen. After explaining in the first annotation all the things he means by "spiritual exercises," Ignatius promptly points out in the second that all prayer on Scripture must be rooted in the unadorned narrative of the Gospels. Additionally he directs that retreatants begin each contemplation by locating each mystery in the course of Jesus' life. When Ignatius suggests materials not found in Scripture, he regularly suggests history or life-story material: regarding sin he tells not only about the angels and Adam and Eve, but also about one person who committed one sin and went to hell for it. He tells the surprisingly successful story of Three Couples which helps reflection on genuine indifference. He introduces the incarnation with a story about the Holy Trinity hovering over the whole globe; the Two Standards, with the scene-painting narrative of Jesus gathering people around him on the sweet green fields of the promised land; and so on. Some story is commonly a presupposition to entry into Ignatian prayer.

You could make a successful case, I think, that those of us who were trying to practice it year after year found the five-point examen problematic precisely here. After thanksgiving and a prayer for light, we moved through a quick survey of the story of the last few hours. We found that helpful as long as we felt that the deed done was vastly more important than how we felt about it or what motivated it. But, once we grew keenly aware of the layers of motive, desire, emotion, perspective, and habit that interweave in any single experience, we could no longer find much good in skimming along over the deeds done in the last hours. As a consequence of this and of other changes, only a very few of us now find this quick survey helpful. Yet in the Ignatian tradition we still feel the need for story, for moving along in a narrative. Without intending in the least to denigrate the practice, I find nothing in the Ignatian tradition about sitting still for a while and letting Jesus call attention to the day's graces and failures. Ignatian practice has been a little more active, and it focuses on story. *Story* here means *incident* (like a screeching near-accident in a car) or *experience* (like a diffused feeling of anxiety in traffic).

The conjunction of all of these developments drew the more mature and practiced in the interior life promptly to adopt George Aschenbrenner's consciousness examen, which called our attention to the story of the spirits moving us during the day. All of these developments affect the beginner as well, and also those whom God calls to a life according to the commandments. In my limited experience, these also need a way of connecting their stories with their human gifts, qualities, and achievements. The method which will suit them is unlikely to require serious discernment of spirits and probably ought to give them a little more focus and explicitness than the consciousness examen offers.

A second pertinent characteristic of prayer in the Ignatian tradition is this: Prayer is not an end in itself, nor even a kind of end-means, in the sense that this is where we go to find God and finding God in this prayer is what we intend. Prayer is, indeed, a kind of end in itself in some other contemplative traditions: it is that to which everything else in the day and in life is ordered. Not in Ignatian spirituality. The first intention here is to find out what God hopes in me and in my lifeworld, what Ignatius called "God's will," and everything in the day is ordered to that discovery and enactment. The whole intention in Ignatian prayer, including the examination of conscience, is to find what God is hoping for and wishes and wants at this time and this place. This is one way to explain the expression "contemplative in action."

Hence, in the Ignatian tradition, to find devotion does not mean to find sweetness in prayer. Richard Rolle wrote, "From my study of Scripture, I have found that to love Christ Jesus above all else will require three things: warmth, and song, and sweetness." Ignatius could not have written that. For him, to love Christ Jesus above all else will require these different things: to reach some sureness about what God hopes and wants in this time in my self and in my world, to be prompt to do what I discover is God's will, and to find God in the enactment of it.

I have just stated a third characteristic of Ignatian prayer in all its modes. Ignatian prayer grows along with an understanding of God's action in the world: God always creating my gifts and self, the Spirit raising my desires out of the divine love, God giving the gift of enactment. Hence, in all its modes Ignatian prayer hovers between the felt sense that God has hopes in me and the enactment of my own authentic desires. This dynamic tension appears in the very first colloquy in the Spiritual Exercises. At the end of the contemplation on the Triple Sin, as I stand next to Jesus fixed to his cross, I ask myself: "What have I done for Christ? What am I doing for Christ? What might I do for Christ?" I am asked, in the presence of the Crucified—who symbolizes all of God's passionate, loving hopes for me and for all humankind—to elicit my own authentic desires to collaborate with Christ in his enterprise. The full meaning of this colloquy surely reveals a good deal about the examen of conscience.

How I am to imitate Christ hanging on a cross? What is this imitation about? Perhaps others remember struggling with the question: Am I supposed to want crucifixion? If not, then what? In other great spiritual traditions, the person doing the imitating concentrates wholeheartedly on Jesus of Nazareth, who became the Christ. In the initial tradition it is this: Christ is there on his cross, offering all of his human gifts to the Father in praise and obedience because of his love for each single human; I stand next to him, full of gifts from the Father, wondering what I am to do. The metaphysics of the love Ignatius describes pithily in the Contemplation for Attaining Love must illuminate this scene if we are to comprehend the examen. Love, the little prenote states (§230), is done, not talked about. And love is the mutual sharing of gifts, the lover and the beloved giving and receiving, both doing both. This is the imitation of Christ in the Ignatian tradition. Notably, it demands of us an awareness of our specific gifts at this moment so that we may share them in building the reign of God. This surely is going to make a difference in the kind of self-examination called for here.

Among those who have been serving God longer, this imitation requires discernment because human love as we experience it reaches not only our thoughts and feelings and behaviors, but most emphatically also our desiring. But the church has always known, and postmodern Christians most emphatically know, that even beginners in the interior life have to examine their desiring. It is useful to recall, therefore, that *discreta caritas* marks any well-made examen, so that mature Christians living the life of the commandments will live good lives without Ignatian discernment. Directors who urge it on those who do not need it or cannot use it are doing them no favor; they may be projecting onto the interior lives of ordinary Christians a need that only the more advanced feel. To do so is to break a good general principle in working with ordinary Christians (and with annotation 18).

Desiring is the dynamic heart of what our postmodern culture calls "freedom."

Few of us managed to explore our desires when we were using the five-point examen (except perhaps that we harped on fleshy desires we considered reprehensible). Yet examining our desires is important for several reasons: the *other* "standard," to begin with—advertising, conformity, consumerism. And, to continue, at the end of this century *desiring* is the dynamic heart of what our postmodern culture calls "freedom": "I gotta be me; I gotta do my own thing; you asked for it, you got it." Such desiring needs careful assessment. But desire was of consummate importance in Ignatian prayer before this century even began. The most common phrase in the *Spiritual Exercises* is "what I want." The whole purpose of the thirty-day retreat is to discover what I want (§1). Behind this is the church's conviction that God our Creator and Lord shapes our freedom by shaping our desiring. Were we all to exact our most authentic desiring—that desiring in us that rises pure and clear from the passionate creative love of God at the core of our selves—we would in an instant inaugurate the reign of God. More modestly, if each of us kept a steady, well-ordered connection between our authentic desiring and our examen, we would have no problem with the church's leading—say, in the matter of the faith that does justice. If God our Creator and Lord wants faith and justice, then God is raising desires in each of us for faith and justice, including the middle class of the U.S.A. The problem is that we have not learned a method for listening to our authentic desires.

In the Ignatian tradition that is sin; so now we talk about sin.

The Focus on Sin as Failure

Far from being limited to the estimation of sin apparent in the General and Particular Examens in the *Spiritual Exercises*, which are meant for people just beginning an interior life, the Ignatian realization of sin develops in several complex ways. From the consideration of the triple sin, through the noble response to the call of the King, to the "Take, Lord, receive" prayer in the Contemplation for Love—I believe it can be argued—sin unfolds both as guilt and as shame. As this unfolding occurs within Ignatian prayer, there arises, at least in people today, an understanding of sin as failure.

In the church's immediate past, we were vaguely convinced that we thwarted God, kept God from doing what God intended. With our postmodern sensibilities we now come up against more than one serious confusion in that way of thinking about sin: How can a puny, limited creature contravene the divine will of God, all-powerful, all-wise, and eternal? And about this puny creature: After absorbing depth-psychological insights, we tend to feel that by our sin we thwart ourselves rather than God. Again, aware of our utter brokenness, we hold that God is forgiving us—poor creatures that we are—even as we sin. The upshot of all this is that we now tend to feel that we are *letting God down, disappointing God,* holding back from God what Father, Son, and Spirt graciously hope for in us and our lifeworld. This is to think of sin not so much in terms of contradicting God's will, but rather—and more fruitfully—in terms of failure. In my own mind (and in the hearts of many others when they speak of their grave failures) an extraordinarily powerful metaphor for sin is a fetus failing and withering in a woman's womb, bitterly disappointing the mother. We are such a failure in God when we sin.

Why failure? Well, Christian iconography, for one thing: the prophet telling David, "You are that man"; the Magdalen's seven devils; the seated figure in Michelangelo's "Last Judgment," staring stark through dirty fingers. Failure as a metaphor for sin is not new; the church has always thought that going against our consciences, the commandments, legitimate laws, is moral failure. Ascetics and mystics have gone further, seeing themselves as failing by not reaching ideals they had set for themselves, though all too often they name ideals of moral behavior ("I will not judge others harshly, I will not tell fibs, I will not . . , and so on").

At the end of this century, however, failure covers a much broader area than morality: physical, aesthetic, political, and economic failures, career failures, medical, grammatical, mechanical, even computer failures. Many prophets about the green earth make lists of these failures: the air we breathe brings death from Chernobyl, the pleasures of love carry AIDS, cars suffer mechanical failure, magazines suffer circulation failure, and (may God avert the evil) computers are subject to hard-disk failure. Every human person knows failure: a friendship fades, a position does not materialize, a debt does not get paid, siblings or children misbehave gravely. We overeat, escape into drugs, grow addicted to harmful substances like tobacco or harmful activities like gambling. We suffer physical failures like diabetes, psychic failures like acrophobia, aesthetic failures like ugliness or awkward manners. And, of course, in the end we fail to live forever as we would like, but die instead. Humankind is intimately, incessantly, incurably acquainted with failure.

Humankind is intimately, incessantly, incurably acquainted with failure.

Some matters regarding these failures have a crucial bearing on the examen of conscience and deserve our notice. At times the failures are not willful, but are sin handed down to us from our forebears. At other times we seem to fail by error or through tiredness, but on closer examination we find the failure hiding some habit or quality or personality trait that needs our attention. And at other times, of course, we suffer one or another of myriad failures because of our own sin. Humankind even tends to believe that certain specific failures are accounted for by sin: leprosy and blindness among the Jews of Jesus' day, AIDS among the Christians of our day. "Who sinned, this man or his parents, that he is blind?" We are not likely to shake that belief because it is partially true. But how is it true? We have to face that question if we take failure as the metaphor for sin.

We have not had to answer that question as long as we have taken sickness as the basic metaphor. And the matter is important because we have not been connecting all kinds of evils with sin. Think of a serial killer. Instinctively, postmodern humankind feel that a serial killer is very sick, inhumanly driven by unconscious motives to madness. "Oh, that's *sick!*" cuts off any further inquiry into the morality of the murders and really implies that they are not sin.

But, when we take failure as a metaphor for sin, we have to inquire further. Finally we get to the heart of the matter of sin: the original sin. We all know the larger theological truth, of course, that we are deeply affected by the original sin. But, as long as we consider sin as a sickness, we who work in theology immediately cede the explanation to the psychologists. We never get to the spiritual significance of the original sin in our own actual lives, and its truth means little more to us than the truth about Pluto's orbit.

This is a crux matter in the lives of many ordinary Catholics. In the American tradition believing a truth means accepting its consequences in real life. Well, are the consequences of the original sin in my life the ones I suspect—negative self-image, neuroticisms, childhood abuses of all kinds, compulsions, addictions, schizophrenia? How can I accept any of these, harsh as they are and even harmful? How do I put together self-acceptance and my own acceptance of God's acceptance of me with the fact that I am from a dysfunctional family, work in a dysfunctional job, am surrounded by neurotics, with whom I fit perfectly? None of us will continue the examen of conscience for long or go any deeper than, yes or no, I did or did not sin, unless and until we find a way to give an account to ourselves of these live urgent issues. And ordinary Christians living the law written in their hearts—much vexed with compulsions, prejudices, inveterate habits, reflex responses to advertising—inevitably face these issues. In sum, these issues are their "dark night of the soul," and ordinary Christians need serious adult catechesis about handling these interior faith issues (and hope issues), and they need a way of self-examination that allows them to apply it.

The examen must be able to help me make this distinction: Is an experience my sin, a sin, or sin in me? The question begs for long study in a church plagued by narcissistic individualism. Perhaps, even more, it begs for some method of prayer that will allow each of us to probe the Christian self, a method available to the merest beginners as well as to someone who falls in love with God again on every starry night. ⟲

In the Ignatian context, we sin when we fail to enact powers and virtues and holy desires that God is creating in us, when we are carelessly unaware of them or enact them neglectfully or refuse to be aware of them for lack of love. Considering sin as failure offers the great advantage of emphasizing simultaneously the interior and the external, an important consideration when we come to the examen of conscience. When a spring fails to bring out sweet water, the spring must be clogged or fouled in itself and the fields around it are deprived of water. When the fig tree fails to bring forth good fruit, the tree is suffering some internal disease or defect and the world around it is deprived of figs. When we sin—it is extraordinarily useful to notice at this juncture in Christian history—we simultaneously suffer some internal fault or defect and our lifeworld suffers some lack or positive injury. Were I to make a false claim against a neighbor in a grave matter, I would suffer internal falseness and dishonor and my neighbor would suffer some concrete injury. That case is obvious; some cases are less so. For instance, when I do not pray according to the specific gifts God is giving to me (time, desire, opportunity for ministry), I fail to enact many of my gifts and my lifeworld is deprived in some way. When spouses fail to nourish regard for each other and starve their married love, their children suffer in ways we can now name. Clearly, ordinary people living ordinary lives need ways to connect their interior failings with their relationships and their lifeworld.

Ordinary people living ordinary lives need ways to connect their interior failings with their relationships and their lifeworld.

The Recovery of Shame

Another great advantage of thinking of sin in terms of failure is the recovery of shame. A hundred years ago Freud concluded that shame is subsumed into guilt, and depth psychology has not had much to say about shame ever since. More recently, popularizers have urged that all shame is "toxic" and insisted that we should spew it out as we would a gulp of hemlock. Both of these stances seem extreme and seem to be connected with modern and postmodern individualism. For guilt can be entirely secret and internal, but shame always reaches both individuals and society. The Oxford English Dictionary finds that for centuries shame has meant "a painful emotion arising from the consciousness of something dishonoring, ridiculous, or indecorous in one's own conduct or situation"; the "fear of offense against propriety or decency"; and the threat of "disgrace, ignominy, loss of esteem or reputation." (Notice that this language brings forcibly to mind the language of the Kingdom and the Contemplation.) In all of these senses, shame hovers between individuals' self-appreciation and what their society considers honorable, proper, decent, and gracious. Shame has been repudiated as an outmoded burden of a "shame culture," in which what we pejoratively called "conformity" is maintained through the fear of being shamed. But we are mistaken to repudiate shame, for it is that repudiation (along with much else) that has given scope in our culture to narcissistic individualism.

Guilt is connected with transgression, with breaking law or violating conscience; shame is connected with failure, with falling short of an ideal. That ideal is a reality which transcends the individual self and which individuals have chosen to make their own. Hence, shame belongs in the Ignatian examen of conscience. For the examen, like all prayer in the Ignatian tradition, is connected with the *magis,* and the *magis* refers to an ideal. Even if I am examining whether I broke a commandment, in the Ignatian tradition I am holding up a higher ideal than mere conformity—some kind of *magis* that calls me, considering the gifts I am given, at least to keep the commandments all the more perfectly. Hence, failure in the Ignatian tradition commonly means falling short of an ideal. The result of that is not guilt; it is shame, which connects me to those in my life and to my lifeworld.

Understanding sin as failure, then, supports the examen of conscience in the Ignatian tradition. It does so for one final reason: I cannot know my failures unless and until I have known my gifts. This is surely why Ignatius begins the five-point examen with an act of thanks to God. I cannot know specifically and concretely how I failed unless and until I know my gifts in all their specificity and concreteness. In the Ignatian context, a failure of any kind (fiscal, physical, aesthetic) transmutes into sin when we have failed at what we have all the gifts to succeed at because we either refuse to use those gifts or actually reject them. Failure transmutes into sin when we fail to use gifts that we have when and as our experience and our lifeworld call on us to use them. We sin when we fail to enact powers and virtues and holy desires that God is creating in us, gifts we are aware of and yet neglect or gifts we refuse to be aware of for lack of love. This brings me to the third thing that the Ignatian examen entails. I can cover it briefly.

The Stress on Gift and Giftedness

I have suggested that the Ignatian examen, like all the prayer in that tradition, is an ongoing search of our life story for what God hopes in us. It entails knowing our authentic desires. It results in a felt sense that a given act or experience is holy or sinful and, if sinful, whether the sense is of guilt or shame or the sorrowful playing out of sin in ourselves. Above all, this examen grows from a graced union with an active God.

Nowhere in the Ignatian tradition is God so transparently active as in the Contemplation for Love. There the focus on what God wishes me to do, and on how God's wishes come to be expressed in my self ontologically, emerges in an almost fiery concentration on the gifts that God continually shares with us in the created world. The one praying recounts the gifts, then God's presence in the gifts, and then God's present action in them and finally embraces the gifts and their enactments as a share in God's Self. The prayer verges into being a quasi-ontological invitation to enact the gift I am aware of in order to collaborate with God in creating not only my own self but also my lifeworld. "Moral action" transmutes into a particular in the divine action—utterly holy in itself. After such a prayer, particularly if this way of praying should become habitual (as it surely does among Ignatian practitioners), an authentically Ignatian kind of examen of conscience will focus on giftedness and the enactment of gifts.

The Ignatian examen, in fact, presupposes a sense of collaborating with God in bringing myself and my lifeworld into existence and giving them definition. This sense results from the Principle and Foundation properly explained and adequately grasped. Though this spiritual sense is not unrelated to Iñigo's profoundly mystical illumination at the Cardoner, many ordinary Catholics are able to appreciate it. We can surely come to this understanding: God has hopes and desires for me regarding my life and my lifeworld overall and even in the smallest details. Within that awareness is the faith conviction that God my Creator and Lord is creating me moment by moment. Of course, the collaboration of creature with Creator God is totally asymmetrical, the finite with the infinite, the failed sinner with the Holy One. But it is truly a collaboration. How does God conduct this collaboration if not by creating in each one gifts to enact, the freedom to choose among those gifts, and the very enactment of those gifts?

The precise failure of modernity, from which we all still suffer, has been people's dim or even nonexistent awareness that every concrete existential reality in my life and lifeworld is God's giving at that and this very moment. Within this modernity the church has seemed commonly to believe in the rationalists' "watchmaker" God, infinitely transcendent, the first cause in a vast long line of secondary causes ending in each one of us. That belief had permeated so many people that the First Vatican Council felt impelled to define as a doctrine of the faith that God directly, personally, as First Cause, created each human soul. The definition left problems behind it, the first of which was, What about the body?

The reasons for the failure of modern Christians to keep mindful that God is always Creator are dense and many, but we ought to note several of the more obvious because they are pertinent to the examen of conscience. We have become aware, to begin with, how human behavior is defined by genetic preconditioning, childhood neglect, and various abuses. We wonder—to visit this same issue in another place—how compulsions and addictions can be gifts. We have grown so used to noting our unconscious motivations that we use them as excuses. Who has not heard such remarks as "I can't help it, I'm an ENTJ" and "Well, I'm a two on the enneagram"? More positively, we think of the self as the product of our own choices; we feel responsible for making ourselves. We know that we must be authentic and express our true self. Well, in what sense are the *me* and *my own self* gifts if I achieve them?

If these grounds for our failure to walk humbly as creatures before our Creator and Lord are even partially true, we well need an examen of conscience that facilitates the connection of our gifts with our actions both graced and failed. I do not mean "in a general way"; I mean a method of connecting our concrete gifts with concrete enactments. How does my gift of intelligence connect with my failure to get a job I applied for? What responsibility have I, son of alcoholic parents, for yet another enactment of dependency? What was the Spirit of Jesus Christ trying to tell me in a consolation I suddenly received and distrusted during a conversation with someone I do not like?

We have so much knowledge about the inner workings of the human psyche that we are being irresponsible not to ask, What is going on here? We once demanded of ourselves the motivation behind our behaviors: What made me say no? What am I doing graduate studies for? Why did I not tell the whole truth? We must now recognize that in every so-called motive there converge contexts, perspectives, perceptions, values, desires, prior decisions, and habits. We cannot give an account of this complexity by asking ourselves, even very earnestly, What was my *motive?*

We need an examen of conscience that facilitates the connection of our gifts with our actions both graced and failed.

To know failure for what it is requires that one know one's skills, gifts, capacities, abilities, habits, and so on. After all, what fails? Hence, the most helpful examen of conscience will require that I examine in detail my gifts. Not in general, not unconnected to my current experience, as though I were making a catalogue of all my gifts and all my achievements. Rather, the exercise will demand that I inquire, with precision and thoroughness, which of my gifts, skills, achievements, habits. and so on are involved in what I am examining, for this is the way God draws me into cooperation in creating my own self and my lifeworld.

And this is how we can reach for fervent ongoing conversion that really addresses ourselves and our situations. In the Christian tradition the examen has been integral to ongoing conversion; in fact, it could almost be called the expression of ongoing conversion. It is integral as well to growing deeper in holiness by accepting more and more into every part of myself my redemption in Christ. For *conversion*, contrary to popular image, does not mean an action done once and forever. Conversion is perhaps best thought of as accepting responsibility for my self—my thoughts, feelings, behaviors, and even my desiring—at this time and in some particular realm of human experience. Thus, a recovering alcoholic accepts responsibility in the realm of moral experience by acknowledging his own drives and needs and responding to them in Christian freedom. All of us have to accept responsibility for ourselves in the realms of intellectual development, moral judgment and action, affective and emotional functioning, appreciation of beauty and development of taste, and active civil engagement for the sake of good order and justice. Obviously, we each go through many, many experiences in every one of these realms, and at each step we all are called on to take greater and greater responsibility for ourselves. That is what conversion means, and obviously it is an ongoing process.

In the Ignatian tradition, conversion does not deal with the minimum. As I have said before, we who follow this tradition feel that the Spirit of Christ calls steadily to the *magis*. This *magis*, however, will never be an abstraction; the Spirt of Christ does not invite us to "holiness" or to "heroism." Rather, the Spirit calls in concrete matters one after another, which grow out of and actualize a fundamental option to follow, and perhaps even to imitate, Jesus Christ. The *magis* will continually involve further insight into my own thoughts, feelings, behaviors, and desiring and into how these are or are not realizing God's hopes in me. That is the point of the incarnation.

The Examen of Particulars

Let me recall what gives Ignatian shape to an examen of conscience. First, any method of self-examination in the Ignatian tradition, like all prayer in that tradition, stays close to story. It is about finding God's wishes in me and in my lifeworld. Or to put that another way, it is about finding my most authentic desiring, which is God's way of shaping both my self and my lifeworld. Then, insofar as it deals with sin, this examen works well when the metaphor for sin is failure. The original sin is the failure of my humanness, bred into me by dysfunctional family, friends, society, and schools, not to mention air, food, and technologies. The failure is both in me and in my lifeworld, so that when I feel it with any clarity I feel shamed as much as guilty, or even more. The typical Ignatian image is of the knight who has failed his Lord or the handmaid who has failed her mistress.

Now, what kind of examen of conscience might respond to these three points about Ignatian prayer and spirituality at the beginning of the 21st century? This examen will proceed in an intimate relationship with God creating me moment by moment. It will help find what God is hoping for me to do. It will focus on experiences as totalities (their contexts, perspectives, perceptions, values, desires, decisions, habits), on things done and undergone both in their externals and in my own thoughts, feelings, and inner behaviors. It will connect external and internal events with actual gifts being created in me by God. The examen will keep me mindful of what I have chosen to do for Christ, or what I believe I might do for Christ. Rather than retail a series of events, this examen will help me unpack both my successes and my failures, bringing me to feel accurately and generously any guilt I have incurred and to assess shame, the failure to reach my own ideals. Throughout, the examen will work on the basis of gratitude to God for gifts, hours, life, everything. This means that, though I may feel sharp shame because in some concrete way I have failed, I still will not allow the tempting thought to seize me that I am a failure.

Here is what might prove to be a useful scheme: Always begin by recalling that God is creating you moment by moment. Each time you decide something that shapes you as a person, God, too, is deciding to shape you. Each time you relate to another or others, the Spirit of Christ is relating you to your entire lifeworld and creating it in you and through you. And, while you are looking at the past, over which you have no further control, God is always acting in the *now*, the Master of history to whom past and future are present. Be mindful that you are now in God and that God loves who you are—not who you might be or could be or even should be. Let the Father's gaze rest on you in all of its complaisance.

The examen of particulars has five moments. First, recall an incident or an experience. Second, remember your response. Third, recall which of your gifts were or might have been involved in this concrete experience. Fourth, examine the particulars: What was really going on? And, fifth, ponder in Christ, What comes next?

1. *Recalling an incident or an experience.* What happened? Recall some incident or experience during your day. For a moment, just remember what happened. Recall an incident (an encounter, for instance, or a friendly gesture): what was done and said, by whom,

where, and when? Or recall an experience (an achievement, for instance, or a feeling of fear): what happened? You can finish this in just a minute even if you jot down a bit of description.

This moment is parallel to entering an Ignatian contemplation: you notice who was there, what was done, and what was said. At first you might take any experience that stands out, whether holy, harsh, or hollow (by which I mean ambiguous). Often enough some incident or some habitual or characteristic action stands out as holy or unholy. You might, however, ask about how Christ is redeeming you, or what the experience of a consolation signifies, or what a failure signifies. After a while you may well find yourself concentrating on one kind of incident or experience: on getting angry rather often, on almost always being late or not finishing things, on feeling restless or touchily anxious, on handling a new kind of success. When you note that, be aware that the Ignatian tradition has valued the examen of a particular virtue or failing as a signpost of how the Spirit of Christ is inviting you to spiritual growth.

2. *Remembering your response.* How did you, yourself, act and react? Remember your thoughts and feelings and behaviors, what you did and said. Remember also what you wanted to do and say, and then how you felt about what happened. Take enough time to recall these interior phenomena. If you are like the rest of us, you too often let thoughts, feelings, and desires go unnoted. Yet they are important connectors to your lifeworld and to your God, and you would do well to write down what you find. After finishing these two phases, let the incident or experience, itself, rest while you turn to your own self.

3. *Recall your gifts.* In every single action and reaction, you act as a whole person, interrelated in concrete ways to other persons. Yet you are complex, with five senses and certain physical qualities; with gifts of intelligence, education, and rearing; and endowed with a certain limited number of abilities and talents. You are graced with certain qualities and characteristics, and you have realized certain achievements and developed certain skills. God your Creator and Lord has been and continues creating all of these complexities in you—or, rather, creating you in all these complexities—and they are all gifts, even your skills and achievements.

In any given action or reaction, certain of your gifts contribute or are called on. As you listen to a friend, your empathy, skill in discernment, availability, freedom to spend the time as you choose, and fidelity as a friend all come into play. Your accomplishment with a guitar, while remaining present, probably would not come actively into play, nor your computer proficiency either. But, if you are looking into an incident of getting angry at a computer, that proficiency would be relevant, and your gift of empathy perhaps less so. In one way or another, though, you do bring every one of your gifts into every incident or experience. If you have gifts of intelligence and articulateness, you may, at the moment of noticing a fellow worker's error, consciously keep your mouth shut so as not to offend. That is to say, in any experience you will have acted out some of your gifts and not others.

In the incident or experience that comes to the fore during your examen, which of your gifts were involved or could have been involved? Among your gifts, note abilities, talents, characteristics, qualities, skills, achievements, strengths. Take plenty of time to do this part of the exercise, and insist with yourself that you be complete in cataloguing the gifts. You may well find this part of the examen somewhat difficult; many do. Part of the reason is that through and in those gifts God connects you to the people in your life and lifeworld and raises in you those desires which, enacted, will bring justice, peace, and love to you and your lifeworld. A plea to the Spirit of Jesus Christ for light will help.

4. *Examining particulars.* What was really going on? Having looked into your concrete gifts and characteristics and achievements, you are in a position to see more fully (and perhaps more accurately) what was going on in your whole *self*. Go back over the first and the second points and examine them in all their particulars. Take your time doing this, especially if you started it while you were listing your gifts. For what seemed a mere burst of temper may prove to be sinful self-reliance and lack of trust in God. What appeared a simple consolation may, on closer examination, signalize a major invitation by the Spirit to growth. You thought at first that you were being humble, and you turn out to have been cowardly. You feared that you had failed in courage, and turn out to have exercised a maturer and deeper prudence than you had been exercising before. An action that you justified may in truth have been a failure; you acted tough when your gifts and the circumstances called on you to show greater compassion. All depends on the particulars.

◀ Realize that you are asking: What is God telling me in this incident or experience? What is God hoping in these gifts that I enacted or failed to enact? Where is the Holy Spirit leading me? How was I interacting in it with Jesus Christ, my redeemer? Done correctly, this exercise is the opposite of narcissistic self-regard.

5. *What comes next?* As you discover more clearly what was going on in the incident, you will come to see clearly what you might do next. So you may have to repent and have sorrow and beg God's forgiveness, or you may need to rejoice and give God praise and thanks. You may be called on to do something or to wait upon the Lord. No matter what you discover in truth, God is hoping in you, for love of you and of your lifeworld.

Summary

This examen puts me into contact with my real thoughts, feelings, desires, and behaviors, allowing me to decide whether I consider them Christlike or not. Better: this is a wonderful way to open to the Spirit of Christ. The Holy Spirit can teach anxious people to trust God the Father much more readily if they have become aware of their anxiety and of how it permeates all their feelings, thoughts, behaviors, and desiring and begs for healing. The Spirit can more readily teach slothful people who have not spoken out against injustice if now they are growing aware of their gifts of clear thinking and articulateness and also aware that they are not using those gifts.

These are spiritual tasks that ordinary Christians feel attracted to and can keep at. This form is surely only one of many possible ones, and imperfect at that. Perhaps it will move forward the quest of finding God in all things, even in self-examination.

A Call for a Bespoke Revival
of a Hijacked Tradition

The impish twinkle in his eye and the spring in his step made the old man seem ever youthful. The unfeigned courtesy, charm, graciousness, and breadth of interest were from a gentler age. The joy he spread, the compassion he showed, his acuity of mind and felicity of phrase, his commitment to the task—all this inspired. To live with him, I am told, was a special blessing. It was indeed a wholesome spirituality which made this brother a saint with such impish, charming, compassionate, and human ways. We wondered about the source of his deep spirituality. Certainly there was the daily Mass, faithfulness to community prayer, and spiritual reading. But, as they pondered, those who knew him saw his rosary as the special resource within. Not so much a routine rosary recited out loud with others—though that was there—but the silent refuge, a default mode which allowed him to ponder, like his mother of old. And like Mary's son he grew "in wisdom and in years, and in divine and human favor" (Lk 2:52).

The rosary can be a source of spirituality. It was for Maurus. Why then is there a wariness, in some, about this prayer? Maybe it is the routine, the blandness, the task-centeredness of this highly structured prayer that does not speak to many moderns. Maybe it became nearly compulsory for the family, and that can kill a devotion. For some it did not fit in with their meaning world.

I contend that this misunderstanding may be an aberration of the essence of the rosary and that too many have not found its empowering spirituality. The personal, reflective way that brings people closer to their God is central but is not visible in the more strident practices of common experience. I contend that the rosary may have been understood only as a complex routine that does not meet the individual in the richness of a personal, reflective mantra.

I suspect the spirituality within the rosary has been hijacked. There is a danger for anything that is good to be formalized. The insight is lost. The intuition is institutionalized. The core is disguised except to those who can penetrate to the essence. The reflective mantra that was life-giving for many an individual was recognized as an enriching prayer. It was isolated, restructured, simplified, and systematized for mass consumption. A personal reflective prayer was routinized for public recital, and the spirit which inspired it was lost to many. Unfortunately, it is the way of many good things in life. The idea is defined. The steps lose flexibility and become *de rigueur*.

The rosary has a long history—a history of experiment and innovation. There was a call for a nonmonastic prayer form that reflected something of monastic prayer tradition but would suit the lay reality—a psalter of 150 Paternosters emerged. Prayers based on repetitions of a Marian antiphon—such as Gabriel's *ave*—caught the fervor of others and Marian chaplets developed to help. Mysteries evolved in time. Suitable scriptural antiphons became the mantras for different mysteries—joys first but later sorrows. The forms became more complex, so fixed formulas were called for to simplify the prayer. Uniformity of pattern would assure that heretical or extravagant practices were controlled. In 1569 Pius V officially approved the rosary we are familiar with. The fixed, uniform formula was beatified even if it meant reducing some of the intuition that was central to it.

The first half of the Hail Mary appears in the seventh-century liturgy as the Offertory antiphon of the Annunciation—though the *Jesus* at the end was not added till later. It appealed and became a feature of the chaplet prayer. It was not till the sixteenth century that the second half was fixed in its present form. They were prayers that grew out of insights and concerns of the culture and the times—though maybe sometimes they were the conserving reaction to preserve ideas from being extended or challenged! Today people may be allowed to tinker with the odd word, but the formula is so sacralized—carved deeply on tablets of stone—it may seem impertinent to question the time-tested formula, though well over a millennium of Christianity was able to survive without the current formula.

What could be some of the features that irk people today?

Hail as used in the prayer is not used seriously in this sense in today's English. Catholic biblical research tells us that a more appropriate translation for Luke's Greek is *rejoice*. So the biblical basis needs to be looked at while the linguistic appropriateness could be questioned. There are other phrases in the prayer based richly on Scripture—the Vulgate at least—that require interpretation. The meaning is no longer transparent.

As for the second half, it is possible that a Catholic today relates to Mary more as the "Faithful Disciple," "Woman of Faith," or "Mother of the Church." With absolutely no questioning of the "Mother of God" title, they may prefer to express a different relationship. Many may find that the focus on the need for support "at the hour of our death," while a very valid concern, is not at the core of their life. Today "as we live our life" is at the center for many. Even while we are aware that "us sinners" need to be prayed for, a more positive approach is the orientation of many. It is not just a matter of the language, it is the ideas in themselves. Today we have other values and different perceptions just as valid as the earlier and particularly relevant for the age. Is it good for a culturally based prayer to be fossilized for future cultures?

The rosary has a long history—a history of experiment and innovation.

Of course, for community recitation an agreed formula must be used. But, if the community form is seen to be prior to the personal way, then there is an unnecessary restraint. The personal experience should inform the community way rather than conform to it.

Then there are the mysteries, reduced and refined to the fifteen we have today. But there are other mysteries that may speak more deeply to the individual. And there may be a need to nuance.

Crowning of queens, in the age of beauty competitions and the irrelevance of monarchies in much of the world, might make the fifth glorious mystery somewhat anachronistic. For it is indeed a reflection on a symbolic act rather than a real act. However, to reflect on "Mary Mother of the Church"—serving, simple, honest, and at one with all—might be an enriching, relevant reflection for today.

The tendency of the glorious mysteries' becoming the triumphal mysteries could be off-putting in a society that likes to think it is egalitarian. The glorious mysteries provide us with challenging reflections as well as the opportunities for triumphal satisfaction.

The tendency for artists to reduce the joyful mysteries to a "Sweet Jesus" spirituality, while helpful to some, can turn others away. A scriptural understanding of the events goes beyond such a limited understanding. The whole understanding of God's intervention, God's way of intervening, the spirituality of those involved, and the deep symbolism challenge the listener to the Good News, not just to a pious thought but to a radical reaction, as well as to rejoicing.

The sorrowful mysteries are more than a reflection on "the precious blood." Mark does not reflect on this aspect of the mysteries; neither do the other evangelists. The bloodied face of Jesus crowned with thorns is pious development—likely enough, but not the center of the mystery. Again artists have helped with the suffering focus and the more emotional reaction, and there is no doubt that it is helpful to many. In the last century the development of such a devotion was a healthy reaction to Jansenist extremes. However, some find the extremes of emotionalism hard to live with. It would be a shame if they left the practice of the rosary, unaware of other depths to be plumbed.

Of course, great men like Maurus could in time cut their way through the hindrances and make the rosary a source of a developed spirituality. It is for us lesser beings to take courage. We now cut the cloth of our contemplative prayer so that the mix of praying our experiences, centering, mantra, lectio divina, and the Jesus prayer can inform the Ignatian method we grew up with and draw us to the Father. So a bespoke (that is, tailor-made) rosary can be integrated into our prayer life—even dominate in some ways. It is a rich prayer, and at times it may be good for us as a community to break from our prayer of Scripture sharing or the church's prayer and pray together this prayer that has its roots deeply in Catholic culture.

Maybe the personal rosary with reformulated prayers, readjusted mysteries, and reflections that are gospel-based is called for. It is to be seen as having a natural rhythm rather than a fixed formula. The mystery, and hence the mantra, is not to be lost in a contrived pattern. It is a simple prayer avoiding mental contortions.

Listening as the Foundation for Spirituality

> Each morning he wakes me to hear,
> to listen like a disciple.
> The Lord Yahweh has opened my ear.
>
> *Isaiah 50:4-5*

personal paths

Have you ever noticed how little *explicit* emphasis there is on listening in the Rules of communities, in the standard manuals the spiritual life, and even in the classics? One searches in vain for a chapter on listening in the writings of St. Benedict or St. Ignatius or even in the writings of very practical, concretely oriented saints like Francis de Sales and Vincent de Paul. One comes up empty too in Luis de Granada and Rodriguez and in later widely used treatises on spirituality like Tanquerey. Listening, of course, enters these writings implicitly under many headings. But if one considers *listening* the foundation for spirituality, one might have expected it to stand out in greater relief.

This article proposes some reflections on listening as the foundation of spirituality. It will examine, in a preliminary way: (1) listening in the New Testament; (2) listening as the foundation for all spirituality; (3) some echoes of the theme in the history of spirituality; (4) the contrast between an implicit and an explicit theme; (5) some ramifications today.

Christian listening begins, of course, with the Old Testament, where listening plays a vital role, especially in the Deuteronomic and prophetic traditions. Yahweh often complains that, when he speaks, his people "do not listen." Conversely, the prophets are preeminent listeners; they hear what Yahweh has to say and then speak in his name. "Speak, Lord, for your servant is listening," says the boy Samuel as he begins his prophetic career. Listening recurs again and again in the New Testament, where a study of Johannine literature, for instance, would reveal listening as the key to eternal life. "Whoever is of God listens to every word God speaks. The reason you do not hear is that you are not of God. . . . If someone is true to my word he shall never see death" (Jn 8:47, 51).

Listening in Luke's Gospel

In Luke's Gospel the listening theme is quite explicit. For Luke, as for the entire New Testament, God takes the initiative through his word, which breaks into the world as good news calling for human attention and response.

Mary the model listener. As with almost all the important themes in Lukan theology, the listening theme is introduced in the infancy narratives. These narratives provide a summary of the theology that Luke will weave through his Gospel. The listening theme is among the most prominent Lukan motifs (parenthetically, one might add that in Luke's Gospel another theme is at work in many of the listening stories; contrary to the expected cultural patterns of the writer's time, a *woman* is the model listener presented to the reader).

Mary is evangelized in Luke's first two chapters. She is the first to hear the good news. She is the ideal disciple, the model for all believers. Mary listens reflectively to Gabriel, who announces the good news of God's presence and tells her of the extraordinary child whom she is to bear; to Elizabeth, who proclaims her blessed among women because she has believed that the word of the Lord would be fulfilled in her; to shepherds, who tell her and others the message which has been revealed to them about the child, the good news that a Savior is born; to Simeon, who proclaims a song of praise for the salvation that has come to all nations and a prophecy that ominously forebodes the cross; to Anna, who praises God in Mary's presence and keeps speaking to all who are ready to hear; to Jesus himself, who tells her about his relationship with his heavenly Father, which must take precedence over everything.

Luke pictures Mary as listening to the Angel Gabriel with wonderment, questioning what it might mean, deciding to act on it, and afterwards meditating on the mystery of God's ways, reflecting on them in her heart.

The theme of listening later in Luke's Gospel. Luke uses three brief stories to illustrate this theme of listening discipleship, namely, that those who listen to the word of God and act on it are the true followers of Jesus.

> (1) His mother and brothers came to be with him, but they could not reach him because of the crowd. He was told, "Your mother and your brothers are standing outside and they wish to see you." He told them in reply, "My mother and my brothers are those who listen to the word of God and act upon it" (8:19-21).

In this story Luke changes the Markan emphasis (cf. Mk 3:31-35) radically. While Mark depreciates the role of Jesus' mother and relatives, Luke extols it, echoing his first two chapters and showing that Mary is the ideal disciple, who listens to God's word and acts on it.

> (2) On their journey Jesus entered a village where a woman named Martha welcomed him to her home. She had a sister named Mary, who seated herself at the Lord's feet and listened to his words. Martha, who was busy with all the details of hospitality, came to him and said, "Lord are you not concerned that my sister has left me to do the household tasks all alone? Tell her to help me." The Lord in reply said to her: "Martha, Martha, you are anxious and upset about many things; one thing only is required. Mary has chosen the better portion and she shall not be deprived of it" (10:38-42).

Even though Jesus' statement about the one thing necessary has been subject to innumerable interpretations, there is little doubt about the point of this story in the context of Luke's Gospel. Mary has chosen the better part because she is sitting at Jesus's feet and listening to his words, just as any true disciple does. While there are many other themes in the story (such as the role of women and the role of the home-church in early Christianity, which is reinforced here through a Lukan addition), Luke emphasizes the basis of discipleship: listening to the word of God. That is the better part (see Lk 8:4-21).

> (3) While he was saying this a woman from the crowd called out "Blessed is the womb that bore you and the breasts that nursed you!" "Rather," he replied, "blest are they who listen to the word of God and keep it" (11:27-28).

This passage interrupts, rather puzzlingly, a series of controversies that Jesus is involved in during the journey to Jerusalem. But Luke inserts it to clarify the meaning of discipleship once more: real happiness does not lie in physical closeness to Jesus, nor in blood relationship with him, but in listening to the word of God and acting on it.

Listening as the Basis for Spirituality

All spirituality revolves around self-transcendence. As a working definition for spirituality, we might use one proposed by Sandra Schneiders: "The experience of consciously striving to integrate one's life in terms not of isolation and self-absorption but of self-transcendence toward the ultimate value one perceives."[1]

For Christians spirituality involves "putting on the Lord Jesus Christ" (Rm 13:14), "giving away one's life rather than saving it up" (Mk 8:35, Mt 16:25, Lk 9:24, Jn 12:25), and other phrases that imply self-transcendence. The self is not obliterated through self-transcendence; rather, it becomes fully actualized.[2] That is the Christian paradox: in giving oneself, one finds one's true self. In that sense authentic love of God, of the neighbor, and of self come together.

Authors put this in different ways. For Bernard Lonergan self-transcendence occurs in the radical drive of the human spirit, which yearns for meaning, truth, value, and love. Authenticity, then, "results from long-sustained exercise of attentiveness, intelligence, reasonableness, responsibility."[3] For Karl Rahner the human person is the event of the absolute self-communication of God. In his foundational works Rahner describes the human person as essentially a listener, one who is always awaiting a possible word of revelation. Only in Jesus, the self-communication of God, is the human person ultimately fulfilled. At the core of the historical human person is a gnawing hunger for the other, for absolute value. A particular spirituality is a way in which this longing for the absolute is expressed.[4]

But this inner yearning for truth and love, this "reaching out," as Henri Nouwen expresses it, can only be satisfied by a word from without—spoken or enfleshed—that reveals what true humanity really is. In the human person the fundamental disposition for receiving that word or Word is listening.

It is worth noting here that Genesis, the wisdom books, and the Johannine tradition all seize on the concept of the Word as the way in which God initiates and breaks into human history. The creating word bears within it its own immediate response: "Let there be light, and there was light." But the word spoken to the human person, who in God's image and likeness rules with freedom over all creation, must be listened to and responded to freely.

Of course, listening here is used in the broadest sense. It includes seeing, hearing, sensing, feeling, perceiving. "Attentiveness" might serve as the term for the various ways in which the human person is ready to grasp what comes from without. Listening in this sense is the indispensable precondition for self-transcendence. Without it the word that comes from without goes unheard, the truth that draws the human mind to a vision beyond itself goes unperceived, the love that seeks to capture the heart goes unrequited.

Is this why the saints have so stressed the importance of listening in prayer? Is this why obedience has played such an influential role in the tradition of religious communities? Is this why the seeking of counsel has always been regarded as one of the signs of true wisdom? Is this why the Word made flesh and the word of God in the Scriptures are at the center of all Christian spirituality? Is this why the reading of the Scriptures in the liturgy and communion with the Word himself in his self-giving, sacrificial love are "the source and summit" of genuine Christian living?

Listening in Vincent de Paul

One can find echoes of the listening theme in many traditions. Ignatian discernment, which has exerted such a forceful influence on the countless people who have made the Spiritual Exercises since the sixteenth century, is a means of listening attentively to what God is saying and allowing God's word to work conversion within us. Francis de Sales, whose *Introduction to the Devout Life* has been read by millions since its first publication in 1609, spoke of the need to "be devoted to the word of God whether you hear it in familiar conversation with spiritual friends or in sermons." He urged his readers, "Always listen to it with attention."[5]

Here, however, I will focus briefly on another seventeenth-century figure, Vincent de Paul, whose writings are less well known, but whose charism has influenced enormous numbers of men and women, not only in the two communities he founded (the Vincentians and the Daughters of Charity), but in other communities that have sprung up under his inspiration, and also in the hundreds of thousands of Ladies of Charity and St. Vincent de Paul Society members throughout the world.

The central place of listening in spirituality is not explicit in the conferences and writings of St. Vincent. But the spirituality he proposes includes several key themes in which the importance of listening is evident.

Humility the Foundation of Evangelical Perfection

Vincent calls humility "the foundation of all evangelical perfection and the core of the spiritual life."[6] For him truly humble people see everything as gift. The humble recognize that God is seeking to enter their lives again and again so that he may speak to them. They are alert, they listen for God's word, they are eager to receive God's saving love. The humble know that the truth which sets them free comes from without: through God's word, through the cries of the poor, through the church, through the community in which they live.

There is probably no theme that St. Vincent emphasized more. He described humility as the origin of all the good that we do.[7] He told the Daughters of Charity: "If you establish yourselves in it, what will happen? You will make this company a paradise, and people will rightly say that it is a group of the happiest people on earth. . . ."[8]

Humility and listening are closely allied in that listening is the basic attitude of those who know that fullness of life, salvation, wisdom, truth, and love come from without. Brother Robineau, Vincent's secretary, whose reflections about the saint have just been published, notes that this attitude was especially evident in Vincent's conversations with the poor, with whom he would sit and converse with great friendliness and humility.[9]

St. Vincent loved to call the poor the real "lords and masters"[10] in the church. It is they especially who must be listened to and obeyed. In the reign of God, the world of faith, they are the kings and queens; we are the servants. Recognizing the special place of the poor in the new order established by Jesus, Vincent was eager not only that his followers would serve and evangelize the poor, but also that they would hear God speaking in those they served or, as we would put it today, that they would allow themselves to be evangelized.[11]

Reading Sacred Scripture

St. Vincent was convinced that the word of God never fails. It is like "a house built upon rock."[12] He therefore begins each chapter of his rule and many individual paragraphs with a citation from Scripture. He asks the members of the Congregation of the Mission to read a chapter of the New Testament every day. He wants them to listen to the word of God and to make it the foundation of all they do: "Let each of us accept the truth of the following statement and try to make it our most fundamental principle: Christ's teaching will never let us down, while worldly wisdom always will."[13]

Abelly, Vincent's first biographer, notes in a colorful passage how devoted the saint was to listening to the word of God: "He seemed to suck meaning from passages of the Scriptures as a baby sucks milk from its mother, and he extracted the core and substance from the Scriptures so as to be strengthened and have his soul nourished by them—and he did this in such a way that in all his words and actions he appeared to be filled with Jesus Christ."[14]

"Obeying" Everyone

The word "obedience" (*ob* + *audire* = to listen thoroughly) is related etymologically to the word "listen" (*audire*). For St. Vincent the role of obedience in community was clearly very important. But he also extended obedience beyond its usual meaning, that all are to obey the legitimate commands of superiors. Using a broadened notion of obedience, he encouraged his followers to listen to and obey *everyone*, so that they might hear more fully what God is saying and act on it:

> Our obedience ought not limit itself only to those who have the right to command us, but ought to strive to move beyond that. . . . Let us therefore consider everyone as our superior and so place ourselves beneath them and, even more, beneath the least of them, outdoing them in deference, agreeableness, and service.[15]

Obedience moreover, is not the duty of subjects alone, but

of superiors too. In fact, superiors should be the first to obey, by listening to the members well and by seeking counsel: "There would be nothing more beautiful in the world, my daughter, than the Company of the Daughters of Charity if . . . obedience flourished everywhere, with the sister servant the first to obey, to seek counsel, and to submit herself."[16]

An Implicit Theme vs. an Explicit One

It is clear that listening plays a significant, even if unaccented, role in each of the themes described above. The importance of listening is not, therefore, a "forgotten truth" (to use Karl Rahner's phrase) in the writings of Ignatius Loyola, or Francis de Sales, or Vincent de Paul, or in the overall spiritual tradition; neither, however, is it a central one. Therein lie two dangers.

First, truths that remain secondary or merely implicit run the risk of being underemphasized or distorted. For example, reading a chapter of the word of God daily can degenerate into fulfilling an obligation or studying a text unless listening attentively retains its preeminent place. Likewise, the practice of humility, when distorted, can result in subservience to the voices without and deafness to the voices within, where God also speaks. In such a circumstance, "humility" might mask lack of courage in speaking up, deficient self-confidence, or a negative self-image. A distorted emphasis on obedience can cause subjects to listen exclusively to superiors, no matter what other voices might say, even voices that conscience demands that we listen to. Conversely, it could cause a superior to insist loudly that he only has to "listen" to the advice of others, not follow it (whereas in such instances he may usually listen to almost no one but himself). But when listening retains a place at the center, the danger of distortion is lessened. Reading the word of God, practicing humility, and obeying are seen as means for hearing what God is saying. The accent remains on attentiveness.

Second, when the importance of listening is underemphasized, there is a subtle tendency to focus on particular practices to the detriment of others or to be attentive to certain voices while disregarding others. For instance, a member of a community might pray mightily, seeking to discern what God is saying, but pay little attention to what a superior or spiritual director who knows the person well is trying to say. He or she may listen "transcendentally" or "vertically," so to speak, but show little concern for listening "horizontally." Along similar lines, a superior might be very confident that, because of the grace of his office, God lets him know what his will is, while other persons, by the grace of their office, are desperately trying to signify to the same superior that God is saying something quite different. The simple truth is that we must listen to many voices since God speaks to us in many ways. Some of these ways are obviously privileged, but none has an exclusive hold on the truth. *0*

Some Ramifications

In his wonderful book on community, Dietrich Bonhoeffer wrote:

> The first service that one owes to others in the community consists in listening to them. Just as love of God begins by listening to his Word, so the beginning of love for the brethren is learning to listen to them. It is because of God's love for us that he not only gives us his Word but also lends us his ear. So it is his work that we do for our brother when we learn to listen to him. Christians, especially ministers, so often think they must always contribute something when they are in the company of others, that this is the one service they have to render. They forget that listening can be a greater service than speaking. Many people are looking for an ear that will listen. They do not find it among Christians, because these Christians are talking where they should be listening. But he who can no longer listen to his brother will soon be no longer listening to God either, he will be doing nothing but prattle in the presence of God too. This is the beginning of the death of the spiritual life.[17]

If listening is so crucial to healthy spirituality, then how might members of communities grow in it, both as individuals and in common?

Listening as Individuals

From reflection on the church's long spiritual tradition, one might glean a number of qualities that characterize good listeners. Here I will touch briefly on four, which seem to me crucial for better listening.

The first indispensable quality for good listening is humility. It is "the foundation of all evangelical perfection, the core of the spiritual life," as Vincent de Paul put it.[18] Humble people sense their incompleteness, their need for God and other human persons. So they listen.

Humility acknowledges that everything is gift; it sees clearly that all good things come from God. St. Vincent writes to a priest of the Mission: "Because we recognize that this abundant grace comes from God, a grace which he keeps on giving only to the humble who realize that all the good done through them comes from God, I beg him with all my heart to give you more and more the spirit of humility. . . ."[19]

But consciousness of one's incompleteness has a further dimension. It is not only "vertical," so to speak, but "horizontal"; we depend not only on God directly, but on God's creation around us. Truth, then, comes from listening not only to God himself, but to other human persons, through whom God's presence and words are mediated to us. The hunger for truth and love that lie at the heart of the mystery of the human person is satisfied only from without. We are inherently social, living within a complex network of relationships with individuals and with society.

It is only when what is heard is pondered that its full meaning is revealed. The second quality necessary for better listening, then, is prayerful reflectiveness. While at times one can hear God speak even in a noisy crowd, it is often only in silence that one hears the deepest voices, that one plumbs the depth of meaning. The Psalmist urges us: "Be still and know that I am God" (Ps 46:10).

The Gospels, particularly Luke's, attest that Jesus turns to his Father again and again in prayer to listen to him and to seek his will. Prayer is then surely one of the privileged ways of listening. But it must always be validated by life. One who listens to "what God is telling me" in prayer, but who pays little heed to what others are saying in daily life, is surely suspect. Prayer must be in continual contact with people and events, since God speaks not only in the silence of our hearts, but also (and often first of all) in the people around us.

Because prayer is a meeting with God himself, what *we* say in prayer is much less important than what God says to us. When there is too much emphasis on what *we* say or do during prayer, it can easily become a "good work," an "achievement," a "speech," rather than a "grace," a "gift," a "gratuitous word" from God. Naturally, prayer, like all human activities, involves structures, personal discipline, persevering effort. But the emphasis must always be on the presence of the personal God, to whose word we must listen attentively as he speaks to us the good news of his love for us and for others.

In an era when there is much noise, where the media, if we so choose, speak to us all day long, one must surely ask: Are we able to distinguish the voice of God among the many voices that are speaking? Is God's word able to say "new things" to us? Are we still capable of wonder? As may be evident to the reader, the word *wonder* has an etymological kinship, through German, with *wound*. Is the word of God able to wound us, to penetrate the membrane that seals us off, that encloses us within ourselves? Can it break into our consciousness and change us?

Prayer must be in continual contact with people and events, since God speaks not only in the silence of our hearts, but also in the people around us.

The third necessary quality is respect for the words of human persons. It is here perhaps that the tradition was weakest. It did emphasize humility. It did accent the need to hear what God is saying and to discern his will. But it rarely focused explicitly, in the context of spirituality, on the central place of listening to other people.

Many contemporary documents put great emphasis on the dignity of human persons and on the importance of hearing the cries that come from their hearts. Vatican II's *Gaudium et spes* and the encyclical *Redemptor hominis* see the human person as the center of creation.[20] *Centesimus annus* puts it strikingly: "Today the church's social doctrine focuses especially on *man*...."[21]

Respect for human persons acknowledges that God lives in them and that he reveals himself in and through them. It acknowledges that words of life come from the lowly as well as the powerful. In fact, St. Vincent became gradually convinced that "the poor have the true religion" and that we must be evangelized by them.[22]

Many of the recently published texts of Brother Louis Robineau, which relate his personal experience of Vincent de Paul, attest to the saint's deep respect for persons of all types. Robineau notes how well Vincent listened to them: poor and rich, lay and clerical, peasant and royal.[23] In this context, the process of questioning persons that is involved in the quest for truth takes on a new light. When there is deep respect for all human persons, questioning involves a genuine search for enlightenment, rather than being, in some hidden way, refutation or accusation. Questioning is a tool for delving deeper, for unpeeling layers of meaning, for knowing the other person better, for digging toward the core of the truth.

As we attempt to develop increasing respect for human persons, surely we must ask some challenging questions. Are we really able to hear the cries of the poor, of the most oppressed: the women and children, who are often the poorest members of society; those discriminated against because of race, color, nationality, religion; the AIDS victims, who are often shunned by their families and by the physically healthy; those on the "edges of life," the helpless infants and the helpless aged, who are unable to speak for themselves? Are we able to hear the counsel given to us by others: by spiritual directors, by members of our own communities, by the documents of the church and our own religious congregations? Are we sensitive to the contributions that come from other sources of human wisdom (like economics, sociology, the audiovisual media, the massive data now available in computerized form) that often speak concretely about the needs of the poor, that can help us find and combat the causes of poverty or that can assist us in the new evangelization called for by the church? Are we alert, "listening," to the "signs of the times": the increasing gap between the rich and the poor and the repeated call for justice made by the church; the movement toward unity within global society, which is now accompanied by an opposite movement toward separatism and nationalism; the growth of the church in the southern hemisphere, which contrasts with its diminishment in many places in the northern hemisphere.

Attentiveness is an indispensable means for creating authentic communities.

The fourth quality needed is attentiveness, one of the most important signs of respect for the human person. It is the first step in all evangelization, the prerequisite for serving Christ in the poor. It is only when the servant is attentive to the needs of the master (in this case, the poor person) that he really knows what to bring him. It is only when the evangelizer is alert to the needs of the listener that she is able to communicate genuinely good news.

Attentiveness is an indispensable means for creating authentic communities. If community members do not pay close attention to the opinions and needs of those they live with, each person becomes isolated even if still physically present to others. Those living in community must therefore continually seek renewed ways of listening to each other and of sharing their prayer, their apostolic experience, their struggles in community, their successes and failures, their joys and sorrows.

Attentiveness is also of the greatest importance as one seeks counsel. Robineau relates how often St. Vincent asked others their opinion about matters at hand, "even the least in the house." He often heard him say that "four eyes are better than two, and six better than four."[24] Robineau relates an interesting incident in this regard:

> One day he did me the honor of telling me that it was necessary to make it our practice, when consulting someone about some matter, always to recount everything that would be to the advantage of the opposing party without omitting anything, just as if it were the opposing party itself that was there to give its reasons and defend itself, and that it was thus that consultations should be carried out.[25]

Listening in Community

Meetings, along with consultations and questionnaires of various sorts, are among the primary means of listening in community. Like most realities, meetings are "for better or for worse." Almost all of us have experienced some that we find very fruitful and others that we would be happy to forget about. To put it in another way, meetings can be a time of grace or a time when sin threatens grace.

Communities, like individuals, can become caught up in themselves. A healthy self-concern can gradually slip into an unhealthy self-preoccupation. Outgoing zeal can be replaced by self-centered security seeking. Communities can be rescued from this state, in a way analogous to that of individuals, only through corporate humility,[26] a communal effort to listen to God and communal attentiveness to the words of others.

Meetings can be a time when sin threatens grace. When there is no listening, they create strife and division. They disrupt rather than unify. They deepen the darkness rather than focus the light. Among the signs that sin is at work in meetings is *fighting*. When participants do not listen, there is inevitable strife, bad feelings, disillusionment, bitterness. Such meetings result in *fleeing*. The group backs away from major decisions, especially those that demand some conversion; it refuses to listen to the prophets; it seeks refuge in the status quo. A further consequence is *fracturing*. When participants do not listen, badly divided splinter groups form; the "important" conversations take place in the corridors rather than in the meeting hall; politics, in the worst sense, takes the place of discernment.

Meetings can be an opportunity for grace. They provide us with a wonderful opportunity for listening and discernment. They enable communities to work toward decisions together, as a community. In order for this to happen, those who meet must be committed to sharing their common heritage, creating a climate of freedom for discussion, and planning courageously for the future.

In meetings where God is at work, we recall our heritage in order to renew it. We listen to and retell "our story." We recount and rehear the deeds of the Lord in our history. We celebrate our gratitude in the Eucharist and let thanksgiving fill our hearts, for we have heard the wonderful works of the Lord. We share communal prayer and reflection because the faith of others strengthens us.

The atmosphere will be grace-filled if all are eager to listen to each other. If all arrive without hardened positions and prejudices, convinced that the group must seek the truth together, then the groundwork for the emergence of truth has already been laid.

The content, no matter how concrete or seemingly pedestrian, will be grace-filled if all hear the word of God together, listen to each other's reflections on that word, and make decisions on that basis. The decisions of a listening community will flow from its heritage while developing the heritage in the light of contemporary circumstances.[27]

Meetings play an important role within God's providence. God provides for the growth of communities through wise decisions that govern their future, especially the training of the young, the ongoing formation of all members, and care for the aging. But such decisions can be made only if the members of the community are willing to listen to the data that describes its present situation and projects its future needs. Communal decision making, based on realistic projections, is one of the ways in which providence operates in community life. Failure to listen to the data—difficult though it may sometimes be to "hear" it honestly—results in calamitous "blindness" and "deafness."

The listening individual and the listening community will surely grow, for listening is the foundation of all spirituality. To the listener come truth, wisdom, the assurance of being loved. To those who fail to listen comes increasing isolation.

Jesus, like the prophets, knew that listening made demands and consequently was often lacking. He lamented its absence: "Sluggish indeed is this people's heart. They have scarcely heard with their ears, they have firmly closed their eyes; otherwise they might see with their eyes, and hear with their ears, and understand with their hearts, and turn back to me, and I should heal them" (Mt 13:15). He also rejoiced in its presence: "But . . . blessed are your ears because they hear" (Mt 13:16).

In recent years many congregations have attempted to assist individuals, local communities, and assemblies to listen better. In workshops much effort has been put into fostering practical listening skills. But are there ways in which communities, particularly during initial formation, can better communicate the importance of listening as foundational for growth? If listening is the foundation of all spirituality, as this article has tried to show, then it is crucial for personal growth and for the vitality of all communities.

Notes

[1] Sandra Schneiders, "Spirituality in the Academy," Theological Studies 50 (1989): 684.

[2] See Ga 2:19-21: "I have been crucified with Christ, and the life I live now is not my own: Christ is living in me. Of course, I still live my human life, but it is a life of faith in the Son of God, who loved me and gave himself for me." The Greek text identifies Jesus as the self-giving one. It also makes it clear that self-transcendence does not wipe out true humanity, but fulfills it.

[3] Bernard Lonergan, A Third Collection, ed. Frederick Crowe (New York: Paulist, 1985), p. 9.

[4] See K. Rahner, Grundkurs des Glaubens (Freiburg: Herder, 1984), pp. 35f, 42f.

[5] Francis de Sales, Introduction to the Devout Life, trans. John K. Ryan (New York: Doubleday, 1972), pp. 107 and 108.

[6] Common Rules II, 7.

[7] SV IX, 674; see *Common Rules II*, 7.

[8] SV X, 439.

[9] André Dodin, ed., *Monsieur Vincent raconté par son secrétaire* (Paris: O.E.I.L., 1991), §46 and §54.

[10] See SV IX, 119; X, 332.

[11] See *Evangelii nuntiandi*, §15.

[12] *Common Rules II*, 1.

[13] Ibid.

[14] Abelly, Book III, 72-73.

[15] SV XI, 69.

[16] SV IX, 526.

[17] D. Bonhoeffer, *Life Together* (London: SCM Press, 1954), p. 75.

[18] *Common Rules II*, 7.

[19] SV I, 182.

[20] *Gaudium et spes*, §§9, 12, and 22; *Redemptor hominis*, passim.

[21] *Centesimus annus*, §54.

[22] SV XII, 171.

[23] André Dodin, ed., *Monsieur Vincent raconté par son secrétaire* (Paris: O.E.I.L., 1991), especially §§71-83.

[24] Ibid, §52.

[25] Ibid, §118.

[26] Vincent de Paul repeatedly emphasized the need for corporate humility if the congregations he founded were to grow. See SV II, 233: "I think the spirit of the Mission must be to seek its greatness in lowliness and its reputation in the love of its abjection."

[27] In his essays on spirituality, Karl Rahner distinguishes between "material" and "formal" imitation of Christ. In material imitation, one seeks to do the concrete things that Jesus did, ignoring the extent to which everything he did was influenced by his social context. In formal imitation, one seeks to find the core meaning of what Jesus said or did and apply it within the changed social context.

That God Might Be Father

*P*erhaps the only question more problematic than that of the possibility of prayer is the question of its genuine significance and necessity. Surprisingly, however, this is also a question we generally fail to consider explicitly or face squarely. More typically, the meaningfulness and requisiteness of our prayer are matters we tend to take for granted, even though the notion of prayer may lie at the heart of important or even fundamental expressions of self-understanding and definition. But the question is an important one, and one we cannot easily afford to avoid or carelessly dismiss, if we intend to take prayer seriously or maintain a proper sense of its place and role in our daily lives.

After all, why really are we called to pray? What, if anything, is truly and uniquely at stake in our prayer? Is there any reason to regard our own personal prayer as a matter of compelling urgency and real necessity, or is the matter really more nugatory? Clearly, as Christians we are called to believe that our prayer is a meaningful, even indispensable activity, vital to the transformation and healing of all we know, and the realization of all we are made and hope for. But how do we justify such a belief? What is it about prayer that makes such claims credible? The answers to all of these questions are based in our recognition that in prayer something deeper and even more fundamental is at stake, something in which all healing and human growth in wisdom and sanctity are rooted, and upon which all our hope depends.

Like Christianity in general, and like God himself, prayer is profoundly paradoxical, and this is particularly true of the question at hand. Although we must acknowledge that prayer is the gift and activity of God attended to by sinners (that is, by persons whose lives are fundamentally marked and marred by fragmentation and alienation), we must also affirm that the deeper truth is the paradox that prayer is primarily something we undertake on God's own behalf, insofar as prayer is the experience of God as the One he wishes to be for us. Quite simply, what is truly and uniquely at stake in our prayer, at each and every moment we pray, is nothing less than the life and destiny of God himself. As Christians, as persons who pray—that is, as persons who share as heirs of God in the obedient Sonship of Jesus Christ, we do so primarily that God might truly be the Father he has willed to be from the beginning.

This insight is easy to lose sight of, something that occurs particularly whenever God's paradoxical nature is obscured or forgotten, and an immutable or even (as commonly misunderstood) "triune" God is substituted for a Living One. Most of us are well aware that on the one hand, our God is the "High and Holy One," the one who reveals himself in sovereignty and self-sufficiency. Indeed he is Yahweh, "the one who will be who (he) will be,"[1] in absolute authority and awesome autonomy. But this dominant Old Testament image is just one side of the paradox whom we Christians know as God; and if on the one hand he is the High and Holy One who is absolutely self-sufficient, he is also the one who has determined not to remain so, but rather has resolved to make his own destiny subject to the responsiveness of his creation. Our God

> is on the one hand without beginning or end, absolutely self-sufficient, in need of no one and no thing. Yet on the other hand he has willed from all eternity not to remain alone but to turn to another—a person who will be his counterpart. He is the eternal decision to speak to this other and to hearken to the word which this other speaks. He is the eternal decision to love this other and to accept this other's love. [The God of the New Testament] who is eternally self-sufficient wills not to be; God who is eternally of and for himself wills to be for another.[2]

This means quite simply that God has determined to be for us as well as dependent upon us. We must allow this determination to be realized, and let God be who he wills to be for us. This is indeed the most human thing we can do, just as it is the most loving. Those who truly appreciate that our own destiny is dependent upon the proper exercise of human freedom should not be surprised that God too is dependent upon it. In fact, we should be aware that the Christ event reveals that it is human freedom which is the true counterpart to divine omnipotence. For many, this will be an astounding assertion. However, if we reflect on precisely what occurred in the Christ event, perhaps this critical point will become more acceptable to most people. Certainly such reflection is necessary if we are to truly appreciate the importance and urgency of our prayer.

It is true that in the Christ event—in the life, death, resurrection, and ascension of Jesus—God drew near to every moment and mood of his creation. This is truth but the truth cuts far more deeply than even this awesome reality. In the Christ event something absolutely singular and unsurpassable occurred. For the first time in human history someone, in this case Jesus of Nazareth, in living a life wholly responsive to the God who would be Father, accomplished two things. In the first place, he lived the first genuinely human existence ever known in the history of humankind, and secondly, *in his proper exercise of true human freedom he allowed God to become the Father he had willed to be from the beginning*. In the dialogue which existed between Father and Son, both human and divine life reached a fullness for which they had yearned and groaned through time and eternity, the realization of human and divine destinies were forever linked, and divine omnipotence and human freedom were inextricably wed as counterparts of one another. Nor is this all. In Jesus' resurrection from the dead, this abundant life was made a continuing and unconquerable reality in our world. It is in prayer that we enter most deeply into participation into this abundant life, and in prayer that Jesus' Sonship becomes our own and the Fatherhood of God is further realized.

It is in prayer that Jesus' Sonship becomes our own and the Fatherhood of God is further realized.

Through our participation in the Sonship of Jesus, we come to know genuine human life, and we become aware that it is a life characterized and constituted by an ongoing and all-consuming dialogue with the Father, who is in turn constituted as Father in this dialogue. In the Christ event Jesus responded to God as Son. He allowed God to be the author of his life, and he allowed God to be authored as Father in the process. Truly human existence is nothing less and nothing other than daughtership or sonship to the Living God *whose own inner truth and dynamism is realized in Fatherhood.* Prayer is simply and always the mutual outworking of these inextricably linked divine and human destinies.

ø God is Father neither before nor apart from the response of Jesus as Son; neither is he our Father apart from our participation in that definitive Sonship which we call prayer. (Note well, in all of this it is important that, according to the prologue to John's Gospel, we are very clear that it is not the Logos that is Son; rather it is Jesus as Son in whom the Logos is incarnate. The two realities are quite different, and are often tragically confused. As the term is commonly but perhaps naively used, the Logos is "preexistent"; the Son is not, and whenever this confusion occurs, it becomes impossible to appreciate the true significance of the obedient Sonship of Jesus or of our own prayer.) Although he is the one "who will be who (he) will be," the God of the New Testament turns to the world as the one who would be Father, that is, as one who would find his counterpart and true completion in those who would turn in response as daughters and sons (that is, as those who are *of him* and *from him*) and as one whose deepest identity would remain unrealized and unrealizable apart from this response.

What are the implications of all this for our prayer? In the first place, we must concede that our prayer has real meaning and urgency, not only and not even primarily because we are saved through God's activity in our lives, but because in our prayer we concern ourselves with the very life of God. Whether or not prayer is a profound experience for us, it is a significant experience for God since it is in prayer that he is allowed to achieve Fatherhood and truly realize himself. Whatever we perceive happening or not happening in our prayer, we must not lose sight of the fact of what does occur there. In prayer God is given the chance to love fully, and thus to fully *be.* It is not simply the case that God is love; it is also true that, in loving, God is (and it is this fact which allows us to speak of prayer in terms of the glorification or magnification of God).

Prayer is possible only to the extent that our God has willed not to remain remote, that is, only to the extent that he has drawn near. But prayer is meaningful and necessary for the most part because the God who has refused to remain remote has also willed not to remain self-sufficient and has, in a very real way, put his own destiny into the hands of those to whom he would be Father, and whom he has thus willed to respond to him as daughters and sons. Without our prayer, God remains the High and Holy One who has drawn near to us in all of life's moments and moods, but who remains deprived of real presence, and thus whose deepest will and identity remains unrealized and frustrated in our regard.

It is particularly telling that the first word and entire Lord's Prayer is contained in the invocation "Father." Jesus' whole life and prayer, which were essentially synonymous, were devoted to allowing God's will to Fatherhood to be accomplished. Claiming this realization of the Fatherhood of God is the heart of all prayer. Allowing him to love us in the way he wills is the heart of all truly human activity. It is important that our prayer remain the God-centered activity it is meant to be. This is the reason Jesus gave his life and his way of praying as a "paradigm of perspective," and in fact, in what is most essentially and profoundly the lesson of the New Testament, taught his followers to pray. We lose proper perspective if we forget that God has drawn near, but it is at least as tragic to forget that prayer is the way nearness is transformed into real presence. We said in an earlier essay[3] that prayer begins, ends, and is sustained by our concern for and commitment to the life of God. Let us remember why we are present to him and what our appreciation of his nearness means for him, and may this knowledge sustain us in even the driest of moments.

Notes

[1] The usual translation of "Yahweh" in Exodus 3:14 as "I am who am" or even the more cryptic "I am" is inadequate insofar as it disregards the dynamic element, the promise of active and effective presence contained in the Hebrew (see Ex 3:12). A better translation is "I will be who I will be."

[2] John C. Dwyer, *Son of Man and Son of God: A New Language for Faith* (New York: Paulist Press, 1983).

[3] Laurel M. O'Neal, "Prayer, Maintaining a Human Perspective," Review for Religious, 46, no. 6 (November-December 1987): 883.

Prayer

*P*rayer is the lifting of the mind and heart to God. I grew up with that definition and missed out on the notion that God wanted to speak to me. Prayer as a love relationship of me to God and of God to me is a much more real definition. It makes prayer into a two-way street. Knowing that traffic can go both ways, one keeps alert for signs.

Relationships can be rocky roads that go nowhere, but they can also be converging roads that bring the minds and hearts of people closer and closer together. A good relationship is not just a falling in step with another. It is a sharing of directions. Prayer is how we share the road with God.

If we are looking for the chance to speak to God, we have to slow down enough to have a conversation. In our prayer we may be going too fast to notice God. The fast track of life demands so much concentration on what we are doing that we may be blind to what happens around us. We have to slow down to smell the roses—or to find God in our amazement at a midnight sky. But the truth about God is that he never passes us by; he is forever waiting for us to slow down and notice his presence.

When I control the direction of my prayer, I am meditating. When I surrender the control, I go in the direction God would take me, and then I am contemplating. My slowing down gradually answers the question of whose journey I am on. It is much better to coast where God takes me than to spin my wheels. Prayer is the chance to discover how God finds me. Meditating is climbing the mountain of the Lord. Contemplation is coming down the other side.

Years ago the miracle of God's presence in my life touched me with the suddenness of lightning. This moment of prayer, which I did not then know as prayer, was like watching a preview of a movie. This vision of my vocation to be a Jesuit was not full of the details that day-by-day living would bring. Rather, it was a confident sense that I would be going in the right direction, no matter how long the journey.

For a moment I belonged to God in a way that I would never quite understand. God would always have to lead me, but my heart knew the goal of my journey, and in prayer that heart knowledge is still there to help me find my way. Life becomes, without my knowing how, the reality of my prayer and gives me in an intuitive way what I have come to call the five P's of prayer.

Presence, Place, Petition, Parachutes, and Person are what make up my prayer. They fit with meditation and with the contemplation to which it leads. They are elements of intimacy, and an absence of one of the P's for too long a time is a likely reason why my prayer is crashing.

Presence

To be in the presence of God is scary. Adoration and fear seem to go together. And moments of the divine touch have a special loneliness about them. Because they are hard to describe to others and therefore seem unique, they also seem unreal. I want them to be true so desperately that the way another hears me talk about them shuts me up, for I notice that the listener is not managing to experience, along with me, the joy of having felt God's touch. I am silenced in the truth of such a moment and find it impossible to go on. I always want, of course, to get back to the presence, but that is not under my control. Conscious awareness of the presence is union.

The Sacrament of the Present Moment is what this is all about. The God who is always there, always everywhere, becomes for me a suddenly realized presence. He is forever creating, but at the same time doing so much more than creating. Usually, though, the presence of God is realized after the fact. God, the same yesterday, today, and tomorrow, has the uniqueness of now. Our hearts are on fire, and even the memory of the memory shares the luster of the moment.

How could I ever leave him who is my very life? As the years go by in my life, I realize whom I was looking for even in my sinfulness. Nothing else but God answers all the needs of my heart and fills me. The echo rings on in my consciousness of all the times I have heard myself saying, "My beloved is gone, and I cannot get my God back." How wrong I was. God seemed easy to adore when I was conscious of his presence. Now I am reduced to silence before the wonder of a God who is so much more than life itself. My emptiness explodes with a cry that is God speaking to God as the Spirit of the living God takes over my prayer. "Hallowed be thy name" becomes the heartfelt prayer of a heart that otherwise lacks words altogether, lost in the emptiness which alone is big enough for God.

Life itself, in its ordinariness, becomes the prayer of adoration. I flunked the car inspection twice and kept having to go back. How could I relate these failures to God's loving mercy for me? I cannot help remembering how obvious God can be when he answers my prayer for his help to be a good teacher. I was teaching my course on Drugs and Alcohol, and the subject for the night was prevention. What had happened to me meshed exactly with the class I taught. My failing inspection gave me a perfect image for prevention. If I do not want a breakdown at a difficult time, I need to pass inspection. This is true of all of life and especially true of prayer.

I look to see where God has been in my day. The gentle presence is unnoticed because love does not force itself on another. I examine my consciousness for God's presence in order to increase my consciousness of that presence. He comes when I least expect him, and I find him all the more when I look to see where he has been. Because I have looked for my God, I find my God all the more easily in my day. My acts of the presence of God are a focusing, and they bring an increasing consciousness of his presence. Looking for his presence brings me to why I am there in my prayer.

Petition or Supplication

The gulf between man and God is the Grand Canyon between daily life and eternity. Touched once by the presence of God, the heart is forever crying for the gulf to be removed. The truth of felt presence is all too quickly followed by the consciousness of absence. "Blessed are those who have not seen and believe" brings little help for those who are caught on the other side of silence. The baby crying for its mother has a counterpart in the spiritual life. The "Come, Lord Jesus" of the early church, which had visual memories of the Christ of the Gospels, becomes the prayer of the loving soul.

Search as one may for a bridge between time and eternity, there is no crossing of the Grand Canyon by one's own power. Unless God permits a vision like Paul's where one is for a time carried out of the body into the mystery of God's eternal love, our prayer keeps us in contact with the drag of daily life. The heaven connection is entirely God's doing. One must wait on the edge of eternity for one's time to cross. One could never make the crossing on one's own. Yet God so loved the world that in the fullness of time he sent his only Son to bridge the gap. And in the humanness of Christ the mystery of divinity has its fullest human expression.

Because I have looked for my God, I find my God all the more easily in my day.

Love and need meet in people who are hurting. And the Christ of God's love identifies with the last, the lowest, and the least. Christ considers what is done for the child as done for himself. Supplication becomes the outreach of love, facing problems bigger than anyone's reach; and heaven is besieged with cries of hearts facing the needs of the world. God created us to be in this world where our cries make a difference because of his Son. Oneness with Christ becomes the faith that does justice. The world in need has been changed by Christ, who died for the sake of all the people in the world. There is no true prayer without the world being faced honestly. Through the Christ of the resurrection, the cry of the poor is forever heard. To face people's needs, to feel their needs, to reach out to help them in their needs is to make life itself into a prayer of supplication. Any cry becomes the cry of Christ reaching the Father and keeping the human race in contact with its Maker.

Place

The Second Person did not hold on to being God, but emptied himself of all the power of God to be like us in everything but sin (Ph 2:6-8). A visit to the cave, the simplicity of the stable, opens one up to finding God in the different places of life. For those who have been blessed with being able to visit the places where Jesus lived and walked and talked, the memory of it lives on and gives a special meaning to "place" in prayer. It is a sad person who lacks the imagination to picture Jesus along the various roads of his life. Jesus made certain places in Israel holy by being there. But we each have our own holy places where we found God or God found us. We remember those places with love, for they put us into the presence of God in both vivid and everyday ways. The local color of my prayer disposes me to be in the presence of God. A return to a place made holy by what occurred for me there in the past puts my mind and my heart in the presence of God once again.

The faith of groups of devout people, or of generations of them, makes some places holy. Where I live we have a beautiful church upstairs and our parish community wants to pray in its own space downstairs, which to me is dark, dank, and dreary. The people are, of course, right to pray where they find God. But, on the other hand, dedicated churches, chapels, and shrines have a distinctive religious goodness which other places that some individuals have found holy may not have. It is important, then, not only to seek out the places we ourselves find holy, but also to adapt ourselves to places that belong to everyone, places where we ourselves may be challenged to get beyond ourselves into a community wisdom, a community generosity and self-sacrifice, that we did not take to at first.

We journey beyond ourselves when we enter into the presence of God, and we shut God out when we limit God to our own point of view. Gradually, through our prayer and our search for God, we make all the places we visit holy. The dichotomy between God's place and ours is ended by the holiness of life we are called to in our prayer. We go initially to prayer and to a holy place so that we can bring the God we find there to every part of our lives. Then we find ourselves praying because our life has become our prayer.

Parachutes

Meditation challenges us to put on the mind and the heart of Christ. By looking at events in the life of Christ in a prayerful way, I discover how Christ looked at life. I also discover how I should look at life if I am going to live my life in his name. For the Christian, the question of the meaning of life is reducible to "Am I willing to live my life just as Christ would have lived his life if he had been lucky enough to be me?" This basic question never goes stale, for each day of my life it keeps raising new questions and new opportunities to find God in what I am doing. I can place them before God and discuss them with him.

Beginners' meditations are usually a systematic study of the Bible in a prayerful way, but that may quickly seem irrelevant or impossible to do as real life poses questions that challenge the way we are living. These questions, which have no easy answers, we need to put before God day in and day out. Prayer touches life even as life touches prayer. After we have learned to find God in some of the odd moments of life, we may learn more and more to find him also in the even moments of life, when he seems not so badly needed.

Still, a person, place, or event may help me to be prayerful, to be aware of God's presence here and now. Or I can let a scripture passage lift me into God's presence on a kind of parachute. I can let the currents of the Spirit move me along, without trying to get back to earth before my prayer time is up. My prayer can also take off from a distraction that I look at in God's presence. How often what comes into my prayer as a distraction is what God wants me to pray about! If something is truly a distraction, I will experience negative vibes. When it comes from God, it helps me make sense out of my day and brings insight about what I should be doing. ☙

We shut God out when we limit God to our own point of view.

Person

I do not try to imagine God when I talk to him in my prayer. Whom I am talking to in my prayer is often obscured in a night-of-faith darkness. What I see when I see Christ praying leads me to his Father, whom I do not see. Christ holds back nothing in sharing his prayer with his disciples, and he promises to send the Spirit. With the Spirit his disciples will be able to understand. I too have to claim the Spirit. When the problems of life become greater than anything I would dare handle by myself, the Spirit becomes important in my prayer. And so do relatives and friends who have gone before me. I welcome their intercession even as I intercede for those who need my prayers.

"There is no right way to pray" becomes the truth of our prayer as we develop a relationship that is entirely our own. Prayer becomes our tenderness with God, a person-to-person relationship. Prayer opens human hearts to one another as well, because the question rings true "How can we love the God we do not see if we do not love the brothers and the sisters we do see?"

Perpetuate is what God does to our prayer. God allows my prayer to live on in my life. What comes up in prayer repeats itself in my awarenesses of God in the ongoing day, and the great moments of prayer are like great moments of love in our lives. They come back again and again. Wherever there is love, God is there.

Prayer becomes life and life becomes prayer. Gradually there are no "formal" times of prayer, no times when I go to prayer only as a duty, for prayer has become the privilege of friends who may talk to each other at any moment. Those moments become the heartbeat of life as we come to live more and more for the God who loved us so much that he was willing to be one of us. Prayer brings us to our destiny of being one with God forever.

Progress in Prayer

O ne day the Apostles came to Jesus with the request, "Lord, teach us to pray like John taught his disciples to pray." Jesus gave them the Our Father. Suppose they had come back twenty years later and made the same request. Would Jesus have given them the same answer? Most probably not. They should have improved during those years, ready for different forms of prayer. What do we understand by progress in prayer? We all know about vocal prayer. But is meditation the only other way to pray? If we have been getting one thought per minute and two acts of the will, do we call it progress because we now have two per minute and an extra act of the will? Just what changes in the spiritual life and in prayer do we expect as a newly baptized infant grows to spiritual adulthood?

Some brief biographical details help evaluate what I say. I am now seventy-six years old and have been a priest for forty-seven years. About forty years ago the Lord started asking for more time in prayer. In 1969 when I was giving about two-and-a-half hours each morning to mental prayer, I read St. John of the Cross and shifted to the prayer of simple regard. In 1987 the Lord brought it sharply to my attention that he had moved me to the passive level. I have since been told that shifting from meditation to full union in eighteen years is an unusually short time.

There is a whole school of spirituality (from Thomas Merton on back) that maintains that if one is called to the active life then that person is not called to contemplation. But the experience of many people denies that theory.

There are no quantum jumps in the spiritual life. We do not

need new powers as we shift from meditation to active and then to infused contemplation. God is involved in every good action that we do, and as we progress his percentage will increase—but we always must do our part. It is well to keep in mind also, when you wonder exactly where you are, that misjudgment will not hurt anything. If you imagine that you are at the top of the mountain when really you have barely reached the first step—no big thing. If you imagine the opposite and you really are at the summit—no big thing either. Listening to the devil and following him as your spiritual guide and being deceived into thinking that it is God who is talking can bring total ruin.

Meditation

At one time or another we were all probably taught to meditate, think about some chosen topic, probably ask questions about it, pray about it and then make appropriate acts of the will. The acts of the will were the more important part of the meditation. Meditation is prayer, but most of us did not realize that meditation is also a process of learning and that God can and does use it to teach us many things. When we meditated on God as our father, we learned more about him, things we had not realized before, while we were also bringing into consciousness and making operative what we already know.

Affective Prayer

After a certain number of meditations on a particular topic, we ought to become so familiar with it that we can easily recall the various ideas with facility. Only a few moments of thinking would supply enough so we can go on for ten minutes making acts of the will. This level is known as affective prayer. Our prayer has begun to simplify so that there are fewer acts of the mind. Our prayer can then be mostly acts of the will with just enough thinking to keep it going. I never got very far in this affective state. A retreat director once pointed out that I was probably trained from childhood not to show emotion. That is probably also why even from the beginning for me the time for colloquy was almost a total blank. It is probably also the reason why at the various stages when the books speak of dryness I never noticed anything special—it was just the usual thing for me.

Prayer of Simple Regard

The next step goes by various names: simple regard, active contemplation, acquired contemplation, or prayer of the heart. After a certain amount of time at the affective level, the action of the will also begins to simplify so that one act of the will can continue for some time before we need to add another to continue praying. Then we will find that life itself begins to simplify as the line between prayer and work begins to get fuzzy. Characteristic of this prayer is the aridity and dryness that makes people think they are falling back. In the beginning they tended to equate fervor and consolation—the Lord teaching them and coaxing them to continue. There was a steady flow of thoughts, affections, acts of the will, and the consolation seemed to be in proportion to our efforts.

Now the consolation has disappeared, even those thoughts and feelings that had meant so much, that had been inspiring and moving, now seem to mean nothing. For most people the tendency then is to imagine that they are getting tepid, even though they cannot seem to be able to put their finger on where they are failing. God does not play guessing games. If they were falling back he would definitely try to tell them so. That they are worried about falling back and are still continuing to try, that it does not seem to be a passing phase but seems to get worse as they go along are good signs. They have reached a state that is often referred to as the desert—a point of normal development in the spiritual life.

As a matter of fact, this state should be expected. With confidence we can assert that sooner or later God will cut down or stop the satisfaction we have been getting in prayer. Provided that we continue making serious efforts and are still working at self-discipline, the lack of satisfaction is almost a sure sign that we are making progress. Everyone should get here sooner or later. After twenty meditations on God as our father, just how many new ideas can we get? Once an orange has been peeled we can try as hard as we can but we will not get any more peelings. The preliminaries are out of the way, and we can eat the orange and enjoy it. So it is with prayer.

Meditation is the preliminary work, but we have barely started. Now that we have learned about God's thoughts and ways, we can begin to reap the results of our labor. But instead of getting easier as we advance, as we try to get closer to him, to know him and not merely know about him, as we learn to give him our hearts and not just a few external actions—suddenly the path will be much steeper and harder than we had expected. Now a total shift in emphasis occurs; no wonder we feel that we are lost. In unfamiliar territory, we will make mistakes and need help. If we want to travel to a new country we must first leave the places that are familiar to us and travel by roads that we have never seen. If a child is to learn to walk it must first be put down from its mother's lap where it was comfortable and protected. Everything then seems to be going wrong. People with poor imaginations will probably get to this stage sooner, or their previous spiritual progress may give them a head start and shorten the time. In any case, as the prayer simplifies, aridity will come because the imagination and other powers will start fighting for a change, not wanting the same old menu day after day.

Time to Shift to Simple Prayer

If we try to shift too soon from meditation to simpler prayer, we will probably end up in daydreaming and idleness. Besides, God has not yet had enough time to teach us all that he wants to. If we delay too long, then we may be resisting God and lose the possible increased benefits that can come from other forms of prayer. At all stages we should always try to pray as we can and not as we think we should. It is important that we follow where God is leading us and not fret too much about the level we have reached.

St. John of the Cross listed three now classic signs that can indicate when we should shift to simpler prayer. When I read about them twenty-five years ago my spiritual life changed. They seemed to fit my situation so well that I decided to try John of the Cross's suggestions for six months and then evaluate. But after only a few weeks I made my decision and have not gone back to meditation as a steady diet since. The signs are: (1) we cannot make discursive meditation as before; (2) we are not inclined to fix our attention on particular ideas, but prefer to dwell on a general idea of God; (3) we like to remain in loving awareness of God without discursive acts of the memory, intellect, and will.

We need all three signs. The first alone can be just a tepid person resolved to sit tight. The first and second signs together may mean that we are tired or sick, a condition that should normally pass. Only when all three signs are present together should we shift away from meditation. When the three are present then

God is probably blocking the action of our intellect and will. That is why we cannot meditate as we did before. He will not let us. God has stopped the consolation; most of us would never change if we continued to receive consolation. God is trying to teach us to grow and serve him for himself, independently of the consolations he might give. If God is not giving us consolations, the reason is that he sees that we do not need them as before.

St. John says that when we find those three signs then we should try to cultivate an attitude of attentiveness to and a loving awareness of God—prayer with only an occasional word or none at all. That does not mean we should be doing nothing, like the quiet of a stagnant pond. God frequently insists that we maintain that attentiveness and awareness until we are conscious that we are being moved passively, something that takes experience and spiritual maturity. Then we should let go even of the attentiveness and awareness and follow where God leads. We may occasionally have to drop back briefly to meditation, but as we gain facility we should hang on even though it seems obvious that we are wasting time and doing nothing! A policeman adds dignity by his presence in a courtroom; no one would say he is loafing because he just stands there and says nothing. I found it helpful at the start of a prayer period to mentally bow my head in a few seconds of adoration before the Lord. See nothing, hear nothing, say nothing—just be totally attentive and listening. Above all do not act like a workaholic model who must always be doing something even while the artist is trying to paint his picture.

A policeman adds dignity by his presence in a courtroom; no one would say he is loafing because he just stands there and says nothing.

Night of the Senses

Toward the end of the time spent at the level of prayer of simple regard, after we have begun to open ourselves more to God and have come closer to him by prayer and penance, after getting some control over tendencies which can lead us away from him, God can begin to take a more direct and a larger part in our purification and prepare us for future progress. This is the period of passive purification known as the night of the senses. We had the more active part with our penances, but now God will take the sandpaper in hand and begin the polishing himself. People in the active life will probably find that God does not have to use a lot of special mystical experiences; there is plenty of material at hand from the events of their daily active life. We know that we cannot be attached to both God and creatures. We know we should use creatures inasfar as they help and leave them if they do not. Now God will more actively help us to leave creatures when necessary and also help us free our hearts from desiring them. The latter is absolutely necessary if we are to progress. Natural feelings and desires are no hindrance in our advance towards God. They are involuntary and cannot be eliminated. Modern psychology tells us how bad the results can be if we try to suppress and repress them. But it is the voluntary defects that can hinder us badly.

St. John says that we have to work towards the point where we incline ourselves to the more difficult, the harder, the least, the unconsoling. He says there will be trials at this stage. There can be strong temptations against faith, chastity, or hope. From our daily life may come misunderstanding by friends or a feeling of worth-lessness that others may notice. Of course these may be just the ordinary bumps in life, but when they are mystical they will come suddenly, be sharp, and produce good results in the soul. Even if they are the ordinary bumps we should not expect God to prevent them just because we are trying to be his friends. God will use these ordinary bumps to sandpaper and file off the rough edges. We will find that his sandpaper can cut pretty deeply sometimes.

Divisions or Levels in Prayer and Union

A standard list of steps in prayer is:

Active Level
    Meditation
    Affective prayer—activity of the mind simplifies
    Simple regard—activity of will simplifies also
Passive Level
    Prayer of quiet—God holds the will
    Full union—at least the mind is also held
    Ecstatic union—senses also blocked
    Transforming union—spiritual marriage.

This list is of some use in noticing what we have already passed, but does not help us much in determining where we are now. It can be useful in guiding someone else. God may not want us to know where we are so that we learn to concentrate on him and follow where he is leading. We have to learn to follow him with the trust of a little child going for a walk. When God made each one of us he broke the mold. God gave us that uniqueness and safeguards it. God works with each one of us individually, taking us from where we are and leading us forward. So my path will not match yours, nor what is in the books.

From the beginning of our life to the end, our actions are always a mixture of active and passive—all the way from 99.9% active to 99.9% passive. At the active level we can easily speak of levels of prayer, but at the passive level it would seem more correct to speak of levels of union with God. With grace, at the active level we can work towards any one of the three forms of prayer, but at the passive level we have no choice. Whether we are even at the passive level at all with its particular type of union depends on God's choice and activity. Even God cannot help us develop to those levels. He can put us there if he chooses, probably after we have worked with him for a long time. Even when we are most active, if it is only wanting to think a good thought—"Without me you can do nothing"—we must accept the help of God's grace or we cannot.

An analogy may help to clarify the difference between "I take the initiative and do something" and "God moves me passively." Suppose I am driving to a big city to visit a friend. I do not know where he lives, and for some reason a map will not help. You know and volunteer to go with me. I drive the car—I am active—but I have to follow your directions; so I am partly passive too. Unfortunately we have to cross through downtown during the rush hour. I have never driven much in city traffic, so you drive or we may never get there. You drive the car and now I am mostly passive, just sitting there accepting what you are doing. It is still my free action and I am responsible. I can always give up and tell you to get out; or I can turn off the ignition and just sit there. Hopefully I do not panic and reach for the steering wheel or the brakes.

So in the spiritual life there are shifts in percentages. In the beginning, though we have a more active part we are also passive; we must have God's grace or we cannot do anything good. But when God puts us at the passive level he becomes much more active, and our activity consists in accepting what he is doing to and with us. "God moves me passively" is the standard statement, but some activity on our side is still necessary. In fact if we take no part at all it is not a human act and we are not responsible. Besides, God will never force us to go where we do not want to go. He will coax, invite, and facilitate. He will offer grace to help; he will let us get into situations where we cannot do it alone so that we learn to ask for his help. God will even stretch us so we can do what we never even thought possible—but he will never force us.

As we discuss the next four levels of passive union it is usually said that from the prayer of quiet to ecstatic union is basically the same grace differing only in degree. The tar-paper shack, the ordinary house, the million-dollar palace are all residences differing only in degree. We can expect to shift back and forth between these three levels as God desires, even in the same prayer period.

Distractions

I have become conscious of three kinds of distractions. In the first two kinds, even though we cannot seem to keep our attention on God because the mind and the imagination seem to be running wild, still somehow there can be a vague desire to continue praying. Even with the wandering mind God can be holding the will in contact with himself, as is shown by our reaction to an outright temptation to quit. Become conscious of that desire to continue, notice that for some reason the prayer somehow still does seem to do us some good, and try not to be too discouraged; God is still working underneath. If God were not holding the will, it would just follow the distractions.

The first type of distraction is light and fluffy; we can often stop it almost with a slight wave of the hand. The second type is a real bother. It is almost like an endless tape that just keeps repeating itself at full volume no matter what we do. Sometimes a mantra may help. "Jesus" or "God, I love you" can be repeated with each breath until the distraction is gone. Sometimes it might be better to shift briefly to spiritual reading or vocal prayer instead. But we should use some discernment too. It might be the Lord trying hard to get our attention when we do not want to listen. In the third type of distraction the will has followed the distraction and we have quit praying. Then we suddenly stop, give ourselves a little shake, and try to get back to praying again.

Again, sometimes we can go for long periods and wonder whether we have been praying or sleeping. With no thoughts in the mind, with no acts of the will, how can we be sure we are praying? We may remember that we did not consciously quit praying and that we did and do not sense the Lord criticizing us. Yet the whole time seemed like one big distraction. But when we check we may realize that we do not seem to have lost ground but in fact have somehow improved a little in our fidelity to the Lord. In a way we cannot account for, we must have been doing some praying or we would certainly have slid backwards during that time. In spite of the distractions, we can learn that God can be working and holding the will united to himself even with a wandering mind.

Another thing to keep in mind is that we cannot stop the mind from thinking, or the memory from remembering, or the imagination from imagining. If we try to stop them by ourselves we will just break our heads. At most we can dampen their activity a little by trying to hold them to one point. We can control the imagination by glancing at the tabernacle or a cross or a picture regularly and control the mind by repeating the same Scripture text or some word or phrase again and again. God can tie these faculties down by keeping them busy elsewhere or by controlling their activity at such a low level that we do not notice.

Mystical Union

The word *mystical* is often used to mean *strange* or *unusual* or even just *out of the ordinary*. By mystical I mean something that even with special graces we cannot reach, that we cannot produce even in a low degree, even momentarily, by our own efforts. It is something that we cannot work up to, that we cannot deserve, that we cannot merit, that we cannot start or intensify or prolong. Sometimes we might be able to prevent or to stop it, but we cannot always do even that. When St. John of the Cross talks about mystical he crosses off almost everything that is popularly labeled as such—visions (and he always includes odors and sounds too), ecstasies, revelations, and prophecies. He says that we should not even waste time trying to decide whether they come from God or the devil or ourselves. He always insists that faith is the only way to get close to God and that the closer something is related to the senses the less sure we can be of its divine origin.

It is only through the senses that the devil can get at us. Even if these visions did come from God, if we ignore them they will have already produced their good effect and we will be putting our hearts on God and not on the sweets that he might offer us. John also says that ecstasies will taper off as the person advances because he or she will no longer be thrown off balance by the sight of spiritual things. An increase in virtue is a truer sign of progress than any of these side effects or personal psychological reactions.

Contemplation

Contemplation means a simple, quiet, peaceful gaze at something without going into all the details. There can be contemplation at a perfectly natural level. I can look at my mother and ignore all the particular details of hairdo and dress. I can take in the general atmosphere of a painting and ignore the brushwork or colors at each particular point.

When spiritual writers use the word *contemplation* we have to check carefully to see what they mean. Some use the word for anything opposed to action (vocal prayer, even a lifestyle), or they may mean any level after meditation (affective prayer), or they may use the word for anything past the active level (prayer of quiet). Modern writers often speak of active contemplation (the prayer of simple regard) and of infused or passive contemplation (all degrees at the passive level). In active contemplation (with God's grace always) I do most of the work. I "look" at God or one of his truths—a simple gaze without moving systematically through a continuing series of steps of acts of mind and/or will. At the infused (passive) level God takes the initiative, determining the moment, the manner, the duration; he moves me passively. When God begins to move me passively, my part is to accept and cooperate with what he does to me. He can work directly on the mind or on the will, infusing knowledge or love, without my being required to follow the usual (natural) steps. Since God does not follow the usual steps (sense to imagination to mind to will) we can easily find ourselves in the position that we know and/or understand or we suddenly grow in love and cannot explain how either to ourselves or to others. In the prayer of quiet and that of full union, the contemplation will often be at such a low level that we will not be conscious of it though we can suspect that it was there by the results in our lives.

I will have to describe this prayer of quiet from the books because in my case I am not sure whether the Lord skipped this level. At least he never brought it to my attention, and I still cannot say that I was ever at this level. The most I can say is that I can verify all of St. Teresa's signs, and for some years I was puzzled by occasional deep absorption where an hour or more of prayer could pass and I would think it was only a few minutes.

At the level of union called the prayer of quiet we have the start of infused contemplation, and we are at the strictly mystical level. Up to now our prayer had depended mostly on our individual initiative, but now God's activity becomes the dominant factor. In the prayer of quiet God begins to hold the will in contact with himself even though the other powers of the soul are free and may continue to function on their own. We will probably find that, since we have to use most of our energy to work with God, we will not have enough left to control these powers and so they often run wild.

The prayer of quiet is a baffling mixture of darkness and light.

The prayer of quiet is a baffling mixture of darkness and light. At the start we may notice only a suddenly deep recollection that soon passes and we are back where we were. Or sometimes there will be some thought of God that recurs often during the day, almost in spite of ourselves. We may slowly realize that it happens and we do not seem to be able to make it happen. It can develop to the point where it is nearly habitual so that we can enter this prayer almost at will. Almost—like any mystical action we cannot start or intensify or prolong it but we can prepare ourselves and be receptive if God decides to move us. At times God does seem to bring some people here briefly and temporarily and then drops them back where they were. Only God knows why he does not keep them here permanently. The biggest characteristic of this prayer is its variability. We can expect the prayer to shift quickly, even during the same prayer period. At times if the union is strong it may interfere even with external activity, or it may persist right in the midst of that activity and neither one hurts the other. St. Teresa gives some signs of this level that we may find growing in our own lives and have not paid attention to. She says that souls will now have more freedom from worry that they might not get to heaven, from fear that penances might hurt their health, from fear of trials that might come. She says they will probably notice that their faith is more alive, that they are starting to withdraw more from worldly delights and are more interested in God. I find that all of these are verified in my own life, though I would be unable to pinpoint when they began to show up clearly. We will also notice that from this level and on, prayer is less strenuous than when we meditated. That is why some of the saints could work sixteen hours a day, and then pray for another three or four, and thrive on it.

We think of faith as believing someone, but faith is also a way of learning and knowing. By supernatural faith we learn things about God that we could never find out by studying creatures. Starting at the prayer of quiet we are getting a new and supernatural way of knowing—infused contemplation. We learn by a special inspiration of the Holy Spirit. Because it is supernatural it does not necessarily follow our previous (natural) ways of learning. Because it is supernatural and comes a different way, there will be no satisfaction to the powers of mind and soul that we have previously used. That is why God has started to block the activity of our minds, and so forth. He does not want them to hold our attention as they previously did and prevent his working directly on us.

Prayer of Full Union

Some authors prefer to omit the word *full* in the label. From here on things will start to get more fuzzy. The person may know perfectly well what has happened but is less and less able to verbalize it. And of course there is always the difficulty of trying to think about some supernatural event when we are back at the natural level afterwards. There will be less and less that we can tell our spiritual directors and that they can tell us. At this level, both the mind and the will are held by God, but the action of the memory and imagination can vary. They may be held so tight that there are no distractions at all, or they may suspect what is going on and so try to cooperate with the will (it will often be a Dennis the Menace cooperation) or they may act like spoiled children who are being left out and declare a veritable war on the will. Sometimes God will hold everything so tight that we will wonder what has happened to the time. We may feel that we were only praying for a few minutes and the clock says that an hour or more has passed.

At this level there will be a growing certitude of God's presence. By faith we know that God is everywhere, but that he is not the same everywhere. Beginning at the prayer of quiet and growing stronger, there can be an experiential realization that God is present in a new and special way. We will experience his presence, instead of merely knowing about it. At first it will be at such a low level that it may not be perceptible, but the sense of nearness will grow and strengthen. Since we can understand sense analogies easiest, this contact is often described as a touch. To modify what St. Teresa said about seeing God, of course we cannot touch a spirit, but there is a method of contact between spirits that is analogous to our sense of touch, an immediate and close contact unlike sight which can contact from a distance.

At first this union will be of short duration and then we are back to the prayer of quiet. Its effects will show as an increased zeal to make God known and loved, an increased detachment from creatures, a more perfect submission to God's will, a greater charity towards our neighbor.

Ecstatic Union☊

At this level there is an intense attention to God or to some spiritual subject, and all the powers of the soul are held by the action of God. The senses, mind, will, imagination, and memory are all blocked so that nothing can get in to them, and they cannot come out even if they wish. This state may come on slowly or it may not be intense, or it may hit suddenly almost with a feeling of violence. St. Teresa says that at times there can be such a strong feeling of transport that it cannot be an error. In the case where it hits suddenly and hard it is often known as rapture rather than simple ecstasy. Usually a full ecstasy lasts for only a short time, though it may take even days to get back to normal. The person will remember clearly what has been learned, even though he or she cannot verbalize it. One check on the authenticity of this union is that while it is going on the person usually will come out at the command of a legitimate superior. If the ecstasy seems to last a long time, it probably is not genuine. Teresa gives the example of a nun who could go for eight hours without a thought of God or of anything else either. Her remedy: reduce the prayer, reduce the penance, put her at work outside in the garden until her health recovers.

Transforming Union

Another common name for this union is spiritual marriage. The note that seems to be common at this stage is some sort of almost permanent intellectual vision of the Trinity or of some divine attribute. This level tends to be permanent and does not shift back and forth like the preceding ones. Some are conscious of God almost taking over their higher faculties so that another name for this is transforming union. This union tends to persist during external occupations, and in some cases even during sleep. In many people this union often starts with visions and with the elaborate symbolism of betrothal, marriage, and wedding ring.

Conclusion

So what do we mean by progress in prayer? Over the years as we progress, our prayer should simplify—fewer and fewer acts of the mind and the will until it becomes an intuitive loving gaze, with God taking the more active part. As we grow closer and closer to God, our prayer should change. It should make a difference to our prayer when we are barely acquaintances of God and afraid to get too near him, and when he is our very dear friend to whom we are completely open. When we are talking to strangers it can get a little embarrassing if no one says anything for a minute, yet we can be comfortable with a friend although no one is saying anything at all. So our prayer should be different when we can just look at God and say nothing, when we no longer have to keep up a constant chatter so that he does not get a chance to tell us something we do not want to hear.

In my own life I now spend almost as much time in prayer as I do sleeping. When I get to bed on time I try to pray three to four hours in the morning before Mass. Though I do not do much with a split attention that can act and pray at the same time, during the more mechanical actions I can keep the attention on God and let the subconscious take care of the activity. Of course the more intellectual actions will demand the whole attention. In my pastoral ministry I celebrate about six hundred and fifty Masses a year, so I am hardly a Carthusian. Fortunately I am not bothered by any tendency to shun action because I want to pray; either one is what God wants me to be doing at that particular time.

PAUL WACHDORF

Leading People into Prayer

*F*or the past six years I have served as a spiritual director for the theologians at Mundelein Seminary, the graduate school of theology of the Archdiocese of Chicago. An increasing number of our incoming students have never been in a seminary. Frequently their knowledge of the history and teachings of the church and of the various prayer traditions of the church is at a very basic level. Some come with no prayer life at all. For others, their experience of prayer is limited to saying prayers, occasionally reading from the Bible, or talking to God. One of the challenges I have faced as a director in working with these students is to lead them into a deeper experience of prayer.

prayer apostolate

Out of my experience of the last six years, I would like to share some of the insights and practical wisdom that I have found helpful in working with these students. Although I have worked primarily with seminary students, I believe that what I have to say can be helpful to anyone working with beginners in prayer: spiritual directors, RCIA facilitators, pastoral-care ministers, homilists, prayer-group leaders, and many others. It is very important to be aware of the special issues and concerns that beginners in prayer face as they seek to come before God.

The Foundational Conviction

The most important insight that I have come to is this: God leads people into prayer. Through God's own invitations, people come to prayer in their own good time and way. As a director I can invite people to a life of prayer. I can walk with them in their attempts to pray. I can help to facilitate their movement into prayer. But I cannot make them pray, and I cannot control the movement or the experience of God in their prayer.

As a director I have had to face my own impatience and desire to have someone become a person of prayer overnight. I have come to see that there are many starts and stops; but, over time, people are given the gift of prayer. Prayer cannot be forced. It is a conversion experience. When people come to experience first-hand the power of God at work in their lives and prayer, then prayer becomes something that they want to do and not something I expect them to do or something they are obligated to do by the church. Until this happens for them, I try as much as possible to affirm their fledgling efforts to pray and to be understanding and accepting of them in their failures, their discouragement, and their resistances as they attempt to pray.

Beginning by Doing

When I meet with prospective spiritual directees, I tell them that one expectation I have of them is that they commit themselves to developing a regular prayer life. Furthermore, within the context of spiritual direction, I want them to talk about what happens to them when they do pray. I also tell them that I am not going to dictate to them how, when, or how often they should pray, nor am I going to scold them in their failures or difficulties with prayer.

I am not indifferent about their prayer life. Within the framework of God's gift and their freedom, I try to be an accountability factor. What is a value to me, I want to be a value for them. In addition, I tell them that their commitment to prayer insures that what we do within the context of spiritual direction becomes more than just guidance and counseling. Some of those I direct have told me that my invitation to prayer has been an important stimulus in their attempts to develop their own prayer life.

In Solidarity and With Support

At Mundelein Seminary, the full-time members of the formation team commit themselves to an hour of personal prayer every morning in our house chapel. We invite the students to join us in our time of prayer, and many of them do. In this hour of quiet time with God, there is a solidarity that develops among us. Many of our students have said that this daily commitment of the formation team to prayer has been an important witness and invitation to them in their own prayer life.

Related to this, on occasion I have invited a student I am directing to join me for this time of quiet prayer. We have used a common prayer form or passage from Scripture as the basis of our prayer. Afterwards we spent some time talking about what we experienced in our prayer. Within the context of direction, I try to share on a limited basis, and whenever I feel it is appropriate, some of the content of my own prayer life and what happens to me when I pray.

These two things have helped some of my beginners in prayer to come to an experiential insight into what can happen when they open themselves up to God in prayer and to understand what prayer in general and what specific prayer forms can be like for them.

The Spiritual Dialogue about Prayer

When I first meet with new spiritual directees, I ask them to spend some time telling me their life history. Among other things, I ask them to tell me about their prayer life and their experiences and images of God. In particular, I ask them if they have ever had what they consider to be a religious experience or a powerful experience of God at work in their lives.

What I have found is not only that many of those I direct have had such experiences but also that these experiences have played an important part in their own vocational discernment and their understanding of God.

I have also found that people feel very shy or embarrassed about having had such an experience, have never told anyone about it before, and have a difficult time articulating just what the experience was like. As a director I find that it is very important for me to listen carefully to what they have to say, to reassure them that they are not weird or crazy, to invite them to explore further what they have experienced, and to give them permission to talk about such experiences as they might occur in the future.

During the course of direction, I ask people to talk about their prayer life in terms of consistency, method, content, and inner feelings associated with praying. Initially they find this difficult since they frequently lack the language to talk about what happens interiorly when they pray. Very often they have not developed the ability to sit quietly for any extended period of time, to notice what they are feeling, and to distinguish the difference between distractions and movements of God.

As we begin, I encourage people to talk about whatever they thought or felt or experienced in their prayer, whether they considered it to be significant or not. I find it important for me to move slowly and to be patient with their attempts not only to pray but also to notice and talk about their experience of prayer. I also find that I need to be sensitive to their desire to please me, to do well in their prayer, or to have something significant to say. I need to reassure them that whatever happens in their attempts to pray is fine with me and is pleasing to God.

Related to these considerations is another question we examine early on: For whom is prayer intended? Is it primarily for my benefit, for what I get out of it? Or is it primarily for God? If prayer is just for my benefit and if nothing seems to be happening, I will feel it is a waste of time and will be tempted to give it up.

On the other hand, if prayer is for God, it does not make any difference if anything "productive" seems to be happening. Even if it feels like a waste of time to me, I am praying because I am giving my time to God in a way that says that my relationship with God is primary. The fact that I am consistently present to God in my prayer is initially far more important than what I do or what happens when I pray. When people come to a different understanding of what prayer is and for whom it is intended, they relax and are more open as they approach prayer.

Resistances, Difficulties, and Dryness

Beginners in prayer are usually eager and enthusiastic as they begin to develop and deepen their prayer lives and to experiment with new prayer forms. They may experience in new and surprising ways the power of God at work in their prayer.

As time passes, however, and they run into resistances, difficulties, and dryness in their prayer, they may become discouraged and disheartened with their prayer life. They may feel as if God has abandoned them. It is important to help them understand the dynamics of what is going on in their prayer. A list of some of the common difficulties that tend to make prayer difficult for beginners follows:

Called to a Different Prayer

Frequently the difficulties encountered by beginners in prayer are connected to being called by God to a different way of praying, to a deeper level of prayer. Although this is true for all prayers, it is especially true for beginners.

My experience with beginners in prayer is that they soon discover that the ways of prayer taught them as children and carried with them into adolescence and young adulthood are no longer satisfying to them. It is important to let them explore their dissatisfactions and new yearnings and to help them see that perhaps God is calling them to a different, deeper way of praying.

Wondering What to Do

Exploring different ways of praying, however, often brings beginners to another difficulty: They do not know how to begin or what to do in their time of prayer. They are intimidated by silence and fear that nothing is going to happen or that they will be plagued by distractions. When they are unfocused as they come to prayer, when they have no sense of how to open themselves up to God so that God can enter into their lives, prayer will be extremely difficult for them.

I find it is important to explore with beginners what prayer is, what attitudes to bring to prayer, how to interpret and deal with distractions, and what prayer techniques may suit them and open them up to God.

If they know their Myers-Briggs type indicator, I offer to go over with them some of the research that has been done on prayer and temperament. One resource I would suggest is the book *Prayer and Temperament* by Chester Michael and Marie Norrisey (Charlottesville, Va.: The Open Door, 1984). The Myers-Briggs type indicator seems to be a limited but useful tool in helping people to understand how they approach the world. This understanding can put them in touch with a favored and a shadow side of prayer, an insight that can open them to a sense of God at work in their lives.

Unworthiness

Another difficulty beginners face is the feeling that they are not worthy to pray. More specifically, they feel unworthy to come before God, that they have nothing worthwhile to offer to God, and that they are not worthy to receive anything from God in their time of prayer. These feelings are often connected with earlier lifestyles which now cause shame. Sometimes they are connected with images of God which portray God as a perfectionist or as a harsh, impersonal, unforgiving judge who punishes wrongdoing. I find that it is important to let people freely explore their life histories, their images of God, and their own sense of unworthiness .

Looking at All Facets of Life

I encourage those I direct to get in touch with their feelings and to tell God in their prayer what they are feeling, thinking, and experiencing. This tends to bring into focus several related difficulties for beginners in prayer.

The first is their image of God as all-knowing. If God is all-knowing, why should they bother to express what God already knows?

A second is that they are often not in touch with what they are feeling or with inner movements which might or might not be of God. They have never cultivated the reflective side of their lives.

A third is that they are frequently suspicious of emotions, especially those they consider to be negative or sinful, such as anger, lust, or despair. They have a difficult time admitting to themselves that they have such emotions. And even when they do, how, for example, could they possibly express to God their angry feelings? Such feelings can be very threatening to them and can reinforce their sense of unworthiness before God.

It is important to help beginners get in touch with their feelings and thoughts, to claim them in a nonjudgmental way, and to begin to express them to God in their prayer. As they do this, God is able to be with them as they are and as he wants to be with them.

The Right Time and Place

Difficulties in prayer can also be related to lifestyle and environment. A poor environment, such as the clutter of their rooms where there are many distractions, can make prayer difficult. I encourage beginners to explore various prayer environments to help them discover a place where they can be with God in peace.

The time of day for prayer is important. "Morning" people or "night" people need to adjust prayer times according to their natural biological rhythms. I encourage people to find a time of day when they can give quality prayer time to God, a time of alertness and concentration.

The general rhythm of life affects prayer. A scattered life or a life out of balance will not help prayer. One needs a regular and rhythmic balance of work, play, and attending to relationships. I encourage people to examine their life patterns because a healthy life is related to healthy prayer.

Difficulties in prayer can also be related to lifestyle and environment.

Consistent Commitment

Inconsistency or not enough time given to prayer can make prayer difficult. The development of a healthy, loving, life-giving relationship between any two people requires that they spend sufficient, consistent, quality time together. Our relationship with God is no different. If God is to be present to us as God truly desires, we have to make time for this relationship to develop. It is important to explore with beginners the discipline of consistent prayer.

Wasting Time with God

In the midst of the hectic pace of modern life, it is difficult to find time to pray. Often, for pragmatic, production-oriented Americans, prayer seems like a waste of time. People can always think of "better" ways to spend their time. The need that beginners have for productive prayer is one that needs to be carefully explored. I encourage them to see prayer as an opportunity to waste time gracefully with God.

Dealing with Setbacks

When people miss prayer for a day or two or three, they become discouraged. They may want to give up on prayer. My response is encouragement. When they miss, they do not need to get upset or give up on prayer as a lost cause. I tell them to come back. Prayer is a decision that continually needs to be renewed. If they fall, they should simply get up and start over again. God, I believe, is not all that interested in how many times they have fallen. God is more interested in how many times they got back up and started over again.

Desolation

In his Rules for the Discernment of Spirits, Week One [322], St. Ignatius suggests three important reasons why we suffer desolation or difficulty in prayer. David Fleming SJ, in *The Spiritual Exercises of St. Ignatius: A Literal Translation and a Contemporary Reading* (St. Louis: The Institute of Jesuit Sources, 1978, pp. 210-211), "reads" the text of St. Ignatius as follows:

> 1. It is our own fault because we have not lived our life of faith with any effort. We have become tepid and slothful and our very shallowness in the spiritual life has brought about the experience of desolation;
>
> 2. it is a trial period allowed by God. We find ourselves tested as to whether we love God or just love his gifts, whether we continue to follow his call in darkness and dryness as well as in light and consolation;
>
> 3. it is a time when God lets us experience our own poverty and need. We see more clearly that the free gift of consolation is not something we can control, buy, or make our own.

These Ignatian guidelines are geared for beginning Christians. When explained properly, they can be helpful in giving beginning pray-ers some insight into what might be happening in their prayer.

Prayer in Direction

I invite those I direct to take time, if they are comfortable in doing so, to join me in prayer at the beginning and/or at the end of our sessions together. My/our prayer might be spontaneous or more formal. As we begin, the prayer is a simple petition inviting God to be a part of our time together and asking for the guidance of the Holy Spirit. As we end, the prayer might be a moment of thanksgiving or praise to God for the ways in which the Spirit works in our lives and in the process of spiritual direction.

It is important not to force this. Beginners in prayer are not usually very comfortable praying out loud or spontaneously. At the same time, such prayer does sensitize beginning pray-ers to the importance of continually inviting God to enter into their lives and of noticing and acknowledging the ways in which God can and does act in their lives.

Conclusion

My experience is that leading people to prayer is an art and not a science. There is no one textbook approach that works for everyone. Prayer is something very personal and unique. It is a special relationship that develops over time between God and the pray-er. People come to prayer in their own good time and way. As a spiritual director, I cannot make prayer happen; but I can help to facilitate this loving relationship. In working with beginners in prayer, I do not apply the suggestions I have offered in this article in any structured or systematic way; but I have found that there are certain common themes and experiences that it is good for me as a spiritual director to be aware of as I seek to lead people under the influence and guidance of the Holy Spirit into a life of prayer.

Called to Unity—Called to Mission

> I pray not only for these but for those who through their teaching will come to believe in me. May they be one, Father, just as you are in me and I am in you, so that they also may be in us, so that the world may believe it was you who sent me. I have given them the glory you gave to me, that they may be one as we are one. With me in them and you in them, may they be so perfected in unity that the world will know that it was you who sent me and that you have loved them as you loved me. (Jn 17:20-23)

*U*nity stands as the principal theme in this section of Jesus' high priestly prayer, it stands as a last will and testament, it stands as an expression of his deepest hopes for his disciples and for all believers throughout the ages. The unity for which Jesus prays is no exercise in mutual admiration, nor even is it the art of living peaceably with others. The unity for which Jesus prays is an apostolic force empowered by love, this unity is born of his "new commandment: love one another; you must love one another just as I have loved you" (Jn 13:34).

In contemporary religious life, community and ministry are frequently viewed and sometimes approached as two separate parts of everyday life. The activities of each are distinct it is true, but both draw time and energy from the same pool, a rapidly depleted one at that. There is much discussion today on the importance of living an integrated and balanced religious life. The temptation, in participating in this discussion, is to make temporary adjustments in daily life, pretending that these will become permanent fixtures. The fact is that integration and balance will never be realized by the juggling of time and energy which attempts to achieve equal distribution among all the essential elements of religious life. Such an attempt fails to recognize the differences of quantity and even quality of time and energy required by each element. True integration and balance are fostered by realistic proportionality, not pretentious regularity.

Underlying the adjustments of time and energy necessary in living an integrated and balanced life of community and ministry is the importance of understanding these two elements of religious life as intrinsically related to and interwoven with one another. The unity for which Jesus prayed is apostolic, the mission to which he calls us is communal. These present reflections will concentrate on the first part of this relationship: the apostolic nature of community.

It must be noted from the outset that apostolic community is not synonymous with ministerial uniformity. The apostolic nature of community has to do with the quality of life among the members, not the quantity of members in the same ministry.

Standard of Unity

At the very beginning of this section of his prayer, Jesus identifies those for whom he is praying: his present disciples and all future believers. Then he prays, "May they all be one, Father, just as you are in me and I am in you." Jesus establishes as a standard of unity nothing less than the caliber of the relationship which unites him with the Father. Even a cursory examination of that relationship in John's gospel reveals unity as its dominant characteristic: "I and the Father are one" (10:30). Jesus and the Father are one in work (5:17), honor (5:23), life (5:26), knowledge (10:15), and possessions (16:15). To know and see the Son is to know and see the Father (8:19; 14:9). The Son sends his disciples even as he has been sent by the Father (20:21). "I tell you the truth: the Son can do nothing on his own; he only does what he sees his Father doing. What the Father does, the Son also does" (5:19).

Such should be the unity among members of a religious community: practical, pervasive, and productive. The practicality of unity lies in its rootedness in everyday life. This is no theoretical unity, existing only in pious words but having little relationship to the routines and struggles of daily life. This unity must be lived in such a way that community members are sincerely involved in one another's lives.

Community is a convocation, not a crowd. Our call from the Lord is to live a particular way of life with others. The pervasiveness of the unity to which we are called lies in its comprehensive approach to life. This is no restricted unity which touches only part of life and abandons the rest as insignificant. This unity must be lived in such a way that community members share their lives and values, their hopes and possessions with one another.

Community is a commitment, not a convenience. It is a choice we make to share who we are and what we have with others in response to the same call we have received. The productivity of unity lies in its natural ability to extend itself. This is no insular unity which rests content with mere camaraderie among members of the community. Unity must be lived in such a way that community members seek always to be involved with and have an impact upon the world around them. Community is a commission, not a clique. It is a channel through which we are an example of love to others.

Such is the unity of Jesus with his Father. Such must also be the unity among religious. Apart from this kind of unity, our life together comes soon to resemble little more than a crowd, a convenience, and a clique. But united in the love to which we are called, our life together rather becomes a means of transformation for each of us, for all of us, for the church, and for the world. This is the apostolic standard of our community life.

Function of Unity

As Jesus continues his prayer we discover that he establishes this high standard: "May they be one . . . so that they also may be in us, so that the world may believe it was you who sent me."

There is a twofold function here. First, unity is the means by which our life together participates in the very life of the Father and the Son. This unity is the verification of our fidelity to Jesus' standard. Second, unity is the means by which others come to have faith in Jesus as the One sent by the Father. Our unity is an invitation for others to follow the Gospel way of life. This verification and invitation have no resemblance to the kind of pharisaism which seeks for itself attention, honor, and glory. Quite the contrary, the function of this unity is to certify the work of God's grace among us.

Such is the task of unity. We cannot support a claim of participation in divine life if our everyday life does not reflect our efforts toward union with one another. "Anyone who says, 'I love God,' and hates his neighbor is a liar; since whoever does not love the neighbor whom he can see cannot love God whom he has not seen" (1 Jn 4:20). In the same way, the call to faith that we proclaim is clearly articulated only if our life together shows evidence of the love underlying that faith. "Everyone will know you are my disciples if you have love for one another" (Jn 13:35). Jesus does not say what others will know if we do not have love for one another—but surely we will not be recognized as his disciples. Possibly, the disparity between the proclamation of our words and the practice of our lives could be so great that we would not be worthy of recognition at all. The Acts of the Apostles records that the early Christian community was looked up to, honored with a respect based upon its unity and its generosity. There is evidence of a sharing in the divine life here, and so "day by day the Lord added to their community those destined to be saved" (2:47). The early Christians lived the love which made them recognizable as followers of Jesus, and they lived the unity which attracted others to their way of life.

Unity is the means by which our life together participates in the very life of the Father and the Son.

Such must be the task of unity among religious. Apart from this unity, our life together closes in on itself, diminishes its sensitivity to the presence and activity of God, and fails to respond to the need and longing of others. United in the love to which we are called, our life together reflects the relationship between Jesus and his Father, even as it invites others to share the life of faith they see with us. This is the apostolic function of our community life.

Means to Unity

Jesus continues to pray: "I have given them the glory you gave to me, that they may be one as we are one." Jesus provides the means by which his followers will be united; he passes on the glory he received from the Father. "Glory" is a rich concept in both the Old and New Testaments; it refers to the visible manifestation of God's presence. In the Old Testament the "glory" of God was manifest in the cloud and the fire which signaled his guidance during the Exodus. "During the day the Lord went in front of the people in a pillar of cloud to show them the way, and during the night he went in front of them in a pillar of fire to give them light, so that they could travel day and night" (Ex

13:21). In the New Testament the glory of God is manifest in Jesus himself. "The Word became flesh and, full of grace and truth, lived among us. We saw his glory, the glory which he received as the Father's only Son" (Jn 1:14). This same "glory" is Jesus' gift to his followers, it is a gift which enables them to incarnate the life of love which unites the Father and the Son. This gift of glory is fully realized in the unity which marks the life of Jesus' followers, for unity is an incarnation of divine life.

Such is the way to unity. The "glory" of religious community is most profoundly evident when the members seek to be united. To the degree that community members are one, to that degree are they reflections of God's presence and activity, to that degree are they truly alive. It is no platitude, then, when the Psalmist declares "how good, how delightful it is, for all God's people to live together in harmony" (133:1). Unity is good and delightful, even blessed, for "there Yahweh bestows his blessing: everlasting life" (133:3). However, if a community is marked by selfishness and division, then it is neither good, nor delightful, nor blessed. It witnesses to nothing but its own myopic interests and petty concerns. It reflects nothing of the presence and activity of God, it does not radiate life. "I know you have the reputation of being alive, even though you are dead!" (Rv 3:1). Community life can be glorious (in the biblical sense of revealing God's presence), or it can be vacuous (in the etymological sense of having no substance).

Such is the call to unity that must be heard among religious. Apart from this unity, our life together drifts, we become a mere conglomerate of individuals whose lives intersect only randomly and accidentally. United in the love to which we are called, our life together moves ever closer to the incarnation of the glory which Jesus gave to us, the glory which is deep within us, the glory which reveals the Lord to others through us.

Goal of Unity

"With me in them and you in them, may they be so perfected in unity that the world will know that it was you who sent me and that you have loved them as you loved me." Jesus brings this section of his prayer to a focal point by indicating the goal toward which unity is directed. It is twofold. First, the world will know that the Father has sent his Son. This echoes a truth which John proclaimed earlier in his gospel: "God so loved the world that he gave his only Son that whoever believes in him will not die but have eternal life" (3:16). This is the heart of Christian faith, it is in this faith that the followers of Jesus first gathered; it is by this faith that they remained one. Through unity, the Father's love in sending his Son is proclaimed anew. Second, the world will know that the Father loves those who are united in him even as he loves his Son. This echoes Jesus' instruction to his disciples: "I have loved you just as the Father has loved me. Remain in my love. If you keep my commandments you will remain in my love, just as I have kept my Father's commandments and remain in his love" (Jn 15:9-10). This is the example of Jesus. As he has loved, so must we love. Thus we will be loved by the Father even as he loves his Son. Through unity, we live the example of love established by Jesus.

This is the summit of unity. The unity among religious is never for themselves alone, it is for those who are served in their ministries. Jesus promises that the world will know of his mission from the Father and that the world will experience the Father's love. But this knowledge and this experience are not academic accomplishments, they are an experiential learning that is communicated primarily through the integrity and example of those who preach the promises of Jesus. If our unity with one another is "perfected" by our responsiveness to the Lord's presence and activity among us, then the world will know of Jesus' mission, then the world will experience the Father's love. We will have preached the Gospel eloquently, as with one voice, by living the faith we profess. Therein lies the heart of the apostolic nature of community.

Such must be the goal of unity among religious. Apart from this unity, our life together is paralyzed in its ability to affect the world around us. United in the love to which we are called, our life together becomes a significant force for evangelization in our world, it symbolizes the possibility of love among all people, and it incarnates anew the presence and activity of the Lord. This is the apostolic goal of our community life.

Every dimension of the unity for which Jesus prayed is apostolic. The standard of this unity places us in mission by calling us to live, among ourselves and with others, the relationship between Jesus and his Father, a relationship of pure love that touches and transforms all of creation. The function of this unity empowers us in mission to proclaim to others the faith which bonds all Christians to Jesus and to his Father. This unity manifests that the Lord is near, and that he continues his mission in this world through us.

This unity forms us into the image of Jesus as one for others, an image which incarnates the example of love between the Father and the Son which is the standard of our life together. This is the fulfillment of Jesus' prayer, "Father, I made your name known to them, and I will continue to make it known, so that the love you have for me may be in them, and I may be in them" (17:26).

The world in which we religious live and minister needs the witness of apostolic community. It needs a demonstration of love. It needs the affirmation of its efforts for justice and peace, however meager they may be in our world. And it needs to know that justice and peace really are practical possibilities not pious platitudes. It is our mission as religious to meet those needs by providing that witness, demonstration, affirmation, and knowledge. We will do that most effectively through the quality of our life together. If we neglect this mission, then we neglect to live the example which Jesus has given to us. If we fail in this mission, then we fail to continue the work of Jesus.

We are called to unity, we are called to mission. Our life together continues Jesus' mission insofar as we are united with one another. We can do our "good works" and perform our professional tasks even when our common life is riddled with discord. But we deceive ourselves if we believe that our lack of amicability is strictly an internal matter. The truth is that we are public figures, and our inconsistencies do not remain tightly sealed within the walls of our local community. Because of its apostolic nature, our community discloses to others (in varying degrees) the characteristics and the quality of our life with one another. If we live together as nothing more than a collection of individuals, then, as community, we will never meet the standard, nor perform the function, nor utilize the means, nor reach the goal of the unity for which Jesus so fervently prayed. Therefore,

> do your utmost to support your faith with goodness, goodness with understanding, understanding with self-control, self-control with perseverance, perseverance with devotion, devotion with kindness to one another, and kindness to one another with love. The possession and growth of these qualities will prevent your knowledge of our Lord Jesus Christ from being ineffective or unproductive. (2 P 1:5-8)

Models of Faith Sharing

One of the frequent complaints about religious life today concerns the superficiality of community life. With different ministries or jobs, different schedules and preferences, religious often feel they have no time or energy to invest in relationships with one another. They look with envy at lay people who are involved in small faith communities or twelve-step groups that foster sharing of personal concerns and spirituality. They say (at least to themselves), "I thought this was what religious life was supposed to be like. What happened? These groups are stealing our fire—and I am feeling left out."

In my work with religious in retreats and spiritual direction, I often hear this longing for some kind of deeper experience of community. Over the years, perhaps, we have grown better at things like assertiveness, respecting individual differences, and communal problem solving. But the missing ingredient appears to be that which ought to bind us most closely: *the sharing of our faith*. Ironically, religious seem to be the least likely people to engage in this kind of exchange. Part of the reason has to do with certain fears, which I will touch on later; the other part is simply a lack of clarity about the purpose and methods of faith sharing—which is what prompted me to write this article.

First we need to distinguish faith sharing from a couple of other endeavors. One is *social analysis*, whereby we look at a concrete problem we have come up against in our community life or ministry and start probing into root causes of the problem. For instance, we notice that more people than ever are coming to our door asking for food, clothing, or shelter. That fact might lead us to examine, as a community, what is happening in our neighborhood, our city, and even our nation to create this situation. Our social analysis may then enable us to take some action beyond sharing our own resources with the needy. We might, for example, get other concerned citizens to help us lobby the city council to organize a holistic community response to the increased unemployment in the area.

Another form of sharing is *theological reflection*. Here we again begin with some concrete experience (either individual or communal) that has generated some emotional response (pleasant or unpleasant) within myself or in the whole community. An experience of success or failure in ministry, getting a bad medical report, loss of a friendship, a conversation that energized us, an event on the news that got us stirred up, a provocative book or conference—any of these can be the occasion for theological reflection. We use the experience (and the feelings it aroused) to search more deeply into the meaning of the event and its connection with God's activity in human history. We discuss with each other questions like: What is the connection between this "story" and the larger story of Christian revelation (Scripture and Tradition)? Does it remind me/us of any biblical passage or theological truth? Can I/we discern the presence and action of God in this event? What might God be calling me/us to through this experience? So theological reflection is just that: an attempt to think theologically (and hence more deeply) about experiences that we might otherwise allow to slip away from our memory. This kind of reflection can be done individually, but it is generally much more valuable when it takes place in a group setting.

> *An experience of success or failure in ministry, a conversation that energized us, an event on the news that got us stirred up —any of these can be the occasion for theological reflection.*

The Notion and Value of Faith Sharing

Faith sharing, in general, is an attempt to share with our brothers and sisters at a deeper level than we do ordinarily. We do not merely "swap stories" about the good old days ("Remember that time when we . . .") or about the present ("I had a bizarre phone call today"); we do not debate the merits and drawbacks of inclusive language; we do not merely reminisce about our growing-up years or our formation days; we do not try to solve all the problems of the church and world. Those are wonderful activities for gathering in the living room or around the kitchen table.

But faith sharing takes a deeper plunge. We let our brothers and sisters in on our inner world of beliefs, values, and commitments—maybe even our doubts and difficulties in believing or in living up to our values:

> "I'm feeling a stronger desire to live poverty more radically."
> "I'm having more and more trouble seeing the presence of Christ in the institutional church."
> "I'm starting to go back and study the Franciscan [or whatever] sources—it's opening me to some new insights and directions for my life."

What is the value of this kind of self-disclosure? For one thing, it is one of the few bases we have left for *bonding* with one another. The religious who went before us—beginning with our founders—had to depend on one another for their very survival. Nowadays, with so many religious having salaried jobs, their own vehicles, credit cards, and so forth, do we need one another?—except for the fact that our brothers and sisters may be the only ones around who care if I am sick, or hurting emotionally, or troubled spiritually. And even then I may have a group of friends outside the community whom I can count on. But—is that what we really want? Have we lost even the desire to be connected to the religious family we once found so attractive? If we have not lost that desire, we will have to find some way to open ourselves to one another and share what is personal and precious to us, so that we may find support for our ideals and values.

Sharing our faith with our brothers and sisters in community can also be a source of healing for our loneliness. Many of us complain that no one in the community really knows us, nor do we know them. Yet we perpetuate the old patterns of superficial relating and avoidance of deeper intimacy. Faith sharing is a way of lowering barriers and reaching that place within each of us where "spirit touches spirit," as I once heard Keith Clark say. Moreover, when we speak and listen to one another at this level, we often find that we are not as alone as we thought we were. As

Carl Rogers used to say, "What is most personal is most general." That is, we often think that we are the only ones who think or feel a certain way. But when we share these inner states with our brothers and sisters, we discover that they have similar experiences, questions, and concerns.

There is one other value in faith sharing: it provides support for our ideals and values. In an increasingly secularized world, such support is not easy to find. The jaded, cynical spirit of our age finds it easy to ridicule gospel values. It is difficult to maintain our commitments and our enthusiasm when so many around us see little sense or meaning in our religious lifestyle. Interestingly, the book *In Search of Excellence* found that corporations which rated high in excellence were characterized by clear vision of goals and purposes. These were articulated often and in appealing ways; they were understood at every level, from the CEO to the maintenance staff; and they were evident in the way people were treated. As a result, workers were enthused about what they were doing because they saw themselves as contributing to some larger project or objective. When I read that, I could not help thinking, "That sounds like what religious life is supposed to be."

Some Basic Assumptions

I am assuming, of course, that there is a desire for this kind of sharing among ourselves. If not, the whole matter becomes moot. But granting that such a desire is present in at least a number of us, there are a couple of other conditions that have to be present if faith sharing is going to be effective. For one thing, religious have to be willing to risk some measure of self-disclosure. Much as I may want to know and be known by others, I do make myself vulnerable when I share some of my personal story and interior states. The risk is that my hearers may not "treasure" what I have shared. They may be threatened by what I say; they may argue with me; they may ridicule me; they may react with indifference.

What will help me overcome my fear of these risks? Some kind of a shared "covenant" that will assure everyone that their disclosures will be received with respect and will be treasured. Moreover, they will be held in confidence, not carried beyond the room. One group I know of uses the image of a "safe house," where each one can feel secure in the pledge of others to maintain confidentiality. All these matters, of course, depend upon such faith sharing's being not mandated, but engaged in freely by people who trust one another.

Another assumption: If faith sharing is seen as a value in the community, it will require some kind of format or structure; it cannot be simply left to chance or spontaneous generation ("Let's just do it around the supper table when we're in the mood"). It probably should not be done as part of the community business meeting, because the purpose is different. It needs to be done with some regularity: weekly, biweekly, monthly. Admittedly, this formal structure may give faith sharing the appearance of artificiality, particularly if community members are not sharing much in other ways. But then— what is the alternative? If we do not opt for faith sharing, what *will* we do to connect with each other more deeply?

It is difficult to maintain our commitments and our enthusiasm when so many around us see little sense or meaning in our religious lifestyle.

Finally, faith sharing will be most effective when it takes place in a small-group setting (3–8 members) and when members have spent some time in personal, thoughtful preparation before the actual sharing. It does not require a trained facilitator, but it is usually helpful to have some kind of format to follow. So, in this final section, I will present several models that can be used as noted or adapted to the needs of the group.

There are two general approaches to faith sharing. One way is to begin with our personal experience and then move to reflection on the experience in the light of the Scriptures or our faith tradition ("from Life to Word"). The other is to read or listen to a passage of Scripture and then connect it with our own experience ("from Word to Life"). In either case it is crucial not to let the sharing slip into an *intellectual* exercise ("head trip") or psychological-theological analysis. What we are trying to share is our *personal faith*, not our fund of knowledge.

The "Critical Incident" Model ✿

This is a form of the first approach mentioned above: reflection on experience.

1. Select an incident from the past week (or two weeks or month) that *stands out* in your memory—preferably one that stirred up some strong emotion (either an "upper" or a "downer").

2. Reflect on questions like the following:
   - What kind of feelings did the incident stir up?
   - How did you respond at the time?
   - How do you feel about the way you responded?
   - What might your response reveal about you?

3. Looking back, how can you see God present or active in the incident and your response?
   - What biblical passages or images come to mind?
   - What response might God be asking of you now (praise, gratitude, wonder, repentance, forgiveness, action)?

As each member shares an experience, the others are free to respond or not respond—give feedback, encourage, question. The session concludes with spontaneous or structured prayer.

Scripture-based Models

Scripture Reflection

Begin with silence or a prayer. Someone reads a scripture passage (either the upcoming Sunday or some other). Then each reflects and shares her or his reflections. Questions like the following may be helpful:
   - How does this passage touch upon my concerns and my feelings at this time?
   - How does it connect with my own experience, past or present? What is this word of God calling me to at this time?

The reflection and sharing may include not only my personal concerns, but also those of our local, provincial, or ecclesial community. The session concludes with prayer.

African Bible Study

This model is based on a method used in some communities in Africa.
   - One person reads the scripture passage aloud slowly.

- Each person shares a word or phrase that caught her or his attention.
- Another person reads the passage again.
- Each shares: How does this passage touch my life today? (It is important that members use "I/me" language rather than "we/us"—to avoid the danger of going on "head trips.")
- Another member reads the passage a third time.
- Members share: What am I being called to be or do this coming week? How is God inviting me to change or conversion?
- As a closing, each one prays for the person on her or his right, naming what that person has shared. As part of the covenant, all commit to praying for the person on their right daily during the week.

The Base Christian Community Model

This method had its origins in Latin America and has been adapted for North Americans. It is action-oriented and tries to apply the scriptural text not only to the individuals but also to the group or community. It calls people to radical conversion and to action on behalf of justice: "That interpretation is best which is the most radical for conversion and gives the most justice to others." (The following is based on notes from a talk by Megan McKenna to *Pax Christi* in 1987.)

After reading the scripture passage aloud and taking time for quiet reflection, members share the following:

1. What word or phrase leaps out at you, and what feeling does it elicit?

2. What affirmed or encouraged you? What challenged you or made you uncomfortable?

3. What are you going to do to concretize the Scripture for yourself?
- What can I *begin* doing?
- What can I *stop* doing?
- What can I *continue* to do better or in a more intentional way?

("You have not really heard the gospel if it does not move you to action.")

4. What can *the group* do together?
- What can we *begin* doing?

- What can we *stop* doing?
- What can we *continue* to do better or in a more intentional way?

(The action must be something concrete that flows out of the reading and reflection, and it should be checked on when the group reconvenes.)

It should be clear that none of these models need be followed slavishly. The religious community will probably have to experiment until it finds a method suitable for the members. The important thing is *to begin*. It has been said that faith sharing, in some form or other, will have to become normative in our parishes if the church is to become revitalized. I would hope that we religious can be leaders and animators rather than latecomers in this process.

The Challenge of Peace:
Prayer in the Nuclear Age

The American bishops' Peace Pastoral addresses the church as a community of conscience called to prayer and penance as part of the labor of peacemaking. To wage peace with all the discipline, passion, self-sacrifice, and heroism of waging war demands profound spiritual force. To marshal this soul force requires courage, patience, and great hope because, in the process, one confronts violence at its source in the human heart—in one's own self.

For this reason the "spiritual warriors" of the early Christian tradition, the desert elders, liken radical prayer to an inner warfare where one encounters all the enemies of the new Christ—consciousness on the true battlefield of one's soul. In this arena, warring is restored to its rightful place. Acted out interpersonally, intertribally, internationally, warfare bears only the curse of literal destruction; enacted intrapersonally, within one's self, the interior struggle bears the blessing of spiritual transformation.

The question of where to put war, aggression, and violence is of profound consequence to people of faith. Their misplacement has left us with a planet bathed in blood, poised for extinction. For Christians, these warring energies are the very stuff to be transfigured by the power of the cross, that transformed instrument of violence, in the paschal mystery of prayer.

The conversion of the peacemaker implies turning toward the sources of violence in our own psyches so that the labor of reconciliation and healing, indeed of salvation, may be realized at the center of us. Only by such renewed and restored human persons can the earth be redirected on the way of peace and justice.

"To approach the nuclear issue in faith is to recognize our absolute need for prayer: we urge and invite all to unceasing prayer for peace with justice for all people" (p. viii). The challenge of peace, therefore, is a call to inner work. It is a call to prayer.

The Call to This Prayer: Personal Conversion

The pastoral situates the peacemaker's call to prayer in the context of personal discipleship. The church is the community of disciples, a "deeply personal . . . society" (John Paul II, *Redemptor hominis*, §21), in which each believer responds to the saving action of the Christ Spirit. The bishops remind us that:

> Convinced Christians are a minority in nearly every country in the world—including nominally Christian and Catholic nations. In our own country we are coming to a fuller awareness that a response to the call of Jesus is both personal and demanding. As believers we can identify rather easily with the early church as a company of witnesses engaged in a difficult mission. To be disciples of Jesus requires that we continually go beyond where we now are. (pp. 85-86)

Personal conversion is the wellspring of the peacemaker's prayer, a deliberate ongoing commitment which involves "separating ourselves from all attachments and affiliation that could prevent us from hearing and following our authentic vocations" (p. 86). The practice of this vigilance and flexibility enables a person to "not simply believe with one's mind, but also to become a doer of the word, a wayfarer and a witness to Jesus" (p. 86). The prayer for conversion of heart, of attitude, of moral awareness and spiritual consciousness requires profound faith in the paradoxical victory of the cross because peacemakers "never expect complete success within history and . . . must regard as a normal event the path of persecution and martyrdom" (p. 86).

It is clear, then, that the peacemaker's call to prayer is no invitation to disengagement, passivity, or other-worldly bliss. It is rather a summons to deep sobriety, fortitude, and intense embrace-of the anguish of our age, accepting the consequences of that engagement. Conversion to this passionate form of prayer brings with it a sense of cultural estrangement which can only be supported by basic Christian community involvement. The call to prayer is at once an invitation to the margins of society and to the heart of the church. As the bishops insist:

We readily recognize that we live in a world that is becoming increasingly estranged from Christian values. In order to remain a Christian, one must take a resolute stand against many commonly accepted axioms of the world. To become true disciples, we must undergo a demanding course of induction into the adult Christian community. We must continually equip ourselves to profess the full faith of the church in an increasingly secular society. We must develop a sense of solidarity, cemented by relationships with mature and exemplary Christians who represent Christ and his way of life. All of these comments about the meaning of being a disciple or a follower of Jesus today are especially relevant to the quest for genuine peace in our time. (p. 86)

The Context of This Prayer:
"A Moment of Supreme Crisis"

The peacemaker takes up this prayer in what the Vatican Council calls "a moment of supreme crisis." The American bishops further specify our historical situation by saying:

The crisis of which we speak arises from this fact: nuclear war threatens the existence of our planet; this is more menacing than any the world has known. It is neither tolerable nor necessary that human beings live under this threat. But removing it will require a major effort of intelligence, courage, and faith. As Pope John Paul II said at Hiroshima: "From now on it is only through a deliberate policy that humanity can survive." (p. 2)

The historical moment of crisis, unparalleled in the memory of our race, has a deeply religious dimension. Our age suffers a profound psychic impasse which severs us from the assurance of a human future. More than a political or strategic crisis, ours, at its very roots, is a spiritual dilemma because we seem to be powerless to redirect our planetary course. The energies of transformation, of wisdom, of right seeing for right doing seem unavailable to us, buried in the threatening abyss of our own souls. We seem to fear the descent to rediscover our bearings, retrieve our center. We have a fear of the depths. Yet awakening to the reality of this age requires that we confront our times and their signs in all their dimensions. History bears the mystery of depth also, and entering into the historical situation urges an inward as well as an outward orientation. Prayer in "a moment of supreme crisis" draws one into supreme depths, into the deeper meaning of events by the labor of disciplined reflection.

The Challenge of This Prayer:
To Contemplate Apocalypse

The challenge of the peacemaker's prayer in the nuclear age is nothing less than contemplating the *apocalypse*—that is, to suffer the revelation of our global situation with its demonic and divine possibilities. The bomb itself is a dark revelation whose threatening light can illumine our reality and teach us profound wisdom about the blindness which has brought us to this impasse. The bomb itself is a revelation of our terror, our disease, our sin. As an idol it manifests our ultimate concerns, values, aspirations, and desires, but in a counterfeit way. It is a god to whom we wittingly or unwittingly pledge our allegiance, and it is of great spiritual importance that we come to understand the demanding god within the bomb or we shall ever be subject to its demonic power.

> *The challenge of the peacemaker's prayer in the nuclear age is nothing less than contemplating the apocalypse.*

But how does one face *apocalypse*—put a face on the great mystery of our age? This is being addressed all over the world by theologians, psychologists, philosophers, therapists, and spiritual directors. To give face to a thing requires images, and images are born in the imagination. Only by facing up to the peril of our situation can we imagine alternatives for our collective survival. Imagination, then, is a key to this prayer, because with it the peacemaker envisions salvific possibilities for the earth. The pastoral notes that this prayer seeks "to penetrate ever more adequately the nature of the biblical vision of peace and relate it to a world not yet at peace" (p. 6).

To place such great value on "the religious vision of peace" implies that it truly lives in the souls of people, that it is a motivating energy and force. But vision, like every other thing upon which we depend, must be honored as a source of life, of nourishment, of direction. It is the challenge of the peacemaker to open one's imagination, conscience, soul to give God access once again to a world from which "the holy" has been expelled. What the bishops say of the theological endeavor can also be said of this, theology's true source: "No greater challenge or higher priority can be imagined than the development and perfection of a [spirituality of] peace suited to a civilization poised on the brink of self-destruction" (p. 72). Peace visionaries, therefore, must be present to the dark process of receiving and articulating what comes to them in the labor of contemplation.

The Characteristics of This Prayer: Polarity and Paradox

The peacemaker's spirituality reflects the features of the multivalent mystery it attends: apocalypse. Apocalypse at once means closure and disclosure; end and beginning; destruction and transformation. The power of this rich symbol rests in its polarity and paradox. So, too, the prayer of peacemakers is grounded in polarity and paradox. They have learned by contemplating the bomb that its lethal physics of fission must be reversed—the metaphysical antidote of nuclearism is fusion. Translated into spiritual understanding, the peacemaker cultivates a consciousness that resists breakup, split-off modes of polarization, but can support the tension of opposites, polarities, difference. Peacemakers especially must learn how to be bridges in the midst of deadly polarization and intolerance, and this can be learned in the school of contemplation where paradox is the rule.

The peacemaker's prayer, then, seeks to reestablish creative polarity so that energy and balance can be restored to the soul of our planet. If the bomb is a detached, antiseptic, rational agent of death, the peacemaker prays to be an intimate, earthy, sensuous servant of life. The bomb preys on abstracts: victims, cultures, ecosystems. The peacemaker prays in the concrete: this person, this polluted river, this Central American town. The power of the specific, the particular, can rescue our souls from the deadening effects of impersonal mass consciousness. Giving faces and names and histories to nuclear hostages intensifies the spiritual power of our prayer and even heals us by the stimulation of our compassion.

The arms race preys on our insecurity; peacemakers pray into a paradoxical security since they know that if everything is already in absolute jeopardy, there is really nothing to lose. New possibilities open up for living as we consciously coexist with ultimate risk, and mysteriously we feel more alive, sense unexpected joy. The bomb, which preys on our first-strike necessity to be sure, secure, and safe is countered by a prayer of unknowing and abandonment. We sacrifice our certainty-lust for faith, and find ourselves much relieved.

❧ The bomb defends our power, pleasures, possessions; the peacemaker moves to the polarity of powerlessness, capacity for pain, for doing without. The bomb defends the patriarchal systems and structures of exploitation and dominance; the peacemaker labors in prayer to rediscover the maternal virtues and values of self-emptying and nurturance. The bomb threatens all created life; peacemakers become defenders of life, upheld by their contemplative intimacy with creation. The bomb steals from God the prerogative of determining the world's course; the peacemaker, in prayer, reestablishes the rights of the Holy One.

The greatest paradox the peacemaker is called to embrace and manifest emerges when another polarity is addressed in prayer. The bomb is the greatest concentration of power known to us, our own creation, megatons of destruction achieved by splitting the smallest particle of matter. But there is another power—the Dynamite of God" as St. Paul might call it—which is the Holy Spirit of the violated/victorious Christ. This power is liberated not by division but by union. It is a bonding power not of our creation, but a power creating us as we are unified, are gathered together in union. It is this great power—the very Christ Spirit—which is the "counterface" of the bomb. The conversion of the dark mystery of the bomb, this anti-Christ, is no other than Christ. In prayer the peacemaker discovers this Christ, revealed in the nonviolent suffering servant, Jesus. In prayer, by the Spirit's anointing, the peacemaker becomes a Christ. In that person the arms race has been radically reversed, the bomb forever dismantled.

The Obstacles to This Prayer: Confronting the Demons

There are many obstacles to be overcome on the road to this deep spiritual empowerment. As Jesus braved the radical self-confrontation his prophetic mission presumed, his disciples enter into the wilderness of self-encounter to face the demons that divide our energies, bind us, oppress us from within. Our inner world mirrors our outer world. The fissioning process idolized in the bomb, goes on in our depths, subtly, subversively splitting our integrity, rending our core. Energy is released and therefore lost, squandered on a million cares, lost in a frenzy of exhausting, dissipating activism. The peacemaker is called to the reverse soul-process, whereby split-off elements of one's person are reintegrated in a healing way. As powerful personal energy gathers and intensifies within the psyche, it is ever available to invest in the vital works of building, constructing, teaching, envisioning, waging peace.

Shalom is the rich, biblical word for peace. It suggests a wholeness, an integrity because a break or rupture has been mended. The task of peacemakers is to discover prayer ways that mend the break in the psyche, whose healing will make available great sources of power for the world. As Jesus named the demons that assailed his wholeness, his *shalom*, so must they who are anointed with him as prophets and peacemakers.

What are the demons that violate our dynamic, creative inner peace? What voices, behaviors, orientations rob us of energizing grace to labor for peace? Although each one's history personalizes the features of these demons, they probably all derive from the same source: fear of being wounded or vulnerable, the result of being wounded or vulnerable. This fundamental human fear has taken on apocalyptic proportions in our own time. "People are frightened," the bishops admit. "As . . . pastors ministering in one of the major nuclear nations, we have encountered terror in the minds and hearts of our people; indeed we share it" (p. 1).

Terror is an explicit, immanent threat to our vital security. Like any overpowering, relentless passion or experience, terror numbs the soul. This psychic numbing, as Robert J. Lifton and others have demonstrated, is a characteristic feature of the modern personality. It is at once revealed and concealed by the faces of despair, denial, selfishness, greed, consumptive materialism, supernationalism, rampant militarism, patriarchal antifeminism. The spiritual deadness effected by psychic numbing has brought our corporate pathology to awesome proportions. Ours is one of the most violent ages in history and its deadly spiral consumes all life in its vortex. Suicide, fratricide, matricide, genocide, biocide, geocide, and even deicide are the effects of soul numbness. It is urgent that peacemakers locate and name the demons of spiritual numbness within themselves so that they can be healed to feel again the anguish of the earth and respond in compassion.

Adversaries of This Prayer: The Inner Opponents

Dr. Mary Watkins is a clinical psychologist and author committed to helping people sustain moral action. She has made an important contribution to this labor in a paper titled "In Dreams

Begin Responsibilities: Moral Imagination and Action." From her extensive research with a broad spectrum of people, Watkins has identified several adversary voices which "benumb" the moral imagination and keep persons aloof from sustained, creative action on behalf of peace and justice. These are the voices of our fear which keep the imagination in a state of paralysis fed by an ongoing interior monologue. Instead of the qualitative interior silence necessary to hear the word of the Christ Spirit calling us to the labor of peacemaking, we hear only these insistent, dominating voices of excuse, denial, and diversion. Their noise within us obscures the more singular voice of our Christ nature. Although these voices sometimes defend an authentic personal value or represent a real human concern, their autonomous, unconscious character is divisive. Split off from our center, they are a problem. Brought into dialogue with the indwelling Word, they can be powerful allies in waging peace. It is the task of the prayerful peacemaker, therefore, to be vigilant toward the benumbing voices speaking in us.

Watkins characterizes six benumbing voices: the Child, the Worker, the Naturalist, the Suburbanite, the Hedonist, the Burdened.

The *Child* is that voice in us which speaks out of our world of play—a relationship of harmony with nature and people. The Child lives in a safe world, far from cruelty and complexity. In this context the Child is secure and happy and resists leaving it for the threatening danger and ambiguity of the adult world. The Child feels small, in need of defense, powerless. The Child cannot deal with the nuclear age. The voice of the Child says "the world and I need to be taken care of by someone older and wiser."

The *Worker* is the voice of the specialist in us. Absorbed in the task at hand, this one gets in the way of action. The specialized concerns of the Worker—teaching, child raising, business and the like—provide a dispensation from involvement and responsibility for peacemaking. The voice of the Worker says, "Peacemaking is not my job."

The *Naturalist* is the one who calls us to live simply. This earthy one tends to hermit-like proclivities: an absorbing solitude that gravitates toward isolation, and an overconcern for the purity of one's diet and environment. This voice calls one to live a secure, circumscribed life in denial of the demands of history. The Naturalist says "I'm going fishing—while there's still time."

The *Suburbanite* is the part of us that wants to live in a world apart, at a safe distance from the violence, poverty, suffering of our reality. This one is on the commute, comfortable in that uniform, stereotypic life that never moves out of the secure or average. The voice of the Suburbanite keeps us at a safe distance from peacemaking.

The *Hedonist* is the one who will not even think of nuclear war, world hunger, or international terrorism. Bound to an ethic of pleasure, this voice draws the personality into a pursuit of self-gratification through overindulgence in art, drugs, food, sex or other modes of exclusive subjectivity. The intense need to live for the present is a dramatic response to the catastrophic dimensions of our age, but this same attitude also breeds violence and exploitation. The voice of the Hedonist talks us out of the self-sacrifice of peacemaking.

The *Burdened* is that one who is already overwhelmed by life and its sorrows. This is the voice of depression and exhaustion and confirms our worst suspicions about the future of our world. This voice wonders if nuclear annihilation would be a relief from the ongoing struggles of existence.

These six voices are some of the benumbing energies that handicap us in our effort to respond to the evangelical call of peacemaking. Dr. Watkins identifies two other interior attitudes which make us aware of our responsibility, but still present obstacles to creative action. These are the voices of the Sufferer and the Activist.

The *Sufferer* is the part of us which, far from being numb to pain, is forever experiencing it. Scarred by the anguish of the world, this voice is a constant outcry, an internal, psychic mourning with everyone who suffers. This one is disfigured by pain, can find no relief from it. It is an awareness bred by personal wounds. But this overwhelming sympathy makes one a victim, too, and ultimately renders one powerless and passive.

The *Activist* aspect reveals itself in two forms, the competent one and the overactivist. The voice of the competent Activist speaks a very self-confident superficial "movement" monologue within us. There is action, yes; but it is not heartfelt compassion. It may be an acting out of any number of unconscious motivations. Therefore, it lacks the soul force of the authentic peacemaker. Overactivists, likewise, are caught up in the labor of justice and peace but are overworked. Their sense of the enormity of the task, their experience of failure and isolation produces a pessimistic depression and loneliness that threatens burnout.

The final voice our Quaker sister, Mary Watkins, discerned from all the subjects she listened to, was the voice of the *Lovers*. This voice was heard mostly in mothers and teachers for whom activism was not a primary goal or necessity but the consequence of their ultimate concern for life. Essentially this is the voice of the one who loves humanity, is in awe of creation, is committed to nature and children and the future. This voice, Watkins found to be the most supportive and attentive to the Indwelling Word of Life. This voice, once located and identified, becomes a link to the others which keep us benumbed.

By inviting these inner voices to dialogue, real peace negotiations can begin. Not only must the dominance of the benumbing voices be modified by the self-sacrificial word of the Lover, but each and every inner voice that speaks its fears and concerns, its dread and denial must be heard by the others. Then, as each voice is honored and valued for its insight, the Specialist can become the ally of the Activist, the Child can become the companion of the Sufferer, and the Hedonist, refreshment for the one on the brink of burnout. Such inner summetry is a creative prayer form that teaches us to honor and listen to our own voices of conflict so that we may be more adept at understanding and reconciling the voices of conflict outside ourselves. Once enlisted in the work of peacemaking these former obstacles to conversion become assets. In prayer our demons can become angels by submitting their power to the task of integration, of making *shalom*, thereby ministering clarity and inner strength to the peacemaker.

The Discipline of This Prayer:
Spiritual Exercises for Peacemakers

The fourth chapter of the bishops' pastoral means to explore "some of the implications of being a community of Jesus' disciples in a time when our nation is so heavily armed" (p. 85). A disciple is one in training with a master. Discipline is the embodied practice which leads to the master's awareness by yoking theory and action in the student. Discipline, then, is incarnating wisdom: it is understanding in the flesh.

The training of the disciple of Jesus is a lifelong process of transformation from image to likeness of Christ. This is true with regard to the study of peacemaking inherent in Christian formation. As the bishops insist:

> Peacemaking is not an optional commitment. It is a requirement of our faith. We are called to be peacemakers, not by some movement of the moment but by the Lord Jesus. The content and context of our peacemaking is set, not by some political agenda or ideological program, but by the teaching of his church. (vii)

The teaching of Jesus' church offers a rich tradition of spiritual exercises designed to effect sustaining power in the disciple. The great triad of Christian discipline has ever been prayer, fasting, and almsgiving. These take on radical significance in an age of spiritual blindness, conspicuous consumption, and global poverty and oppression. These ancient and universal practices, adapted to our reality, are powerful modes of strengthening and developing one's endurance in peacemaking. A fresh look at each of these gives new insight and purpose.

Peacemakers search the Scriptures for Christ's gospel of peace.

It is the challenge of peacemakers to embody ways of prayer that will insert them into the heart of the world and Jesus' compassion for it. Peacemakers search the Scriptures for Christ's gospel of peace. They pray into Jesus' radical sense of security and undefendedness before the god who is discovered to be a loving parent. They pray into reconciliation with their neighbor; they honor the poor, the widow, the orphan, the alien. They pray the Good News.

But peacemakers pray the bad news, too. Drawn from journals, papers, and media, the scriptures and icons of sin and suffering are held in mindfulness. Stations of the Cross are daily revisited as the passion of Christ continues to unfold all about us. The peacemaker conspires with the Spirit of reconciliation by repeating a simple mantra: Peace be to Lebanon (to Ireland, El Salvador . . .)." The peace prayer becomes a deeper way of breathing, inhaling earth's woundedness, exhaling the Spirit of mercy. And in the hands of the peacemaker, the rosary becomes a powerful circle of intercession to the great and Holy Mother, that her compassion, tenderness, and defense of life be embodied in the world.

In this first mode of ancient discipline—prayer—the peacemaker learns to honor those endangered species of the soul:

silence and solitude. Somewhere in their lives, peacemakers concretely designate nuclear-free, nonviolent zones— moments, places, rites, relationships—which they offer themselves and the world as islands of sanity. In these sanctuaries the covenant of peace is reaffirmed with the God of Creation and the holiness of life more deeply known.

The second spiritual exercise of the peacemaker is fasting. This ancient practice takes on radically new significance in a world in which seventy or more percent of its population live with hunger as a constant deadly companion. It takes on new meaning also in a culture where overeating and overdrinking are ravenous diseases consuming the soul of our nation. We stuff ourselves to fill the deep unsatisfied emptiness we feel in our depths. We participate in a materialistic orgy to gratify our every want, in delirious excess of any simple need. And the deeper truth is that the hunger of the poor and the gluttony of the rich are demonstrably connected. We consume the vital resources of the hungry. In some occult way our pathological consumption devours our starving neighbor. In a mystical way, conspicuous consumption is cannibalism. It is a disease all around.

Not just our habits of consumption but the armaments which defend our lifestyle starve the hungry. For this reason the bishops explicitly call the Christian community to fast for the cause of peace.

"We call upon our people to fast and abstain on each Friday of the year. We call upon our people voluntarily to do penance on Friday by eating less food and by abstaining from meat" (p. 91). On this day, held in our hearts as the memorial of Jesus' crucifixion, the peacemaker makes a will-act, volunteers to be in solidarity with Christ's ongoing passion in the oppressed. This is an act of resistance to the arms race and the disordered living it would defend.

Fasting has ever been both a mode of altering consciousness and a method of dramatizing a grievance in religious societies. The fasting of the peacemaker likewise becomes an interior angel, ever announcing the discomforting presence of God in the hungry. It is a faithful companion to peacemakers, accompanying them in the deep, dark process of transformation from the inside out. Fasting is a passivity, a diminishment, a gnawing threat-in-the-gut where we first awaken to the issue of survival. Fasting for disarmament becomes a visceral annunciation, a gut-felt grievance for the starving. "Bread not bombs" our angelic hunger tells us. Bombs must become bread because the holocaust of these unexploded things is already underway in the hungry of Latin America, Africa, Asia. Indeed, the devouring madness of the bomb has its malnourished victims in our own cities, mountains, and reservations. Fasting is the peacemaker's way of coming to the empty table of the poor and tasting its judgment and its strange grace. When peacemakers fast in this way they are not weakened, they are made strong.

The third dimension of spiritual discipline incarnates the other two: "almsgiving for peace." This practice of redistributive justice very concretely and existentially redirects the resources of a defense-oriented nation to the people given priority status in the new society envisioned by Jesus: the poor and oppressed. Those resources are first and foremost our own persons—our time, energy, service, skills, gifts. It is imperative that human connections be made between the affluent and the poor. Matthew's Gospel (25:31-45) makes clear that the poor are the historical presence of Christ in relation to whom we find salvation. He puts on the lips of Jesus a strong indictment of those who failed to feed the hungry, clothe the naked, visit the sick and the prisoner, welcome the homeless. And in our age the major obstacle to doing these works of God's reign is our national priority of defense. Bombs are theft from the poor. The peacemaker enacts Christ's priorities in the works of mercy and as an agent of justice by becoming advocate, evangelist, bridge, and servant of the poor.

Mentors of this Prayer: Saints, Gurus, Bodhisattvas

To learn the ways of the peacemaker, one must study those who have made of their lives a peace offering. Throughout our tradition there have been great nonviolent sages and witnesses. In the wider communion of saints beyond Christianity there are even more avatars of peace. The race is rich in models of transfigured human nature. These peacemakers, known and unknown to us, quietly and dramatically revive the prophetic spirit of our church and world. They have been our forerunners of conscience, teaching, preaching, provoking, and disturbing us to evangelical awakening. These persons and communities, wherever they are found, are the indispensable mentors of peacemaking.

It is imperative that the peacemaker learn from the great nonviolent witnesses. Gandhi, Merton, Dorothy Day, Lanza del Vasto, Daniel Berrigan, Mairead Corrigan and Betty Williams, Daniel O. Dolci, Martin Luther King, Simone Weil, and a host of others offer invaluable instruction to those who would learn the ways of nonviolence. Peace people make study a mode of prayer and devote themselves to the asceticism of reading, reflection, and clarification of thought. Peacemakers learn by the conscious imitation and practice of the virtues of nonviolent teachers. They enter into faithful awareness of the communion of saints and elect from them heroes and heroines who will support their new nonviolent consciousness.

The pastoral honors one person in particular as the patron of peacemakers: our mother and sister, Mary.

> We call upon Mary, the first disciple and the Queen of Peace, to intercede for us and for the people of our time that we may walk in the way of peace. In this context, we encourage devotion to Our Lady of Peace. (p. 59)

Mary keeps surprising us as she dawns evermore radiantly, subtly, insistently in the Christian soul. She is the wellspring of the peacemaker, herself, a revelation of peace.

In Mary we contemplate and imitate the one who's hunger for God's justice was a consuming passion, espoused in the depths of herself. Her inward marriage to the God of Liberation was so singular and intense that she became alive with the fruit of that union. She carried shalom within her, she grew full with it, grew burdened with it, suffered its birth into history through her fierce fidelity, her rugged faith.

The gospel of Mary is a special gift in our tradition because it proclaims the mysterious way authentic peace is conceived and carried, labored and delivered, into a world of violence and oppression. Her gospel casts a revealing light on the Christian vocation because she gives witness to those profound human dispositions without which the Christ Spirit cannot be made incarnate or historical.

Mary is above all the Woman of Peace bound in a special way to the anguish and outrage which war and violence have forever been to women. Mary stands as the source of every feminist initiative for peace. Without her the peace of Christ would be unknown in our world. Her "womb-love" (*rachamin*) for earth's poor and oppressed is the boldest image we have of God's maternal compassion. She spends her eternity reaching into history to touch the powerless with divine power, as the Marian apparition traditions of Guadalupe, Knock, Lourdes, and so many others attest.

Her presence in the church as Mother and Disciple of Christ challenges us to move away from models and attitudes of paternalism, militarism. imperialism, even in our spirituality. She calls us to a passionate defense of life as church. She calls us to enact church's identity of "Mother": Mother Church for Mother Earth revealed in Mother Mary. She teaches Christians how to be midwives of peace in a world hostile to life and therefore to women; hostile to women and therefore to life. She calls all of us to a rediscovery of feminine soul, that the world's inner woman may be liberated in brothers and sisters alike. So empowered, the feminine nature of persons can assert its responsibility "to hold up half the sky." Without the strength which Mary images, the sky will continue to fall upon us.

The Fruit of This Prayer

The prayer of the peacemaker bears abundant fruit. If sustained, sober, and deep, it leads to contemplation where one's consciousness becomes healed by the unifying grace of the Christ Spirit. As the pastoral affirms:

> The practice of contemplative prayer is especially valuable for advancing harmony and peace in the world. For this prayer rises, by divine grace, where there is total disarmament of the heart and unfolds in an experience of love which is the moving force of peace. Contemplation fosters a vision of the human family as united and interdependent in the mystery of God's love for all people. This silent, interior prayer bridges temporarily the "already" and "not yet," this world and God's kingdom of peace. (p. 90)

As contemplatives, we penetrate to the roots of our wounds and fears, and sense an inner reconciliation. We are healed of our anger, our insecurities: we become non-violent. Freed from the gross and subtle ways of our own destructiveness, we become creative. Turned from our covert habits of death-dealing, we become life-giving. We develop patience, the handmaid of hope. And hope gives us tremendous energy for action.

The prayer of the peacemaker heals the moral imagination also. Practiced in the ways of envisioning the great web of life, the interdependent network of all that exists, the Christian becomes obedient to life's greater necessities and humbly serves them. The healed imagination permits one to sense subtleties, live with contradictions and paradox and liberates the peacemaker from the pathology of literalism, fundamentalism, reductionism rampant in our world, driving it to destruction. Prayer has taken the peacemaker out of a static, one dimensional, ideological perspective of reality. Idols give way to symbols that break us out of polarization, lead us to integration. We see the unity of creation, of the human family and its universal struggle for life, justice, and dignity.

The prayer of the peacemaker bears the fruit of connections. We begin to see historical relationships between things and events. Learning to understand from Christ's viewpoint, we move into solidarity with the poor, those who are most violated and exploited. This new connection changes us—mindful of them, we make distinctions between what we want and what we need. This prayer bears the fruit of voluntary simplicity and personal service of the poor.

We also begin to realize there is a community of peacemakers in the church and beyond. We begin to recognize each other, and thereby draw strength and share wisdom. We sense we are not alone, not isolated, not "nuclear" at all. We are corporate, a body, and in that confidence we begin to act, personally and together. We energize each other's labors for peace.

The most sacred fruit of this prayer is the new humanity it effects in us. The peacemaker is transformed at the heart by this saving work of grace which only God can do. Because we are changed at our source and center, so is the world, the work of our hands. But this prayer summons a more powerful energy to be channeled into history: the Spirit of Christ incarnate in a new people. This Spirit alone is ever triumphant over death and violence. Action fueled by our ego, anger, resentment, or fear is not peacemaking. The self-initiated struggle for justice can too easily have recourse to hostility, polarization, violence.

> Christ is our peace, for he has made us both one, and has broken down the dividing wall of hostility . . . that he might create in himself one new (man) in place of the two, so making peace, and might reconcile us both to God. (Ep 2:14-16 and pp. 7-8)

This reconciliation is the life-giving durable fruit of that prayer which makes peace a political objective, a prophetic mandate, a mystical necessity. The challenge of peace is a challenge of prayer: "as it was in the beginning, is now, and ever shall be, world without end"—let us hope. "Amen."